Practice
Book

mheducation.com/prek-12

Send all inquiries to:
McGraw Hill
1325 Avenue of the Americas
New York, NY 10019

ISBN: 978-1-26-580738-2
MHID: 1-26-580738-8

Printed in the United States of America.

7 8 9 SMN 26 25 24 23

A

Contents

iv

Name _____

- A **sentence** is a group of words that shows a complete thought.
- A **sentence fragment** is a group of words that does not show a complete thought: *Climbed a tree.*
- Every sentence begins with a **capital letter**.
- Most sentences end in a **period** (.). The period is a kind of **end punctuation**.

Read each group of words. Write *yes* if the group of words forms a complete sentence. Write *no* if it does not form a sentence.

1. I read a book about sea life. _____

2. The largest mammal. _____

3. I want to see a whale someday. _____

4. Swims quickly through the water. _____

5. A jellyfish is an interesting sea creature. _____

6. Most sharks live in warm water. _____

7. A giant squid can grow to be very large. _____

8. Live off the coast of Japan. _____

9. Dolphins have two flippers. _____

10. A walrus can live in or out of the water. _____

 **In your writer's notebook, write about a sea animal that you have seen or would like to see. Reread your work to make sure you used sentences that show a complete thought.**

Name _____

> - A **statement,** or declarative sentence, tells something. It ends in a period: *I like to play baseball.*
> - A **question,** or interrogative sentence, asks something. It ends in a question mark: *What is your favorite sport?*

A. Write *statement* if the sentence tells something. Write *question* if it asks something. Put the correct end punctuation at the end of the sentence.

1. We learned about fire safety at school today _____

2. It is important to have fire alarms that work _____

3. Do you check your fire alarms each year _____

4. Do firefighters teach safety classes at your school _____

5. Families should plan escape routes from their home _____

B. Reread this paragraph from "Room to Grow." Underline one question. Circle the end punctuation of the question. Then rewrite the question on the lines below.

> All of a sudden, Jill's mother smiled. "Can you help us with a project?" she asked. "Our community wants to plant a garden. Our plot is very small. There is so much we want to grow."

_____

_____

Name _____

> • Begin every sentence with a **capital letter**.
>
> • Use a **period** (.) at the end of a statement.
>
> • Use a **question mark** (?) at the end of a question.

Write each sentence correctly using capital letters and end punctuation. If the group of words does not tell a complete thought, put an X next to it. Then add words to make it a complete sentence.

1. fall is my favorite time of year

   _____

2. i like to see the leaves turn bright colors

   _____

3. pumpkins at the pumpkin patch

   _____

4. do you go to football games in the fall

   _____

5. we take lots of pictures of the colorful leaves

   _____

 **In your writer's notebook, write about your favorite time of year. Then reread your work. Make sure you have used complete sentences and correct end punctuation.**

Name _____

> • Begin every sentence with a **capital letter**.
>
> • A **statement** is a sentence that tells or describes something. A statement ends in a **period**.
>
> • A **question** is a sentence that asks something. A question ends in a **question mark**.

Rewrite the sentences below, fixing any mistakes you might find.

1. we had a terrible storm last night.

_____

2. There was a lot of wind and heavy rain?

_____

3. did you see the weather report this morning

_____

4. Yesterday our town got over three inches of rain

_____

5. Do you think that some streets are flooded.

_____

Name _____

A. Read the paragraph. Then answer the questions.

(1) I went whale watching last week. (2) Our boat set sail on a clear and windy day. (3) I could smell the salty ocean air. (4) Big whales swimming. (5) Have you ever seen a whale?

1. Which of the following is a sentence fragment?
   A Sentence 1
   B Sentence 3
   C Sentence 4
   D Sentence 5

2. Which of the following is a question?
   F Sentence 2
   G Sentence 3
   H Sentence 4
   J Sentence 5

B. Read the student draft and look for revisions to be made.

(1) My family and I went for a walk in the woods yesterday afternoon. (2) Warm and sunny day. (3) We followed a small stream and passed maple and oak trees. (4) Soon we came to a meadow filled with colorful wild flowers. (5) on our way home we saw a deer and even a fox.

3. What is the correct way to write sentence 2?
   A Warm but sunny day.
   B It was a warm and sunny day.
   C Sunny and warm day.
   D No change needed in sentence 2.

4. What change, if any, should be made to sentence 5?
   F Change *on* to *On*
   G Change *deer* to *Deer*
   H Change *fox* to *Fox*
   J Make no change

Name _____

Fold back the
paper along
the dotted line.
Use the blanks
to write each
word as it is
read aloud.
When you finish
the test, unfold
the paper. Use
the list at the
right to correct
any spelling
mistakes.

1. _____
2. _____
3. _____
4. _____
5. _____
6. _____
7. _____
8. _____
9. _____
10. _____
11. _____
12. _____
13. _____
14. _____
15. _____

Review Words 16. _____
17. _____
18. _____

Challenge Words 19. _____
20. _____

1. clap
2. camp
3. hand
4. stamp
5. snack
6. rack
7. grabs
8. glad
9. bill
10. miss
11. click
12. pink
13. sick
14. grin
15. lift
16. cat
17. bit
18. man
19. anthill
20. cramp

Name _____

When a vowel appears between two consonants, it usually makes a short vowel sound.

- /a/ as in *snap, bag,* and *man*
- /i/ as in *rip, trip, fin,* and *swim*

The short *a* sound can appear at the beginning of a word, as in *animal* or *ant*. Short *i* can appear at the beginning of a word, as in *ink* or *insect*.

Read aloud the spelling words in the box. Then write the spelling words that have each short vowel sound below.

sick	stamp	click	miss	snack
camp	bill	glad	grabs	clap
grin	rack	hand	pink	lift

short *a* as in *snap*

1. _____
2. _____
3. _____
4. _____
5. _____
6. _____
7. _____
8. _____

short *i* as in *rip*

9. _____
10. _____
11. _____
12. _____
13. _____
14. _____
15. _____

Look through the selections you read this week and hunt for words with short *a* and short *i*. Read the words you find aloud and record them in your writer's notebook.

Name _____

When a vowel appears between two consonants, it usually makes a short vowel sound.

- /a/ as in *snap, bag,* and *man*
- /i/ as in *rip, trip, fin,* and *swim*

Read aloud the spelling words in the box. Then write the spelling words that have each short vowel sound below.

clap	fan	rack	click	bag
sick	kick	hid	snap	big
bill	grin	miss	sit	band

short *a* as in *snap*

1. _____
2. _____
3. _____
4. _____
5. _____
6. _____

short *i* as in *rip*

7. _____
8. _____
9. _____
10. _____
11. _____

12. _____
13. _____
14. _____
15. _____

 **Look through the selections you read this week and hunt for words with short *a* and short *i*. Read the words you find aloud and record them in your writer's notebook.**

Name _____

A. Write the spelling words that have each short vowel sound below. One word has both a short *a* and short *i* vowel sound.

clap	flicker	stand	click	sick
snack	stamp	grass	anthill	grant
billed	brand	rack	brick	pants

short *a* as in *snap*   **short *i* as in *rip***

1. _____   6. _____   10. _____

2. _____   7. _____   11. _____

3. _____   8. _____   12. _____

4. _____   9. _____   13. _____

5. _____   14. _____

15. Which word has both short *a* and short *i*?

_____

B. Compare the words *clap* and *click*. How are the two words alike? How are they different?

_____

_____

 **Look through the selections you read this week and hunt for words with short *a* and short *i*. Read the words you find aloud and record them in your writer's notebook.**

Name _____

clap	stamp	grabs	miss	sick
camp	snack	glad	click	grin
hand	rack	bill	pink	lift

A. Write the spelling word that completes each sentence.

1. I will _____ for the best pet in the show.

2. Will you help me _____ this heavy box?

3. The monkey _____ for the rope and swings away.

4. Mom will pay the gas _____ today.

5. I put the dishes on the _____ to dry.

6. I always raise my _____ to give an answer.

7. I use this rubber _____ to mark my address.

8. I need my sleeping bag to _____ outside.

9. You know the machine is on when you hear it _____ .

10. I will _____ my friend when he moves away.

B. Write the spelling word that has the same meaning as each word or phrase below.

11. ill _____

12. pleased _____

13. a broad smile _____

14. a light red color _____

15. a light meal _____

Name _____

There are six spelling mistakes in the story below. Underline the misspelled words. Write the words correctly on the lines.

Once there was a girl named Betty. Betty was odd. She had soft penk hair. When she looked in the mirror, a big gran would spread across her face. Her pretty hair made her glade.

One day Betty sat eating a sneck when a big dog came by. He took the apple out of her hend! Betty was so scared! Her hair turned white. She knew she would miess having such pretty hair.

1. _____ 4. _____

2. _____ 5. _____

3. _____ 6. _____

Writing Connection **Write a story about your pet or favorite animal. Use at least four spelling words in your story.**

_____
_____
_____
_____
_____
_____
_____
_____

Name _____

Remember

When a vowel appears between two consonants, the vowel sound is usually short. The words *snap, man,* and *cap* have a short *a* vowel sound. The words *rip, fin, thick,* and *swim* have a short *i* vowel sound.

Circle the spelling word in each row that rhymes with the word in bold type. Read the spelling word aloud and write it on the line.

1. **tap**	stop	big	clap	_____
2. **fin**	grin	wag	kite	_____
3. **pick**	cake	click	like	_____
4. **cabs**	take	nice	grabs	_____
5. **pack**	bake	snack	pie	_____
6. **link**	pine	lake	pink	_____
7. **band**	hand	home	bid	_____
8. **ramp**	roam	come	camp	_____
9. **lick**	look	kind	sick	_____
10. **gift**	lift	gave	raft	_____
11. **back**	bake	rack	king	_____
12. **lamp**	stamp	late	play	_____
13. **hiss**	have	miss	mess	_____
14. **fill**	fold	wall	bill	_____
15. **sad**	glad	seed	made	_____

Name

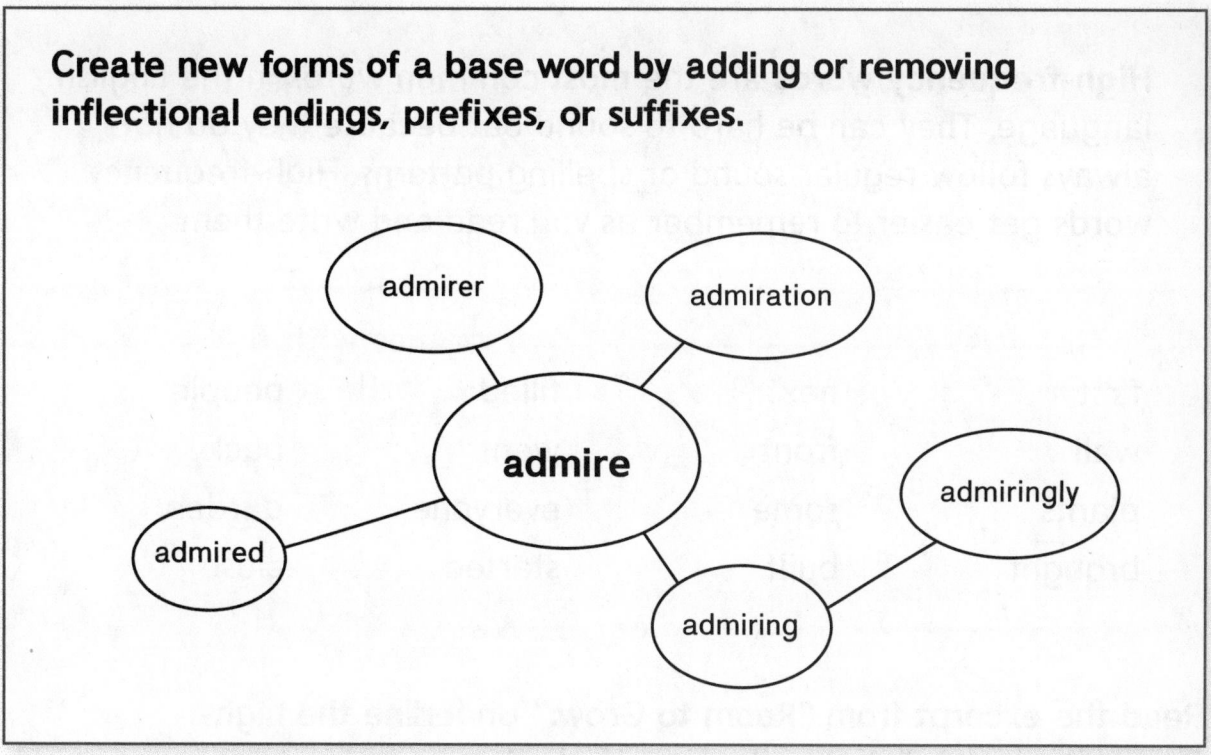

Create new forms of a base word by adding or removing inflectional endings, prefixes, or suffixes.

admirer

admiration

admire

admiringly

admired

admiring

Use your notes from *Gary the Dreamer*. Choose one word and write it on the outside of the watermelon. Then write related words on as many watermelon seeds as you can. Use a dictionary to help you.

Name _____

High-frequency words are the most common words in the English language. They can be hard to sound out because they do not always follow regular sound or spelling patterns. High-frequency words get easier to remember as you read and write them.

first	next	filled	people
wall	front	went	back
plants	some	everyone	garden
brought	built	started	close

Read the excerpt from "Room to Grow." Underline the high-frequency words listed in the box. Underline each word only once.

First we had a meeting with the community. Everyone agreed to contribute. Some people brought seeds, tools, and dirt. Then the next day we met and started our garden.

Papa built long, open boxes. Next, we filled them with dirt. The tallest box went close to the back wall. The boxes got shorter and shorter. The shortest box was in the front. "All the plants will get sunlight without making shade for the others," Mama said.

 **In your writer's notebook, write about a community project you have worked on or would like to work on. How did or could you contribute? When you are finished, use a dictionary to check your spelling of high-frequency words in your writing.**

Name _____

> - A **sentence** expresses a complete thought.
> - A **statement** tells something. A **question** asks something. A question often starts with interrogative words such as *Who, What, Where, When, Why,* and *How.*
> - A **command** is a sentence that tells someone to do something. It ends with a **period**.

After each sentence, write *statement, question,* or *command* for the kind of sentence it is. Then write the sentence correctly. Use capital letters and end marks correctly.

1. we can help you put the groceries away _____

   _____

2. put the cans of food on the shelves _____

   _____

3. do you want me to put the apples in the bowl _____

   _____

4. where should I put the flour and sugar _____

   _____

5. close the door when you are finished _____

   _____

 **In your writer's notebook, write about a game or sport you like to play. Explain the rules of the game. Reread your work to make sure you use complete sentences.**

Name _____

> • A **command** is a sentence that tells someone to do something. It ends with a **period**: *Clean up your toys.*
>
> • An **exclamation** shows excitement or strong feeling. It ends with an **exclamation mark**: *We won the game!*

A. After each sentence, write *statement, question, command,* or *exclamation* for the kind of sentence it is. Place the correct punctuation at the end of the sentence.

1. I want to go to Florida next summer _____

2. What a beautiful state it is _____

3. Have you ever been there _____

4. Wow, my grandmother sent me a free ticket _____

5. Go with me to Miami _____

B. Reread this paragraph from *Gary the Dreamer*. Underline one exclamation. Circle the exclamation mark. Then write the sentence on the lines below.

> I played tag with the neighbor kids. I played hide-and-seek. I played catch with oranges. In our backyard, we had an orange tree. We also had plum, lemon, and apple trees. Lucky me! Anytime I was hungry for a snack, I just went outside and picked a fruit!

_____

_____

Name _____

> • Use a period (**.**) at the end of a **statement** or **command**.
>
> • Use a question mark (**?**) at the end of a **question**.
>
> • Use an exclamation mark (**!**) at the end of an **exclamation**.

Add correct punctuation to the ends of sentences in the letter below.

Dear Aunt Jackie,

    Wow, I was so happy to hear your good news   It will be fun to read your poem in the magazine   Mom says we can frame it   Will you get extra copies   Send me an extra one, please   I want to take it to school to show my class They will see that I have the best aunt ever

    I have a small favor to ask   Would you mind giving me some tips on writing a poem   Find out if you can come for a visit soon   We can have an amazing poetry reading together

Your favorite niece,

Carly

 **Write a letter to a friend or family member. Try to include at least one statement, question, command, and exclamation. Use the letter above as a model.**

_____

_____

_____

_____

_____

Name _____

> • A **statement** tells something. It ends with a **period**.
>
> • A **question** asks something. It ends with a **question mark**.
>
> • A **command** tells someone to do something. A command also ends with a **period**.
>
> • An **exclamation** shows excitement or strong feeling. It ends with an **exclamation mark**.

After each sentence, write *statement, question, command,* or *exclamation* for the kind of sentence it is. Then write the sentence correctly. Use capital letters and end punctuation correctly.

1. what a great day for a parade _____

_____

2. does the parade start at noon _____

_____

3. we can see the parade from Green Street _____

_____

4. walk down Oak Street, then turn down Third Avenue _____

_____

5. wow, here come the marching bands _____

_____

Name _____

A. Read the paragraph. Then answer the questions.

(1) Yesterday I learned how to make bread. (2) I combined flour, water, yeast, and salt. (3) Then I baked the bread in the oven. (4) It smelled so good! (5) Anyone can learn to bake bread. (6) Remember to clean up when you are done.

1. Which of the following is a command?
   A Sentence 1
   B Sentence 3
   C Sentence 4
   D Sentence 6

2. Which of the following is an exclamation?
   F Sentence 1
   G Sentence 3
   H Sentence 4
   J Sentence 5

B. Read the student draft and look for revisions that need to be made. Then answer the questions.

(1) I'm so excited to visit the beach! (2) I'm planning to arrive this afternoon. (3) Would you like to join me! (4) We can go swimming in the ocean and build castles in the sand. (5) Bring your sunglasses and sunscreen.

3. What change, if any, should be made to sentence 1?
   A Change *I'm* to *i'm*
   B Replace the exclamation mark with a period
   C Replace the exclamation mark with a question mark
   D Make no change

4. What change, if any, should be made to sentence 3?
   F Change *Would* to *would*
   G Replace the exclamation mark with a period
   H Replace the exclamation mark with a question mark
   J Make no change

Name _____

Fold back the paper along the dotted line. Use the blanks to write each word as it is read aloud. When you finish the test, unfold the paper. Use the list at the right to correct any spelling mistakes.

1. _____
2. _____
3. _____
4. _____
5. _____
6. _____
7. _____
8. _____
9. _____
10. _____
11. _____
12. _____
13. _____
14. _____
15. _____

Review Words
16. _____
17. _____
18. _____

Challenge Words
19. _____
20. _____

1. step
2. mess
3. head
4. crops
5. stop
6. rock
7. clock
8. sock
9. pond
10. jumps
11. shut
12. luck
13. slump
14. bugs
15. mug
16. clap
17. sick
18. snack
19. ready
20. does

Name _____

When a vowel appears between two consonants, it usually makes a short vowel sound.

- /e/ as in *egg, beg,* and *red*
- /o/ as in *pop, chop,* and *lock*
- /u/ as in *rub, nut,* and *thumb*

SPELLING TIP

Some short vowel sounds can be spelled in more than one way. The short *e* sound is sometimes spelled *ea,* as in the words *bread* and *ready.* The short *o* sound can sometimes be spelled with the letter *a,* as in the word *swap.*

Read aloud the spelling words in the box. Then write the spelling words that contain each short vowel sound below.

jumps	mug	clock	step	rock
sock	stop	mess	shut	bugs
luck	slump	pond	head	crops

short *e* as in *red*

1. _____
2. _____
3. _____

short *o* as in *lock*

4. _____
5. _____
6. _____
7. _____
8. _____
9. _____

short *u* as in *thumb*

10. _____
11. _____
12. _____
13. _____
14. _____
15. _____

 **Look back at the selections you read this week and hunt for words with short *e, o,* and *u.* Read the words you find aloud and record them in your writer's notebook.**

Name _____

When a vowel appears between two consonants, it usually makes a short vowel sound.

- /e/ as in *egg, beg,* and *red*
- /o/ as in *pop, chop,* and *lock*
- /u/ as in *rub, nut,* and *thumb*

SPELLING TIP

Some short vowel sounds can be spelled in more than one way. The short *e* sound is sometimes spelled *ea,* as in the words *bread* and *ready.* The short *o* sound can sometimes be spelled with the letter *a,* as in the word *swap.*

Read aloud the spelling words in the box. Then write the spelling words that contain each short vowel sound below.

pump	stop	pond	yet	top
fed	mess	shut	bugs	jumps
sled	rock	clock	cuts	step

short *e* as in *red*

1. _____
2. _____
3. _____
4. _____
5. _____

short *o* as in *lock*

6. _____
7. _____
8. _____
9. _____
10. _____

short *u* as in *thumb*

11. _____
12. _____
13. _____
14. _____
15. _____

 **Look back at the selections you read this week and hunt for words with short *e, o,* and *u.* Read the words you find aloud and record them in your writer's notebook.**

Name _____

A. Read the spelling words in the box. Then write the spelling words that contain each short vowel sound. One word has two of the short vowel sounds listed below.

gush	ready	check	bathtub	funnel
head	crops	rock	jumps	stop
block	mess	shut	slump	trust

short *e* as in *red*	short *o* as in *lock*	short *u* as in *thumb*
1._____	5._____	9._____
2._____	6._____	10._____
3._____	7._____	11._____
4._____	8._____	12._____
		13._____
		14._____
		15._____

B. Compare the words *head* and *mess*. How are the two words alike? How are they different?

_____

_____

 **Look back at the selections you read this week and hunt for words with short *e, o,* and *u*. Read the words you find aloud and record them in your writer's notebook.**

Spelling · Word Meaning

Name _____

step	crops	clock	jumps	slump
mess	stop	sock	shut	bugs
head	rock	pond	luck	mug

A. Write the spelling word that goes with the other two words.

1. ocean, lake, _____
2. ants, grasshoppers, _____
3. plate, fork, _____
4. stone, pebble, _____
5. hops, leaps, _____

B. Write the spelling word that best completes each sentence.

6. We know to _____ at a red light.
7. Please _____ the door when you go out.
8. I hope to win the game, so wish me _____.
9. I lost one blue _____ in the laundry.
10. I need an alarm _____ to wake up.
11. I need to clean up the _____ in my room.
12. Our new puppy is white with brown spots on his _____.
13. Take a big _____ over that spilled water.
14. Our team started out winning, but now we're in a _____.
15. The farmer spoke to our class about growing _____.

20 Grade 3 · Unit 1 · Week 2

Name _____

There are six spelling mistakes in the story below. Underline each misspelled word. Write the words correctly on the lines.

Kate's alarm clack goes off and she jummps out of bed. She has a job to do. She has to clean the meass in her room today.

She reaches under the bed and finds two shirts, three pens, and a sok. Then her friend Dan shows up. He asks her to go down to the pand with him. They like to catch buges there. Kate can always clean her room tomorrow.

1. _____   4. _____

2. _____   5. _____

3. _____   6. _____

Writing Connection **Write a story about someone who has chores to do. Use at least four spelling words in your story.**

_____

_____

_____

_____

_____

_____

_____

_____

_____

Name _____

Remember

When a vowel appears between two consonants, it usually makes a short vowel sound. You can hear the short *e* sound in *wet, bet,* and *nest.* The short *o* sound is in *fog, clog,* and *pop.* The short *u* sound is in *cub, puppy,* and *bump.*

Circle the spelling word in each row that rhymes with the word in bold. Read the spelling word aloud and write it on the line.

1. **pep**	seem	step	time	_____
2. **tug**	goat	take	mug	_____
3. **drops**	close	crops	days	_____
4. **duck**	luck	lake	done	_____
5. **dock**	state	rock	pool	_____
6. **bumps**	bakes	lunch	jumps	_____
7. **nut**	use	foot	shut	_____
8. **bond**	pond	bank	sand	_____
9. **shop**	shine	stop	skip	_____
10. **less**	mess	lost	rose	_____
11. **bread**	road	bride	head	_____
12. **rugs**	rings	bugs	grow	_____
13. **thump**	thing	name	slump	_____
14. **block**	stick	clock	walk	_____
15. **knock**	nice	took	sock	_____

Name _____

> **Synonyms** are different words that have the same meaning. For example, synonyms for *large* are *big, massive, giant,* and *huge*.
>
> If you come across a word you don't know, you can look for a synonym nearby to help you define it.

A. Read the sentences below. Underline the synonym in the second sentence that means the same thing as the word in bold in the first sentence. Then write the meaning of the word on the lines below.

1. I had thought the rain would never **cease**! But by morning the rain came to a stop and the Sun was shining.

   _____

2. The book I borrowed from the library looks **ancient**. I can't believe something so old is still in one piece.

   _____

3. The train was moving very **rapidly**. We didn't expect to get to the station so quickly.

   _____

4. The young trees in the meadow are very **slender**. I can easily wrap my two hands around the skinny trunks.

   _____

B. Rewrite the sentence using a synonym for the word in bold.

5. The **large** mountains looked beautiful against the blue sky.

   _____

   _____

Name _____

Read the sentences from "Joseph Bruchac." Underline the compound word in each sentence. Then write its definition. Remember to use a dictionary for help.

1. His grandfather showed him how to walk softly through the woods and how to fish in the lakes and rivers.

   _____

   _____

2. Joseph's grandmother kept bookshelves in the house full of books.

   _____

   _____

3. He liked to read storybooks about animals.

   _____

   _____

4. But he still lives in the hometown where he grew up.

   _____

   _____

Name _____

> • A **sentence** is a group of words that tells a complete thought.
>
> • Every sentence has two parts: the **subject** and the **predicate**.
>
> • The **subject** tells what or whom the sentence is about.
>
> • The **predicate** identifies what the subject does or is.
>
> • A **complete subject** is all the words in a subject.

What or whom is each sentence about? Draw a line under the complete subject.

1. The pet store is busy on Saturday.

2. People smile at the puppies and kittens.

3. The goldfish swim in a big tank.

4. Furry rabbits hop around.

5. A long snake coils in its cage.

 **Write about your favorite animal. Describe what you like about it. Remember to use complete sentences that include both a subject and predicate.**

_____

_____

_____

_____

_____

_____

Name _____

> - The **subject** of a sentence tells what the sentence is about. In the sentence *The Sun shone brightly*, the subject is *The Sun*.
> - A **complete subject** is all the words in a subject.
> - A complete subject can be one word, more than one word, or a **compound subject** connected by *and*. In the sentence *Birds and squirrels live in the park*, the subject is *birds and squirrels*.

Reread this paragraph from "The Dream Catcher." Underline one compound subject. Then rewrite the sentence on the lines below.

> Nokomis and Peter worked together and made a dream catcher. That night, as he gazed and looked at the dream catcher over his bed, he made a plan.

_____

_____

Connect to Community **Talk with a parent or another trusted adult about a cultural tradition that you could take part in. Write about why that tradition is important.**

_____

_____

_____

_____

_____

_____

Name _____

> • Every **complete sentence** has a subject and a predicate. It expresses a complete thought.
>
> • A **sentence fragment** is a group of words that does not express a complete thought: *Were barking all night* is a fragment.

Correct each fragment by adding a subject from the box. Then write the sentence correctly on the line.

Skyscrapers	A city	A subway	People	A park

1. _____ is much larger than a town.

   _____

2. _____ may take subways, trains, or buses to work.

   _____

3. _____ is a train that goes under the ground.

   _____

4. _____ are tall buildings.

   _____

5. _____ is a great place for families to have a picnic.

   _____

 **In your writer's notebook, write about some of the things that you find in the town or city where you live. Remember to write in complete sentences.**

Grammar · **Proofreading**

Name _____

> • A **complete subject** is all the words in a subject. It can be one word, more than one word, or a **compound subject** connected by *and*. In the sentence *Lemons and limes are sour*, the compound subject is *Lemons and limes*.
>
> • A **sentence fragment** may be a group of words that does not have a subject. It does not express a complete thought. *Was drinking water* is a fragment because there is no subject.
>
> • Correct some **sentence fragments** by adding a subject.

Underline the complete subject in each sentence. For sentence fragments, add a subject. Then write the sentence correctly. Use capital letters and end marks.

1. my class will go on a field trip to a museum next week

   _____

2. a museum is a good place to learn about the past

   _____

3. can see all kinds of things used long ago

   _____

4. wagons and buggies were once used for transportation

   _____

5. had not been invented yet

   _____

Name _____

A. Read the paragraph. Then answer the questions.

   (1) You can spot many kinds of animals when you visit a swamp. (2) Birds walk through the shallows on their long legs. (3) Snakes and alligators glide across the water. (4) Frogs croak and hop along the banks. (5) Turtles dive underwater to look for food.

1. What is the subject in sentence 2?

   A Birds
   B walk
   C shallows
   D long legs

2. Which of the following sentences contains a compound subject?

   F Sentence 1
   G Sentence 3
   H Sentence 4
   J Sentence 5

B. Read the student draft and look for revisions that need to be made. Then answer the questions.

   (1) Last week, I went camping in the mountains. (2) Brought a tent, sleeping bag, food, and some books. (3) At night, I built a campfire and gazed at the stars above. (4) Owls coyotes called from the dark. (5) When I woke up, it was snowing.

3. What is the correct way to write sentence 2?

   A I brought a tent, sleeping bag, food, and some books.
   B Tent, sleeping bag, food, and some books I brought.
   C Tent, sleeping bag, food, and some books.
   D No change needed in sentence 2.

4. What is the correct way to write sentence 4?

   F Owls coyotes calling from the dark.
   G Owls but coyotes called from the dark.
   H Owls and coyotes called from the dark.
   J No change needed in sentence 4.

Name _____

Fold back the
paper along
the dotted line.
Use the blanks
to write each
word as it is
read aloud.
When you finish
the test, unfold
the paper. Use
the list at the
right to correct
any spelling
mistakes.

1. _____
2. _____
3. _____
4. _____
5. _____
6. _____
7. _____
8. _____
9. _____
10. _____
11. _____
12. _____
13. _____
14. _____
15. _____

Review Words 16. _____
17. _____
18. _____

Challenge Words 19. _____
20. _____

1. date
2. lake
3. skate
4. plane
5. grade
6. fine
7. life
8. rice
9. wise
10. smile
11. rose
12. globe
13. smoke
14. come
15. used
16. step
17. rock
18. luck
19. sneeze
20. stripe

Name _____

A word spelled with a vowel, consonant, and final *e* usually has a long vowel sound. You can hear a long *a* in *late*, a long *i* in *invite*, and a long *o* in *alone*. The final *e* in these words is silent.

DECODING WORDS

The first syllable in *inside* is the prefix *in-*. The second syllable is spelled with a vowel, consonant, and final *e* (VCe). This forms a long *i* vowel sound. Blend the syllables and read the word aloud: *in/side*.

Read each of the spelling words out loud. Then write the words that contain each long vowel sound below.

fine	used	globe	date	lake
smoke	grade	rice	rose	come
skate	smile	wise	life	plane

long *a*	long *i*	long *o*
1. _____	6. _____	11. _____
2. _____	7. _____	12. _____
3. _____	8. _____	13. _____
4. _____	9. _____	**long *u***
5. _____	10. _____	14. _____

15. Which word has an unexpected vowel spelling? _____

Go back through the selections you read this week. Look for words with VCe spellings. Read the words you find aloud, and record them in your writer's notebook.

Name _____

A word spelled with a vowel, consonant, and final *e* usually has a long vowel sound. You can hear a long *a* in *late*, a long *i* in *invite*, and a long *o* in *alone*. The final *e* in these words is silent.

DECODING WORDS

The first syllable in *inside* is the prefix *in-*. The second syllable is spelled with a vowel, consonant, and final *e* (VCe). This forms a long *i* vowel sound. Blend the syllables and read the word aloud: *in/side*.

Read each of the spelling words out loud. Then write the words that contain each long vowel sound below.

date	base	rice	wise	grade
fuse	come	rose	woke	lake
safe	fine	mile	dome	used

long *a*	long *i*	long *o*
1. _____	6. _____	10. _____
2. _____	7. _____	11. _____
3. _____	8. _____	12. _____
4. _____	9. _____	long *u*
5. _____		13. _____
		14. _____

15. Which word has an unexpected vowel spelling? _____

 **Go back through the selections you read this week. Look for words with VCe spellings. Read the words you find aloud, and record them in your writer's notebook.**

Name _____

wise	grade	come	striped	sneeze
envelope	whale	plane	smiled	shapes
skate	smoke	crime	globe	fine

A. Read each of the spelling words out loud. Then write the words that contain each long vowel sound below.

long *a*	long *i*	long *o*
1. _____	6. _____	11. _____
2. _____	7. _____	12. _____
3. _____	8. _____	13. _____
4. _____	9. _____	**long *e***
5. _____	10. _____	14. _____

15. Which word has an unexpected vowel spelling? _____

B. Compare the words *come* and *smoke*. How are the words alike? How are they different?

_____

_____

_____

 **Look at the selections you read this week. Look for words with a long vowel spelled with a final *e*. Read the words you find out loud and record them in your writer's notebook.**

Name _____

date	plane	life	smile	smoke
lake	grade	rice	rose	come
skate	fine	wise	globe	used

A. Write the spelling word that belongs with each group of words below.

1. puddle, pond, _____

2. jet, rocket, _____

3. flames, ashes, _____

4. clever, smart, _____

5. map, atlas, _____

B. Write the spelling word that completes each sentence.

6. The bride had one bright red _____ in her hand.

7. Dad _____ the rake to clear the leaves.

8. Do you know today's _____ ?

9. When I am happy, I always have a _____ on my face.

10. Where is the third _____ classroom?

11. The weather was just _____ for a picnic.

12. He learned how to _____ at the ice rink.

13. She gave a report about _____ in the desert.

14. I helped make a bowl of _____ and beans.

15. I taught my dog to _____ when I call his name.

Name _____

There are six spelling mistakes in the biography below. Underline the misspelled words. Write the words correctly on the lines.

Sarah Hughes can skeate. In 2002 she won a gold medal. Sarah flies around the glob talking about her lief.

Sarah always has a huge smil on her face when talking to kids. She tells them it is wiz to stay in school and work hard. One day she may coome to your school.

Writing Connection | **Write about someone's life. Tell what the person has done. Use at least four spelling words in your story.**

_____

_____

_____

_____

_____

_____

_____

_____

_____

Name _____

Remember

When a word is spelled with a vowel, consonant, and final *e*, the vowel sound is usually long: *mate, alive, alone, inside, rule.*

There are some exceptions to this rule. The words *have, give,* and *love* have the final *e* spelling but no long vowel sound.

Read the words aloud. Circle the spelling word in each row that rhymes with the word in bold. Write the spelling word on the line.

1. **fused**	fussy	used	loose	_____
2. **robe**	globe	cold	stale	_____
3. **tile**	smile	toil	clay	_____
4. **made**	sod	glad	grade	_____
5. **spice**	teach	rice	slick	_____
6. **snake**	sneak	shell	lake	_____
7. **wife**	with	life	soft	_____
8. **crate**	date	crane	dart	_____
9. **pose**	lost	porch	rose	_____
10. **some**	come	storm	cone	_____
11. **spine**	spill	poem	fine	_____
12. **lane**	clean	plane	link	_____
13. **broke**	shook	brake	smoke	_____
14. **rise**	wise	trees	raise	_____
15. **state**	slick	skate	fleet	_____

Name _____

Create new forms of a base word by adding or removing inflectional endings, prefixes, or suffixes.

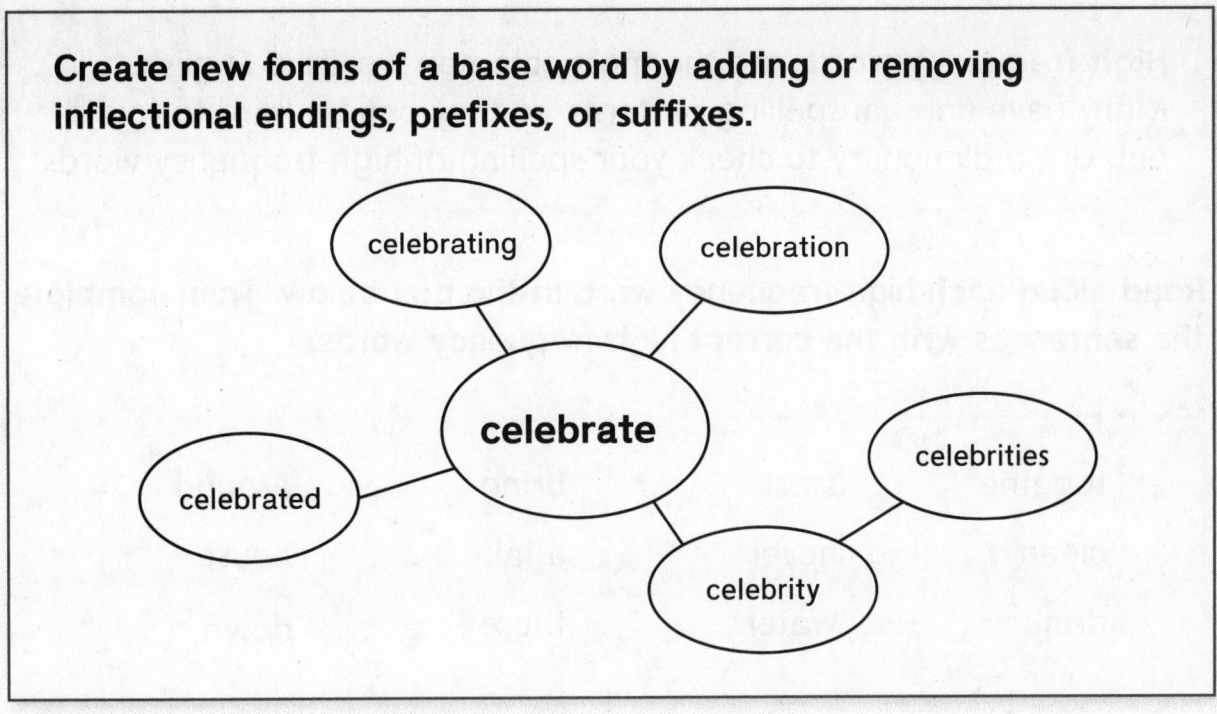

Use your notes from *Yoon and the Jade Bracelet*. Choose one word and write it on the bracelet below. Then write related words on the charms hanging from the bracelet. Use a dictionary to help you.

Name _____

High-frequency words are the most common words in English. Many have unusual spelling patterns, so they can be hard to sound out. Use a dictionary to check your spelling of high-frequency words.

Read aloud each high-frequency word in the box below. Then complete the sentences with the correct high-frequency words.

together	start	bring	around
clean	never	again	house
drink	water	there	down

1. Even though my sister and I went for a run _____ yesterday, we will go _____ today.

2. We _____ get tired of breathing in the fresh and _____ air outside.

3. We'll each _____ a bottle of _____ with us.

4. If I _____ to get thirsty, I will _____ from my bottle.

5. We're going to run _____ the hill to our friend's _____.

6. When we get _____, we'll turn _____ and come home!

 With a partner, divide up the High-Frequency Word Cards. Take turns showing the cards to your partner and reading them aloud. Then take turns using each word in a sentence. Look for more high-frequency words in your writer's notebook.

Name _____

A **sentence** is a group of words that expresses a complete thought.

• Every **sentence** has a **complete subject** and **complete predicate**.

• The **complete subject** tells what or whom the sentence is about.

• The **complete predicate** tells what a subject is or does. Predicates can be more than one word.

Which word or words tell what the subject is or does? Draw a line under the complete predicate.

1. Bears live in many different habitats.

2. Polar bears live in cold places.

3. These bears live on thick ice sheets.

4. Heavy fur keeps the polar bear warm.

5. A grizzly bear is large and fierce.

6. The grizzly likes to catch fish to eat.

7. Grizzlies hibernate when it gets cold.

8. The sun bear is a small bear.

9. Sun bears live in warmer climates.

10. The sun bear steals honey from beehives.

 **In your writer's notebook, write about an animal that you know about. When you're done, check your work to make sure you used complete sentences with a subject and predicate.**

Name _____

- The **complete predicate** tells what a subject is or does. In the sentence *The eagle caught a fish*, the predicate is *caught a fish*.
- Two predicates joined by *and* form a **compound predicate**. In the sentence *The wolves howled all night and slept all day*, the compound predicate is *howled all night and slept all day*.

Reread this passage from "Family Traditions." Underline the compound predicate in the last sentence. Then write the sentence on the lines.

Storytellers bring the old tales to life. The soft notes of a flute may help tell a story. The firm beat of a drum adds power. People from other cultures can watch and listen. Everyone enjoys the stories and learns about the traditions.

_____

_____

Reading/Writing Connection **Write about what you do during celebrations with your family and friends. Reread your work to make sure you used compound predicates correctly.**

_____

_____

_____

_____

_____

Name _____

- Every **complete sentence** has a subject and a predicate.
- A **sentence fragment** does not have both a subject and a predicate. Correct a fragment by adding a subject or predicate.
- A **run-on sentence** joins two sentences that should be separate. Correct a **run-on sentence** by separating the two ideas into two sentences. *I like oranges they taste good* is a run-on sentence.

Read the sentences. Rewrite each sentence and fix any fragments or run-on sentences.

1. I like summer I always go camping with my dad.

_____

2. First, Dad and I.

_____

3. We gather wood for a campfire later we take a swim in the lake.

_____

4. In the evening build a campfire.

_____

5. We sleep great in the tent we have breakfast the next morning.

_____

 **In your writer's notebook, write about things that you like to do in the summer. Check your work for run-on sentences.**

Name _____

> • Correct a **sentence fragment** by adding a subject or a predicate.
>
> • Correct a **run-on sentence** by separating the two ideas into two complete sentences.
>
> • **Compound predicates** are two predicates joined by *and*.

Rewrite the paragraphs below. Correct sentence fragments and run-on sentences. Be sure to use capital letters and end marks.

My grandmother is an artist she lives in New York. Paints pictures and takes photos of birds. her photos are used in books about birds in their natural habitats Some of her paintings can be seen in museums.

> **HANDWRITING CONNECTION**
>
> Be sure to write legibly. Use proper cursive and remember to leave spaces between words.

My grandmother gets to travel all over the world she has even painted penguins in Antarctica. Once Grandmother. climbed a tree to sketch an eagle. I think that my grandmother has the best job in the world I want to have a job like hers someday.

_____

_____

_____

_____

_____

_____

_____

Name _____

A. Read the paragraph. Then answer the questions.

(1) This afternoon I sat by the river. (2) I listened to the crickets and watched an otter swim by. (3) A frog caught a fly. (4) Tall river grass swayed in the wind. (5) The breeze felt good.

1. What is the predicate in sentence 4?

   A Tall river grass

   B river grass swayed

   C swayed in the wind

   D in the wind

2. Which sentence has a compound predicate?

   F Sentence 2

   G Sentence 3

   H Sentence 4

   J Sentence 5

B. Read the student draft and look for revisions that need to be made. Then answer the questions.

(1) Yesterday my class visited the natural history museum. (2) Our tour guide taught us about animals that lived long ago. (3) We saw dinosaur skeletons they were big. (4) Also saw gemstones and learned about different rocks. (5) We had fun!

3. What is the correct way to write sentence 3?

   A Dinosaur skeletons they were big.

   B We saw dinosaur skeletons. They were big.

   C We saw dinosaur skeletons were big.

   D No change needed in sentence 3.

4. What is the correct way to write sentence 4?

   F We also saw gemstones and learned about different rocks.

   G Also saw gemstones and we learned about different rocks.

   H Also saw gemstones and learned about rocks differently.

   J No change needed in sentence 4.

Name _____

Fold back the
paper along the
dotted line. Use
the blanks to
write each word
as it is read
aloud. When you
finish the test,
unfold the
paper. Use the
list at the right
to correct any
spelling
mistakes.

1. _____
2. _____
3. _____
4. _____
5. _____
6. _____
7. _____
8. _____
9. _____
10. _____
11. _____
12. _____
13. _____
14. _____
15. _____

Review Words
16. _____
17. _____
18. _____

Challenge Words
19. _____
20. _____

1. plain
2. braid
3. fail
4. grain
5. snail
6. paint
7. sway
8. tray
9. gray
10. stay
11. state
12. fake
13. same
14. weigh
15. they
16. fine
17. skate
18. globe
19. sleigh
20. afraid

Name _____

> The long *a* vowel sound that you hear in *say* can be spelled in several different ways: *ay* as in *play*, *ai* as in *rain*, *a_e* as in *face*, *ea* as in *great*, *eigh* as in *eighteen*, and *ey* as in *they*.

DECODING WORDS

The first syllable in *eighteen* is a long *a* sound spelled *eigh*. The second syllable is spelled *teen*. The letter *t* stands for /t/. The letters *ee* form a long *e* vowel sound. The letter *n* stands for /n/. Blend the letters and read the word aloud: *eigh/teen*.

Read each spelling word out loud. Then write the spelling words that have each long *a* sound spelling.

sway	fake	plain	stay	paint
they	snail	tray	state	weigh
fail	same	gray	grain	braid

long *a* spelled *ai*

1. _____
2. _____
3. _____
4. _____
5. _____
6. _____

long *a* spelled *ay*

7. _____
8. _____
9. _____
10. _____

long *a* spelled *eigh*

11. _____

long *a* spelled *a_e*

12. _____
13. _____
14. _____

long *a* spelled *ey*

15. _____

 **Go back through the selections you read this week. Look for words that have the long *a* vowel sound. Read the words you find aloud and record them in your writer's notebook.**

Name _____

> The long *a* vowel sound that you hear in *say* can be spelled in several different ways: *ay* as in *play*, *ai* as in *rain*, *a_e* as in *face*, *ea* as in *great*, *eigh* as in *eight*, and *ey* as in *they*.

Read each spelling word out loud. Then write the spelling words that have each long *a* sound spelling.

pail	they	tray	pain	make
same	plain	rail	may	sway
paint	stay	gray	lane	tail

long *a* spelled *ai*

1. _____

2. _____

3. _____

4. _____

5. _____

6. _____

long *a* spelled *ay*

7. _____

8. _____

9. _____

10. _____

11. _____

long *a* spelled *a_e*

12. _____

13. _____

14. _____

long *a* spelled *ey*

15. _____

 **Go back through the selections you read this week. Look for words that have the long *a* vowel sound. Read the words you find aloud and record them in your writer's notebook.**

Name _____

A. Read each spelling word out loud. Then write the spelling words that have each long *a* sound spelling.

eight	explain	weigh	they	plain
painted	radio	state	obey	sleigh
grain	fake	ladies	tray	same

long *a* spelled *ai*

1. _____

2. _____

3. _____

4. _____

long *a* spelled *ay*

5. _____

long *a* spelled *a_e*

6. _____

7. _____

8. _____

long *a* spelled *ey*

9. _____

10. _____

long *a* spelled *eigh*

11. _____

12. _____

13. _____

long *a* spelled *a*

14. _____

15. _____

B. Compare the words *sleigh* and *obey*. How are they alike? How are they different?

_____

_____

 Go back through the selections you read this week. Look for words that have the long *a* vowel sound. Read the words you find aloud and record them in your writer's notebook.

Name _____

plain	grain	sway	stay	same
braid	snail	tray	state	weigh
fail	paint	gray	fake	they

A. Write the spelling word that goes with the other two words.

1. black, brown, _____

2. city, country, _____

3. worm, slug, _____

4. curl, twist, _____

5. wheat, rice, _____

B. Write the spelling word that best completes each sentence.

6. I like _____ vanilla ice cream.

7. I didn't _____ the test because I studied.

8. I hope to _____ my room a pretty blue.

9. As the wind blew, the wheat began to _____ gently.

10. We have to _____ inside until it stops raining.

11. We are so much alike, and we even have the _____ birthday.

12. Do you think _____ will win the race?

13. We placed all the cookies on a large _____.

14. He said the stone was a diamond, but we think it was _____.

15. We had to measure and _____ the fossil we found.

Name _____

There are six spelling mistakes in the paragraphs below. Underline the misspelled words. Then write the words correctly on the lines.

A snale is very small. Its color is usually brown or greay. Thay have only one foot and move slowly.

1. _____ 2. _____ 3. _____

Iowa is a stait in the Midwest. Many farmers grow grayn in large fields. Many fields look the saim because they all have wheat growing in them.

4. _____ 5. _____ 6. _____

Writing Connection **Write about a crop that grows in your state. Tell how it is used. Use at least four spelling words in your writing.**

_____
_____
_____
_____
_____
_____
_____
_____

Name _____

Remember

Sometimes the long *a* vowel sound is spelled with the letter *a* only: *acorn, nation, potato, April, bagel, vacation, bakery.*

Other long *a* vowel sound spellings include *ai* as in *rain, ay* as in *day, a_e* as in *face, ey* as in *hey,* and *eigh* as in *eighteen.*

Read each word aloud. Then circle the spelling word in each row that rhymes with the word in bold. Write the spelling word on the line.

1. **hay**   they   joy   why   _____

2. **grade**   glad   gray   braid   _____

3. **pail**   small   snail   pull   _____

4. **plate**   state   plot   float   _____

5. **say**   sorry   cry   weigh   _____

6. **rail**   rule   fail   boil   _____

7. **faint**   paint   foot   great   _____

8. **spray**   boys   gray   sport   _____

9. **shake**   stock   shook   fake   _____

10. **sleigh** stay   high   bright   _____

11. **stain**   join   grin   plain   _____

12. **jay**   sway   jeep   jeep   _____

13. **crane**   corn   grain   keen   _____

14. **bay**   tray   sorry   buy   _____

15. **game**   germ   same   chime   _____

Name _____

> **Antonyms** are two different words that have opposite meanings.
> For example: *good* and *bad*; *big* and *small*; *hard* and *easy*.
>
> If you find a word you don't know, look for an antonym in the
> same sentence or a nearby sentence to help you define it.

**Read the sentences below. Underline the antonym that has the
opposite meaning of the word in bold. Then write the meaning of the
word in bold on the lines below.**

1. The storm's **powerful** winds easily knocked over the weak fence.

   _____

2. I think the game is **challenging**, but my friend thinks it is easy.

   _____

3. The tall buildings downtown are **massive**! They can make you feel so
   tiny when you stand next to them.

   _____

4. My car's gas tank was **full** when I left New York, but it was almost
   empty when I got to Boston.

   _____

 **In your writer's notebook, compare two kinds of animals. Write
about how the animals are different. Use antonyms in your
writing, such as *tall* and *short*, *big* and *small*, or *fast* and *slow*.**

Name _____

Read the sentences from "Juneteenth." Underline the context clues that help you understand the meaning of each word in bold. Then use the clues and your background knowledge to write the word's meaning on the line.

1. **Communication** was different back then. There were no telephones. There were no computers.

_____

2. "On June 19, 1865, the last **enslaved** people in America learned they were free, here in Texas," said Uncle Bernard.

_____

3. "In Milwaukee we have a **parade** on June 19. They shut down a street for a few blocks. We have music and games. It's like a block party for the whole city!"

_____

4. "Back in 1872, some people here in Texas bought ten **acres**. The land became Emancipation Park."

_____

5. She pointed to **portraits** on a large quilt. The people wore clothes from long ago. Kayla recognized Douglass and Tubman from her books.

_____

Name _____

- A **simple sentence** is a group of words that expresses a complete thought. Simple sentences include a subject and a predicate. *The bear caught a fish* is an example of a simple sentence.

- Combining simple sentences can add variety to writing.

- Two sentences can be combined with a comma and the **coordinating conjunctions** *and, or,* or *but*: *The bear caught a fish, but it slipped through his paws.*

Reread this paragraph from "A Landmark for All." Combine the two underlined simple sentences by using the word *and*. Write the new sentence on the lines below.

> Every year, more than five million people visit the Grand Canyon. They hike the trails and explore the caves. <u>They snap pictures of the magnificent views.</u> <u>They admire the wildlife.</u>

_____

_____

Write about a landmark you have visited. Tell why you thought it was interesting. Check your work when you're done to make sure you used complete sentences.

_____

_____

_____

_____

_____

Name _____

> • A **compound sentence** contains two related sentences joined by the coordinating conjunctions *and, or,* or *but.*
> • These conjunctions have different functions. *And* joins ideas, *but* shows a change in thought, and *or* offers a choice.
> • Place a **comma** before *and, or,* or *but* in a compound sentence.

Combine the sentences to make a compound sentence. Use the conjunction in parentheses. Write the new sentence on the line.

1. Dogs make good pets. Cats are good pets, too. (and)

   _____

2. Dogs learn tricks easily. Cats are not easy to train. (but)

   _____

3. You can teach your pet. You can take your pet to a trainer. (or)

   _____

4. Dogs are eager to please. They like to work for treats. (and)

   _____

5. Cats are very independent. They can also be sweet pets. (but)

   _____

 In your writer's notebook, write about your pet or an animal you think would make a good pet. Use at least one compound sentence in your writing by using *and, or,* or *but.*

Name _____

> • Begin simple and compound sentences with a capital letter.
>
> • End simple and compound sentences with the correct punctuation. If the sentence is declarative or a command, end it with a period. If the sentence is a question, end it with a question mark. If it is an exclamation, end it with an exclamation point.
>
> • Use a comma before the words *and*, *or*, or *but* when forming a compound sentence.

Correct each sentence below. Use capital letters, commas, and end punctuation correctly.

1. did you see the meteor shower last night

_____

2. dad and I drove out to the country and we saw it with some friends

_____

_____

3. it was the most amazing thing I've ever seen

_____

4. we cheered as the last star disappeared from sight

_____

 **In your writer's notebook, write about an exciting moment you had with your family or friends. Use compound sentences in your writing. Check that you used a conjunction to form your compound sentences, and make sure each conjunction is followed by a comma.**

Name _____

> • Begin sentences with a capital letter. End sentences with correct end punctuation.
>
> • Use a comma before *and, or,* or *but* in compound sentences.

Rewrite the paragraphs below. Look for any sentences that you can combine. Be sure to use capital letters and end marks correctly.

Earthworms are interesting creatures They are important to farmers, too. earthworms loosen the soil as they crawl making it easier for farmers to plant seeds As they crawl they make tunnels This helps water and nutrients get to the roots of young plants

do you want to see an earthworm. Lift up a rock on a hot, sunny day Or look under cool damp leaves. Earthworms need to stay away from the hot sun Or they will dry up. Instead of lungs, earthworms breathe through their skin Their skin needs to say cool and moist at all times. an earthworm is an amazing earthmover?

_____

_____

_____

_____

_____

_____

_____

_____

_____

Name _____

A. Read the paragraph. Then answer the questions.

(1) I like to go for long runs. (2) I leave early in the morning when most people are still asleep. (3) I listen to the sound of my shoes on the road, and I breathe in the damp air. (4) When I get back, the Sun is warm. (5) Running is good exercise, and it's a great way to get fresh air.

1. Which sentence is a compound sentence?
   A Sentence 1
   B Sentence 2
   C Sentence 3
   D Sentence 4

2. Which sentence uses a coordinating conjunction?
   F Sentence 1
   G Sentence 2
   H Sentence 4
   J Sentence 5

B. Read the student draft and look for revisions that need to be made. Then answer the questions.

(1) Today I helped my mom make chicken soup. (2) First I gathered carrots and onions from the garden. (3) My mom cut up the vegetables I added them to the pot. (4) We added salt and pepper before letting it cook for a long time. (5) The soup smelled delicious. (6) The soup tasted great.

3. What is the correct way to write sentence 3?
   A My mom cut up the vegetables, or I added them to the pot.
   B My mom cut up the vegetables for me I added them to the pot.
   C My mom cut up the vegetables, and I added them to the pot.
   D No change needed in sentence 3.

4. What is the best way to combine sentences 5 and 6?
   F The soup smelled delicious, but it tasted great.
   G The soup smelled delicious, and it tasted great.
   H The soup smelled delicious, or it tasted great.
   J The soup smelled delicious it tasted great.

Name _____

Fold back the paper along the dotted line. Use the blanks to write each word as it is read aloud. When you finish the test, unfold the paper. Use the list at the right to correct any spelling mistakes.

1. _____
2. _____
3. _____
4. _____
5. _____
6. _____
7. _____
8. _____
9. _____
10. _____
11. _____
12. _____
13. _____
14. _____
15. _____

Review Words 16. _____
17. _____
18. _____

Challenge Words 19. _____
20. _____

1. coast
2. float
3. toad
4. coal
5. soak
6. gold
7. sold
8. scold
9. slope
10. broke
11. note
12. bone
13. slow
14. show
15. foe
16. snail
17. same
18. weigh
19. bowl
20. program

Name _____

The long *o* vowel sound that you hear in the word *so* has several different spellings. Long *o* can be spelled *o* as in *no*, *oa* as in *coat*, *o_e* as in *vote*, *ow* as in *low*, and *oe* as in *toe*.

Read each spelling word aloud. Write the spelling words that contain the matching spelling pattern for the long *o* vowel sound.

sold	coal	coast	scold	soak
float	slow	bone	slope	show
broke	foe	gold	toad	note

long *o* spelled *oa*

1. _____

2. _____

3. _____

4. _____

5. _____

long *o* spelled *o_e*

6. _____

7. _____

8. _____

9. _____

long *o* spelled *oe*

10. _____

long *o* spelled *o*

11. _____

12. _____

13. _____

long *o* spelled *ow*

14. _____

15. _____

 Go back through the selections you read this week. Look for words that have the long *o* vowel sound. Read the words you find aloud and record them in your writer's notebook.

Name _____

The long *o* vowel sound that you hear in the word *so* has several different spellings. Long *o* can be spelled *o* as in *no, oa* as in *coat, o_e* as in *vote, ow* as in *low,* and *oe* as in *toe.*

Read each spelling word aloud. Write the spelling words that contain the matching spelling pattern for the long *o* vowel sound.

soak	boat	sold	show	cold
open	gold	slow	slope	load
coast	home	grows	bone	foe

long *o* spelled *oa*

1. _____
2. _____
3. _____
4. _____

long *o* spelled *o*

5. _____
6. _____
7. _____
8. _____

long *o* spelled *oe*

9. _____

long *o* spelled *o_e*

10. _____
11. _____
12. _____

long *o* spelled *ow*

13. _____
14. _____
15. _____

Name _____

A. Read the words aloud. Write the spelling words that contain the matching spelling pattern for the long *o* vowel sound.

soak	float	folk	window	gold
note	scold	growth	bowl	loaves
coast	slope	program	show	goes

long *o* spelled *oa*   **long *o* spelled *ow***   **long *o* spelled *o***

1. _____   6. _____   10. _____

2. _____   7. _____   11. _____

3. _____   8. _____   12. _____

4. _____   9. _____   13. _____

long *o* spelled *oe*   **long *o* spelled *o_e***

5. _____   14. _____

                                              15. _____

B. Compare the words *soak* and *folk*. How are the words alike? How are they different?

_____

_____

_____

 **Go back through the selections you read this week. Look for words that have the long *o* vowel sound. Read the words you find aloud and record them in your writer's notebook.**

Name _____

coast	coal	sold	broke	slow
float	soak	scold	note	show
toad	gold	slope	bone	foe

A. Write the spelling word that belongs with the other words in each group.

1. shore, beach, _____

2. frog, lizard, _____

3. silver, copper, _____

4. letter, e-mail, _____

5. bought, rented, _____

B. Write the spelling word that best completes each sentence.

6. I learned how to _____ during swim class.

7. You can burn _____ to make heat.

8. Mom had to _____ my pants to remove the grass stains.

9. I had to _____ my puppy when he chewed my shoe.

10. The ball rolled down the steep _____.

11. The wheel on the wagon _____ when we pulled it.

12. On our field trip, we saw a huge dinosaur _____.

13. A rabbit is fast, but a snail is very _____.

14. I want to _____ you the painting I made.

15. The opposite of friend is _____.

Name _____

There are six misspelled words in the paragraphs below. Underline each misspelled word. Write the words correctly on the lines.

A cowst is where the land meets the sea. Lots of plants and animals live there. A bird might nest among the grasses on a sandy slop. Sometimes a fish will sho its silvery fins as it swims by.

You can find shells on the beach. Some shells are white and others are as black as cole. You can soke your shells to clean them. You might even see a sloe turtle walking toward the waves. There are lots of things to see there!

1. _____ 4. _____

2. _____ 5. _____

3. _____ 6. _____

Writing Connection **Write about something you might see at the beach. Use at least four spelling words.**

_____
_____
_____
_____
_____
_____
_____
_____

Name _____

Remember

Sometimes the long *o* vowel sound is spelled with the letter *o* only, as in the words *open, yoyo, oval, yogurt,* and *over.*

The long *o* vowel sound can also be spelled *oa* as in *coat, oe* as in *toe, o_e* as in *nose,* and *ow* as in *know.*

Circle the spelling word in each row that rhymes with the word in bold type. Write the spelling word on the line.

1. **toast**   taste   beast   coast   _____

2. **boat**   beet   float   brought   _____

3. **rode**   toad   ride   said   _____

4. **bowl**   wall   coal   blue   _____

5. **oak**   only   weak   soak   _____

6. **fold**   gold   feed   loud   _____

7. **told**   deal   late   sold   _____

8. **old**   scold   cloud   lead   _____

9. **rope**   pear   slope   ring   _____

10. **joke**   broke   join   king   _____

11. **vote**   trout   stop   note   _____

12. **cone**   count   bone   nice   _____

13. **glow**   glad   slow   look   _____

14. **snow**   show   sneeze   wake   _____

15. **toe**   time   tree   foe   _____

Name _____

> **Content words** are words that
> are specific to a field of study. The
> words *national* and *landmark* are
> social studies content words.
>
> Sometimes you can figure out what
> a content word means by using
> context clues. You can also use a
> dictionary for help.

CONNECT TO CONTENT

"A Landmark for All" gives
facts about the Grand
Canyon and argues that
the Grand Canyon should
be seen by everyone. The
author uses content words
related to this topic to
help you understand this
important landmark.

 Go on a word hunt with a partner. Find content words
related to landmarks in the selections you read this week.
Write them on the points of the Statue of Liberty's crown.

**Pick two words that you were able to figure out the meaning of by
using context clues. Write the words and their meanings on the lines.**

_____

_____

Name _____

Read each sentence. Underline the context clues that help you figure out the meaning of each word in bold. Then write the meaning of the word on the line. Use a dictionary and your background knowledge to help you.

1. The week is almost over! There's just one day **left** before we go home for the weekend.

   _____

2. When you get to the corner you should turn **left**.

   _____

3. In autumn my dad rakes up loose leaves and **sticks** that lie on the front lawn.

   _____

4. When you add glue to the paper, it **sticks** to any surface.

   _____

5. I love when my aunt visits me. She always tells me great **stories**.

   _____

6. This building has four **stories** and I live on the third floor.

   _____

Name _____

> A **noun** is a word that names a person, place, or thing.
>
> • A **common noun** names any person, place, or thing: *apple, library, chair, mother*.
>
> • A **proper noun** names a special person, place, or thing. It begins with a capital letter.
>
> • **Proper nouns** include people's names, towns, states, holidays, days, months, streets, special events, geographical names, and historical periods: *Michael, Dallas, Thanksgiving, July, Main St.*

Read each sentence. Write *common* or *proper* under each underlined noun.

1. William raked the leaves for Mr. Ames.

_____

2. A storm blew down a huge tree on Second Street.

_____

3. Jess planted trees in Gable Park.

_____

4. Sasha bought a large pumpkin at the Janesville Fall Festival.

_____

5. Mom grows colorful flowers in her planters.

 **In your writer's notebook, write about your favorite holiday. When you're done, check that you capitalized the holiday and other proper nouns. Use a dictionary to check your spelling of common nouns or other words you used in your writing.**

Name _____

> • A **concrete noun** names a person, place, or thing that can be seen or identified with the five senses: *New York, banana, book.*
>
> • An **abstract noun** names something that cannot be seen or identified with the five senses. Abstract nouns usually name ideas: *joy, peace, friendship.*

A. Write *concrete* or *abstract* to identify each underlined noun.

1. <u>Nina</u> wrote a report about Dr. Martin Luther King Jr. _____

2. Dr. King wrote a speech about the value of <u>freedom</u>. _____

3. Keely read a <u>book</u> about American presidents. _____

4. She found the book at the <u>library</u>. _____

5. Abraham Lincoln was known for his <u>honesty</u>. _____

6. A <u>firefighter</u> talked to our class about his job. _____

7. We thanked him for his <u>bravery</u>. _____

B. Reread this paragraph from "Every Vote Counts!" Find and circle the abstract noun in the underlined sentence.

> Voting helps kids learn how to be independent and think for themselves. <u>It also gives them the power to share how they feel.</u> Kids Voting USA wants kids to vote now. There's a good reason. They estimate that when these kids grow up, more of them will vote.

Name_____

> • A **proper noun** names a special person, place, or thing.
>
> • **Proper nouns** include names, holidays, days of the week, months, product names, book titles, historical periods, titles with a name, initials, and geographic names and places.
>
> • Proper nouns begin with a capital letter. Capitalize the important words in proper nouns. Short words such as *of* and *and* are usually not capitalized.

Underline the proper noun in each sentence. Write it correctly on the line. Capitalize the first letter of each important word.

1. We went to the park on saturday. _____

2. Later we walked to oakville market. _____

3. The owner is mr. simpson. _____

4. The store only closes on new year's day. _____

5. What time does hill street library close? _____

6. The title of my favorite book is *boxes of bananas*. _____

7. Is mother's day next month? _____

8. We have always wanted to see the grand canyon. _____

 **In your writer's notebook, write about something you did over the weekend. Reread your writing when you're done to make sure you capitalized proper nouns.**

Name _____

> • A **common noun** names any person, place, or thing.
>
> • A **proper noun** names a special person, place, or thing. It begins with a capital letter.

Rewrite the letter so that proper nouns begin with capital letters.

Dear principal ortiz,

    Our class would like to visit the sander's science museum. It is only twenty miles from school. We would like to go on may 1st. The museum will have a special speaker that day. dr. cane will tell us about the oceans. We have been studying the atlantic ocean. We will get to see all kinds of seashells at the museum. It will be fun for our class to take this field trip. Please let our teacher, mr. rahim, know your decision soon.

Thank you,

Alana Teal

_____

_____

_____

_____

_____

_____

_____

_____

Name _____

A. Read the paragraph. Then answer the questions.

(1) The peregrine falcon is the fastest animal on Earth. (2) The falcon soars high in the air to search for food. (3) When it spots its prey, it dives down with great skill and speed. (4) The falcon's teardrop shape allows it to reach speeds of 200 miles per hour.

1. Which word in sentence 2 is a common noun?
   A falcon
   B soars
   C high
   D search

2. Which word in sentence 3 is an abstract noun?
   F dives
   G ground
   H great
   J skill

B. Read the student draft and look for revisions to be made.

(1) My swim team is named the Marlins. (2) We practice every saturday morning. (3) Sometimes the water is cold, but we warm up quickly. (4) Last week, Coach smith showed me how to do the backstroke. (5) I can't wait to swim in our next race!

3. What change, if any, should be made to sentence 2?
   A Change *We* to *we*
   B Change *practice* to *Practice*
   C Change *saturday* to *Saturday*
   D Make no change

4. What change, if any, should be made to sentence 4?
   F Change *week* to *Week*
   G Change *Coach smith* to *Coach Smith*
   H Change *me* to *Me*
   J Make no change

Name _____

Fold back the
paper along
the dotted line.
Use the blanks
to write each
word as it is
read aloud.
When you finish
the test, unfold
the paper. Use
the list at the
right to correct
any spelling
mistakes.

1. _____
2. _____
3. _____
4. _____
5. _____
6. _____
7. _____
8. _____
9. _____
10. _____
11. _____
12. _____
13. _____
14. _____
15. _____

Review Words
16. _____
17. _____
18. _____

Challenge Words
19. _____
20. _____

1. sky
2. fry
3. pie
4. tied
5. tight
6. right
7. bright
8. grind
9. child
10. cube
11. cute
12. mule
13. music
14. drew
15. few
16. coast
17. scold
18. bone
19. mighty
20. Utah

Name _____

The long *i* vowel sound can be spelled in a few different ways: *i* as in *wild*, *y* as in *try*, *ie* as in *lie*, and *igh* as in *high*. Long *u* can be spelled *u_e* as in *tube* and *ew* as in *grew*.

COMMON ERRORS

When a word is spelled with a vowel, consonant, and final *e*, the vowel sound is usually long: *take, bone, slide.* Be careful of exceptions that do not have a long vowel sound: *give, move, have, come.*

Read aloud each spelling word in the box. Then write the spelling words that contain the matching long vowel spelling.

right	mule	music	fry	bright
cube	tight	tied	cute	grind
pie	sky	child	drew	few

long *i* spelled *y*

1. _____
2. _____

long *i* spelled *ie*

3. _____
4. _____

long *u* spelled *u*

5. _____

long *i* spelled *igh*

6. _____
7. _____
8. _____

long *i* spelled *i*

9. _____
10. _____

long *u* spelled *u_e*

11. _____
12. _____
13. _____

long *u* spelled *ew*

14. _____
15. _____

Name _____

The long *i* vowel sound can be spelled in a few different ways: *i* as in *wild*, *y* as in *try*, *ie* as in *lie*, and *igh* as in *high*. Long *u* can be spelled *u_e* as in *tube* and *ew* as in *grew*.

COMMON ERRORS

When a word is spelled with a vowel, consonant, and final *e*, the vowel sound is usually long: *take, bone, slide*. Be careful of exceptions that do not have a long vowel sound: *give, move, have, come*.

Read aloud each spelling word in the box. Then write the spelling words that contain the matching long vowel spelling.

sky	mule	bite	cute	cube
unit	find	few	right	fly
might	child	use	huge	pie

long *i* spelled *y*

1. _____

2. _____

long *i* spelled *ie*

3. _____

long *i* spelled *igh*

4. _____

5. _____

long *i* spelled *i_e*

6. _____

long *i* spelled *i*

7. _____

8. _____

long *u* spelled *ew*

9. _____

long *u* spelled *u*

10. _____

long *u* spelled *u_e*

11. _____

12. _____

13. _____

14. _____

15. _____

Name _____

A. Read aloud each spelling word in the box. Then write the spelling words that contain the matching long vowel spelling.

grind	human	tied	rude	music
few	cube	firefly	fume	mild
child	tightly	mighty	right	menu

long *i* spelled *i*

1. _____

2. _____

3. _____

long *i* spelled *igh*

4. _____

5. _____

6. _____

long *i* spelled *ie*

7. _____

long *u* spelled *u_e*

8. _____

9. _____

10. _____

long *u* spelled *u*

11. _____

12. _____

13. _____

long *u* spelled *ew*

14. _____

15. Which word has two long *i* spellings? _____

B. Compare the words *few* and *menu*. How are the two words alike? How are they different?

_____

_____

Name _____

sky	tied	bright	cube	music
few	tight	grind	right	drew
pie	cute	child	mule	fry

A. Write the spelling word that matches each definition below.

1. young person _____
2. half horse, half donkey _____
3. opposite of wrong _____
4. round dessert _____
5. not many _____

B. Write the spelling word that best completes each sentence.

6. We learned to _____ fish at camp this summer.

7. The coat I wore last year is too _____ now.

8. We saw a man _____ wheat into flour at the mill.

9. I think the puppy with the long, floppy ears is so _____.

10. In art today, I _____ a picture of my big brother.

11. I listen to all kinds of _____ on the radio.

12. Let's refill the ice _____ trays with water.

13. The flashlight sent out a _____ signal in the dark.

14. I _____ my little sister's shoes for the third time.

15. Dark storm clouds gathered in the _____ over the city.

Name _____

There are six spelling mistakes in the paragraphs below. Underline each misspelled word. Write the words correctly on the lines.

Once there was a little boy who had a pet mewle. One day they went to town to buy some apple pigh. The skiye was clear and blue that day.

On the way home, the boy heard mewsic. He saw a cewte kitten playing a horn. The boy drue a picture of the kitten and put it on his wall.

1. _____   4. _____

2. _____   5. _____

3. _____   6. _____

Writing Connection **Write a story about an animal that can play music. Try to use at least four of the spelling words in your story.**

_____

_____

_____

_____

_____

_____

_____

Name _____

Long *i* can be spelled with the letter *i* only, as in *idea* and *final*. It can also be spelled *y* as in *try*, *ie* as in *lie*, *igh* as in *light*, and *i_e* as in *kite*. Long *u* can be spelled with the letter *u* as in *unit*, *ew* as in *flew*, and *u_e* as in *mute*.

Circle and read aloud the spelling word in each row that has the same vowel sound as the word in bold. Then write the word on the line.

1. **mild**	willed	child	coin	_____
2. **use**	cute	until	run	_____
3. **ice**	inch	pie	kit	_____
4. **kite**	paint	hint	tight	_____
5. **fume**	some	drum	few	_____
6. **find**	wink	grind	found	_____
7. **hide**	hand	slid	tied	_____
8. **zoo**	book	gown	drew	_____
9. **white**	wait	right	wheat	_____
10. **use**	cube	tub	would	_____
11. **rice**	rich	sky	stray	_____
12. **mute**	duck	sunny	music	_____
13. **shy**	fry	silly	ship	_____
14. **huge**	thumb	mule	wool	_____
15. **high**	swing	grill	bright	_____

Name _____

Content words are words specific to a field of study. *Government* and *voting* are social studies content words.

Authors use content words to explain a concept or an idea. You can figure out what a content word means by using context clues or a dictionary.

CONNECT TO CONTENT

"Every Vote Counts" explains how voting works. The author uses content words related to this topic to help you understand how important it is to vote on issues in your community.

Go on a word hunt with a partner. Find content words related to voting and elections. Write them on the ballot box below.

Pick two words that you can figure out the meaning of by using context clues. Write the words and what they mean on the lines.

_____

_____

Name _____

Use the words and clues below to solve the crossword puzzle.

classmate	monument	traces	clues
scared	grand	massive	admires
landmark	contribute	carved	national

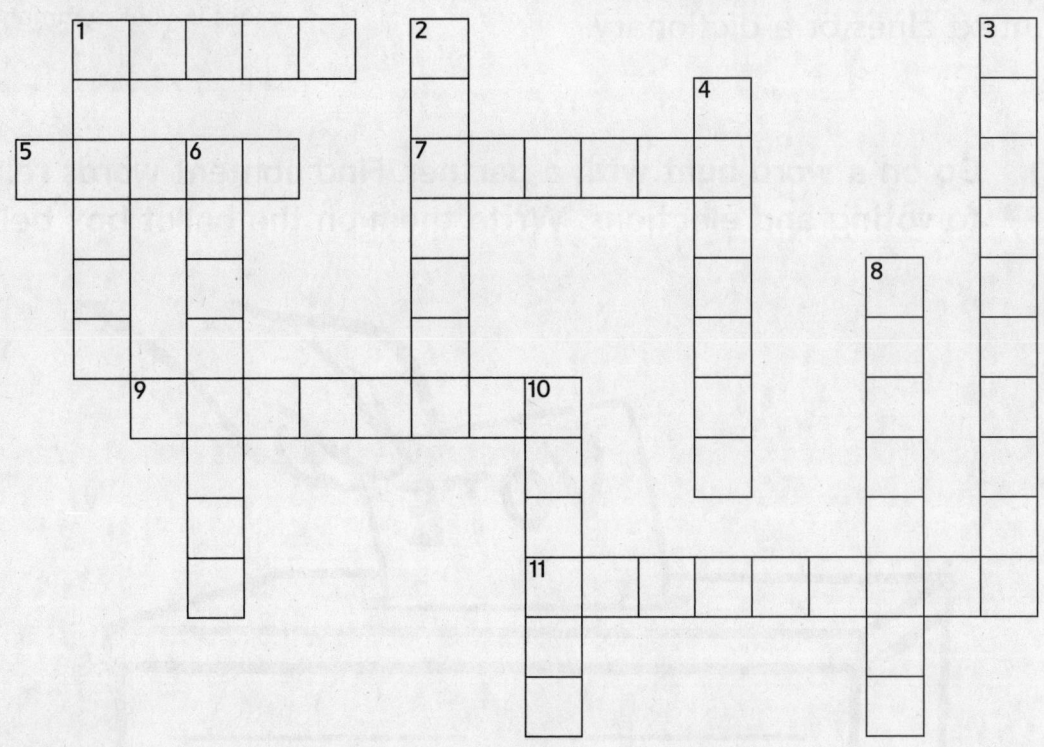

Across

1. Hints

5. Great or large

7. Afraid

9. Something built to honor someone

11. Who you go to school with

Down

1. Cut or etched into

2. Very big

3. Add to something

4. Likes or respects

6. Relating to a country

8. An important object or place

10. Remains of something

Name _____

> A **singular noun** names one person, place, or thing. A **plural noun** names more than one person, place, or thing.
>
> • Add **-s** to form the plural of most singular nouns: *dogs, cars, cats*.
>
> • Add **-es** if the singular noun ends in **-s, -ch, -sh,** or **-x**: *gases, beaches, dishes, foxes*.
>
> • Singular and plural nouns can be compound words: *sandboxes*.

Write the correct plural form of each singular noun.

1. coat _____

2. wish _____

3. box _____

4. bench _____

5. tree _____

6. cupcake _____

7. patch _____

8. bus _____

Writing Connection **Write about what you like to do when you get home from school. When you're done, use your knowledge of spelling rules and patterns to check for spelling errors in singular and plural nouns. You can also use a dictionary.**

_____

_____

_____

_____

_____

Name _____

> • A **singular noun** names one person, place, or thing. A **plural noun** names more than one person, place, or thing.
>
> • To form the plural of a noun that ends in a consonant and **y**, change the **y** to **i** and add **-es**: *city/cities, baby/babies, fly/flies.*

A. Change each singular noun to a plural noun.

1. library _____   6. butterfly _____

2. puppy _____   7. supply _____

3. party _____   8. family _____

4. sky _____   9. pony _____

5. army _____   10. cherry _____

B. Reread this passage from "A Plan for the People." Find the singular noun ending with a consonant and *y*. Rewrite the word on the line, and then write the word's plural form.

> Some delegates wanted one person to run the new government. Others thought a group should be in charge. They all agreed on one thing. A group should make laws for the country.

_____

Name _____

• A **statement** is a sentence that tells something. It ends in a period: *I went to the store today.*

• A **question** is a sentence that asks something. It ends in a question mark: *What is your favorite book?*

• A **command** is a sentence that tells someone to do something. It ends in a period: *Please wash the dishes.*

• An **exclamation** is a sentence that shows excitement or strong feeling. It ends in an exclamation mark: *I can't wait to get home!*

After each sentence, write *statement, question, command,* or *exclamation.* Rewrite sentences using capital letters and end marks.

1. do you know what time the library opens _____

_____

2. i need to check out a book about sea life _____

_____

3. what amazing creatures sharks are _____

_____

4. get my library card for me, please _____

_____

5. let's go wait out front until the library opens _____

_____

 **In your writer's notebook, write about the next book you would like to check out from your school or community library. Say why you're excited about reading the book.**

Name _____

> • Add **-s** to form the plural of most singular nouns.
>
> • Add **-es** if the singular noun ends in **-s, -ch, -sh,** or **-x**.
>
> • To form the plural of a word that ends in a consonant and **y**, change the **y** to **i** and add **-es**.

A. Read the poster. On the lines below, write the correct plural form of the underlined nouns.

> **Nature Walk**
>
> do you want to learn some new <u>thing</u> Come to the Waterfront Park on Saturday for a nature walk. you will learn the names of all kinds of <u>tree</u> and <u>bush</u> in the park We will help you identify the <u>bird</u> that live there This is a great way for <u>family</u> to spend the day together

1. _____ 2. _____ 3. _____

4. _____ 5. _____

B. Rewrite the paragraph above using the correct plural nouns. Use capital letters and end marks correctly.

_____

_____

_____

_____

_____

Name _____

A. Read the paragraph. Then answer the questions.

(1) Yesterday I watched my sisters run a marathon. (2) A marathon is a very long run. (3) My sisters and the other runners ran more than 26 miles through the city. (4) A big clock was set up at the finish line to show the runners how fast they ran the race. (5) It took most people more than four hours!

1. Which word in sentence 3 is a singular noun?
   A sisters
   B ran
   C through
   D city

2. Which word in sentence 4 is a plural noun?
   F clock
   G line
   H runners
   J race

B. Read the student draft and look for revisions that need to be made.

(1) I have a small garden to grow my own fruits and vegetables. (2) I grow carrots, onions, and strawberrys. (3) I also grow herbs and flowers. (4) I love to watch the bees, butterflys, and hummingbirds dance around the flowers.

3. What change, if any, should be made to sentence 2?
   A Change *carrots* to *carrotes*
   B Change *onions* to *oniones*
   C Change *strawberrys* to *strawberries*
   D Make no change

4. What change, if any, should be made to sentence 4?
   F Change *bees* to *bee*
   G Change *butterflys* to *butterflies*
   H Change *hummingbirds* to *hummingbirdes*
   J Make no change

Name _____

Fold back the
paper along
the dotted line.
Use the blanks
to write each
word as it is
read aloud.
When you finish
the test, unfold
the paper. Use
the list at the
right to correct
any spelling
mistakes.

1. _____
2. _____
3. _____
4. _____
5. _____
6. _____
7. _____
8. _____
9. _____
10. _____
11. _____
12. _____
13. _____
14. _____
15. _____

Review Words

16. _____
17. _____
18. _____

Challenge Words

19. _____
20. _____

1. heel
2. week
3. creek
4. free
5. green
6. street
7. freeze
8. seal
9. weak
10. bean
11. speaks
12. team
13. clean
14. cream
15. field
16. tight
17. tied
18. cute
19. sixteen
20. peanut

Name _____

> The long *e* vowel sound can be spelled *ee* as in *seen*, *ea* as in *deal*, *ee_e* as in *cheese*, and *ie* as in *yield*. Read each word aloud to hear the long *e* sound.

Read aloud each spelling word in the box. Then write the spelling words that contain the matching long *e* spelling.

seal	freeze	free	bean	clean
week	green	weak	street	cream
field	speaks	heel	team	creek

long *e* spelled *ee*

1. _____
2. _____
3. _____
4. _____
5. _____
6. _____

long *e* spelled *ea*

7. _____
8. _____
9. _____
10. _____
11. _____
12. _____
13. _____

long *e* spelled *ee_e*

14. _____

long *e* spelled *ie*

15. _____

 Look back at the selections you read this week, and look for words that have the long *e* vowel sound. Read the words aloud, and record them in your writer's notebook.

Name _____

The long *e* vowel sound can be spelled *ee* as in *seen*, *ea* as in *deal*, *ee_e* as in *cheese*, and *ie* as in *yield*. Read each word aloud to hear the long *e* sound.

SPELLING TIP

In most cases, *i* comes before *e* except after *c*, as in the words *thief* and *receipt*. The letter *i* also comes after *e* in words spelled *eigh*, as in *weigh*, *neighbor*, and *height*.

Read aloud each spelling word in the box. Then write the spelling words that contain the matching long *e* spelling.

heel	green	tree	street	feel
clean	seal	team	teen	week
free	need	meet	bean	leak

long *e* spelled *ee*

1. _____   6. _____

2. _____   7. _____

3. _____   8. _____

4. _____   9. _____

5. _____   10. _____

long *e* spelled *ea*

11. _____

12. _____

13. _____

14. _____

15. _____

 **Look back at the selections you read this week, and look for words that have the long *e* vowel sound. Read the words aloud, and record them in your writer's notebook.**

Name _____

A. Read aloud each spelling word in the box. Then write the spelling words that have the matching long *e* spelling.

heel	clean	weekly	creek	peanut
repeat	weakest	seal	street	freeze
sixteen	field	speaks	free	chief

long *e* spelled *ee* **long *e* spelled *ea*** **long *e* spelled *ee_e***

1. _____ 7. _____ 13. _____

2. _____ 8. _____ **long *e* spelled *ie***

3. _____ 9. _____ 14. _____

4. _____ 10. _____ 15. _____

5. _____ 11. _____

6. _____ 12. _____

B. Compare the words *heel* and *seal*. How are the two words alike? How are they different?

_____

_____

_____

 **Look back at the selections you read this week, and look for words that have the long *e* vowel sound. Read the words aloud, and record them in your writer's notebook.**

Name _____

heel	free	freeze	bean	clean
week	green	seal	speaks	cream
creek	street	weak	team	field

A. Write the spelling word that matches each definition below.

1. seven days _____

4. type of vegetable _____

2. small stream _____

5. opposite of strong _____

3. opposite of dirty _____

B. Write the spelling word that best completes each sentence.

6. He hurt his _____ on a sharp stone.

7. Every Monday you can skate for _____ at the ice rink.

8. We bought _____ paint for the fence.

9. We watched the school band march down the _____.

10. We can _____ water to make ice cubes.

11. I like to watch the baby _____ play in the pool.

12. When the coach _____, we must listen.

13. We sent letters to the coach of our favorite _____.

14. I put milk, butter, eggs, and _____ on my grocery list.

15. We like to play softball in the open _____ near my house.

Name _____

There are six spelling mistakes in the paragraphs below. Underline each misspelled word. Write the words correctly on the lines.

Sam liked helping Pa plow the feeld to grow corn and grean peas. But Sam liked to have fun, too. After a weak of helping out, Sam decided to go fishing.

He started down to the creak with his fishing pole. As he walked down the streat that led away from town, he saw President Abraham Lincoln. The president was talking to a crowd of people. He said that everybody should be frea. Sam never forgot that special day.

1. _____ 4. _____

2. _____ 5. _____

3. _____ 6. _____

Writing Connection **Write a story about meeting someone famous. Use at least four spelling words in your story.**

_____
_____
_____
_____
_____
_____
_____

Name _____

> **Remember**
>
> The long *e* vowel sound has several different spellings. It can be spelled *ee* as in *feet* and *sleet, ea* as in *cheat* and *neat, ee_e* as in *cheese* and *sneeze,* and *ie* as in *yield* and *shield.*

Circle the spelling word in each row that rhymes with the word in bold type. Read the spelling word aloud, and write it on the line.

1. **lean**   plane   loan   green   _____

2. **healed**   should   field   helped   _____

3. **she**   free   stem   show   _____

4. **squeaks** square   speaks   soaks   _____

5. **leak**   weak   lock   cloak   _____

6. **seem**   stump   team   storm   _____

7. **queen**   crane   quite   clean   _____

8. **sneeze**   freeze   steel   snooze   _____

9. **peek**   spark   week   peep   _____

10. **teen**   bean   spine   tune   _____

11. **real**   stroll   boil   seal   _____

12. **heat**   short   street   heart   _____

13. **dream**   cream   drink   ramp   _____

14. **meal**   loom   heel   smell   _____

15. **beak**   brick   steak   creek   _____

Name _____

The best way to learn the definition, or meaning, of an unfamiliar word is to look up the word in a **dictionary**. A dictionary lists words in the English language in alphabetical order.

- The **entry words** show the spelling and number of syllables of each word. **Syllabication** separates the syllables by bullets.

- The **pronunciation** of each word is shown in parentheses.

- The **part of speech** is shown after the pronunciation guide.

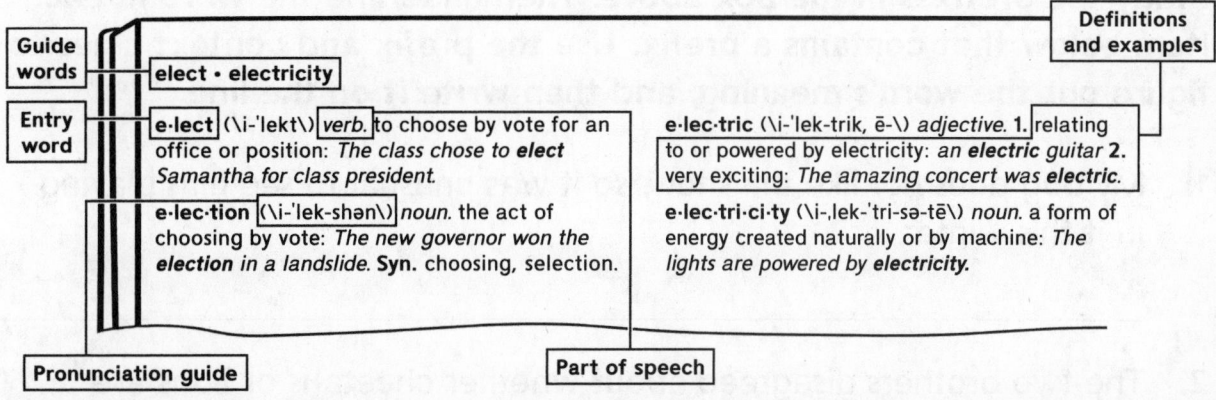

Guide words

Entry word

elect • electricity

e·lect (\i-'lekt\) *verb.* to choose by vote for an office or position: *The class chose to **elect** Samantha for class president.*

e·lec·tion (\i-'lek-shən\) *noun.* the act of choosing by vote: *The new governor won the **election** in a landslide.* **Syn.** choosing, selection.

Definitions and examples

e·lec·tric (\i-'lek-trik, ē-\) *adjective.* **1.** relating to or powered by electricity: *an **electric** guitar* **2.** very exciting: *The amazing concert was **electric**.*

e·lec·tri·ci·ty (\i-,lek-'tri-sə-tē\) *noun.* a form of energy created naturally or by machine: *The lights are powered by **electricity**.*

Pronunciation guide

Part of speech

Use the dictionary entry and context clues to learn the meaning of the words in bold. Write the meaning and part of speech on the lines.

1. On Tuesday people from around the city will cast their ballots and **elect** a new mayor.

_____

2. The US presidential **election** occurs once every four years.

_____

Read aloud the entry words in the dictionary entry with a partner. How many syllables are in each word?

Name _____

> • A **prefix** is a word part added to the beginning of a word. A prefix changes the meaning of the word it is added to. You can use prefixes to figure out the meaning of new words.
>
> • *re-* means *to do again*: *retry* means *to try again*.
>
> • *dis-* means *not* or *opposite*: *disappear* means *to go out of sight*.
>
> • *un-* means *not* or *opposite*: *unhelpful* means *not helpful*.

Study the prefixes in the box above. Then underline the word in each item below that contains a prefix. Use the prefix and context clues to figure out the word's meaning, and then write it on the line.

1. My dog does not like the snow, so it was unusual to see him playing in it this winter.

   _____

2. The two brothers disagreed about whether cheetahs or lions are faster.

   _____

3. We are reviewing Chapter 1 for the test on Monday.

   _____

4. The jungle is full of wild animals, so it is unsafe to walk there alone.

   _____

5. If you don't wear knee pads when you skate, your knees are unprotected.

   _____

Name _____

> Some nouns have special plural forms. They do not add *-s* or *-es* to form a plural.
>
> - The words *men, women,* and *children* are the **irregular plural noun** forms of *man, woman,* and *child.*
> - The word *mice* is the **irregular plural noun** form of *mouse.*
> - **Collective nouns** name groups of people, places, or things: *class, team, band, family.*

A. Complete each sentence with the correct plural form of the noun in parentheses.

1. The (man) _____ who coach the soccer teams talked to our class.

2. The library invited all the (child) _____ to the story hour.

3. I wrote a poem about three small (mouse) _____.

4. We talked to the (woman) _____ about their jobs.

5. I read about the (life) _____ of the presidents.

B. Read each sentence. Underline the collective noun.

6. There are four people in my family.

7. That movie is about a brave army.

8. A jury makes important decisions in a courtroom.

 **Pick one of the irregular plural nouns above. Use that word in a sentence in your writer's notebook. Then pick two more irregular plural nouns, and write two sentences using each.**

Name _____

> • A few plural nouns have the same singular and plural forms. The singular and plural forms of the words *sheep, deer, scissors, fish, moose,* and *salmon* are spelled the same way.
>
> • A few plural nouns change spellings but do not add *-s* or *-es.* The plural form of *tooth* is *teeth*. The plural form of *goose* is *geese*.

A. Write on the line if the underlined noun is *singular* or *plural*.

1. We saw five <u>deer</u> behind our house. _____

2. Do we have enough <u>scissors</u> for everyone? _____

3. I painted a picture of a beautiful <u>trout</u>. _____

4. The <u>fish</u> have been jumping all afternoon. _____

B. Read the excerpt from "Sailing to America." Then answer the questions.

> "Maybe you'll be glad it isn't Ireland," Nora said. "There will be enough <u>food</u> to eat. Mama and Da can relax and not worry so much. We'll all have a better <u>life</u>. America will be the land of our dreams."
>
> Then Da carried a <u>bag</u> into the room. "Cheer up, my little loves! Why, in no time at all, you'll be joining me."
>
> A year later, Da had saved enough money to send for his <u>family</u>. Mama, Danny, and Nora packed what little they had. They got on a crowded <u>steamship</u> and began their voyage.

5. Which underlined noun has an irregular plural form? _____

6. Which underlined noun is a collective noun? _____

Name _____

> • Some plural nouns change spellings but do not add *-s* or *-es*.
> • Some plural nouns have the same spelling as the singular form.

Rewrite the sentences. Use the plural form of the underlined noun.

1. The <u>child</u> swam in the pool.

_____

2. Sometimes my <u>tooth</u> chatter when I am cold.

_____

3. Did you see the blue <u>fish</u> swim by?

_____

4. The <u>mouse</u> hid under the refrigerator.

_____

5. I know the <u>woman</u> who work at the bank.

_____

Writing Connection Pick one of the underlined words above, and write a sentence using the singular form of the word. Then write a new sentence using the plural form.

_____

_____

_____

_____

Name _____

> • Some plural nouns change the spelling of the singular form:
>   *man/men, child/children, goose/geese, wolf/wolves.*
> • Some plural nouns have the same spelling as the singular form:
>   *fish, scissors, pants, deer, moose.*

Proofread the sentences for incorrect plural nouns. Circle each incorrect plural noun, and write its correct form on the line.

1. I think astronauts have exciting lifes. _____

2. The childs had fun building a snowman. _____

3. How many mouses did you see? _____

4. Be careful with the sharp knifes. _____

5. The womans helped with the toy drive. _____

6. The gooses are making too much noise! _____

7. Salmons like to swim upstream. _____

8. Did you know ducks have webbed feets? _____

9. Brush your teeths before going to bed. _____

10. I want to read a book about mooses. _____

Name _____

A. Read the paragraph. Then answer the questions.

(1) Last summer I traveled to the state of Wyoming. (2) My family and I visited Yellowstone National Park. (3) We saw a herd of bison eating some grass in a meadow. (4) We also spotted bears, foxes, moose, and eagles. (5) I've never seen so many beautiful animals.

1. Which word in sentence 3 is a collective noun?

   A herd
   B bison
   C grass
   D meadow

2. Which word in sentence 4 is an irregular plural noun?

   F bears
   G foxes
   H moose
   J eagles

B. Read the student draft, and look for revisions that need to be made.

(1) I'm writing a school report on snakes. (2) Snakes can range in size from just 4 inches to over 22 foots! (3) Smaller snakes eat insects like ants or termites. (4) Larger snakes can eat mammals like mouses, rats, and rabbits. (5) Some snakes, like the water snake, even eat frogs and fish!

3. What change, if any, should be made to sentence 2?

   A Change *foots* to *foot*
   B Change *foots* to *feet*
   C Change *foots* to *feets*
   D Make no change

4. What change, if any, should be made to sentence 4?

   F Change *mouses* to *mice*
   G Change *rats* to *rates*
   H Change *rabbits* to *rabbites*
   J Make no change

5. What change, if any, should be made to sentence 5?

   A Change *frogs* to *froges*
   B Change *fish* to *fishes*
   C Change *fish* to *fishies*
   D Make no change

Name _____

Fold back the paper along the dotted line. Use the blanks to write each word as it is read aloud. When you finish the test, unfold the paper. Use the list at the right to correct any spelling mistakes.

1. _____
2. _____
3. _____
4. _____
5. _____
6. _____
7. _____
8. _____
9. _____
10. _____
11. _____
12. _____
13. _____
14. _____
15. _____

Review Words 16. _____
17. _____
18. _____

Challenge Words 19. _____
20. _____

1. wrap
2. wrists
3. wrote
4. wreck
5. wring
6. write
7. wreath
8. knit
9. knife
10. knight
11. knock
12. knee
13. gnome
14. sign
15. gnaws
16. heel
17. weak
18. field
19. wristwatch
20. knapsack

Name _____

> Some words have silent letters. When *k* is followed by *n*, the *k* is silent: *knew*. The letter *w* is silent before *r*: *wrong*. The letter *g* is usually silent before *n*: *gnaw*.

SPELLING TIP

Silent letters don't always appear at the beginning of a word. The letter *g* is silent in the word *design*. The *w* is silent in the word *sword*.

Read aloud each spelling word in the box. Then write the spelling words that have the matching silent letter spellings.

knee	knife	wreath	knight	gnome
gnaws	wring	knit	knock	write
wrote	sign	wreck	wrap	wrists

wr

1. _____
2. _____
3. _____
4. _____
5. _____
6. _____
7. _____

kn

8. _____
9. _____
10. _____
11. _____
12. _____

gn

13. _____
14. _____
15. _____

 **Look back at the selections you read this week. Hunt for words with the silent letters *k*, *w*, and *g*. Read the words you find aloud, and record them in your writer's notebook.**

Name _____

> Some words have silent letters. When *k* is followed by *n,* the *k* is silent: *knew.* The letter *w* is silent before *r*: *wrong.* The letter *g* is usually silent before *n*: *gnaw.*

SPELLING TIP

Silent letters don't always appear at the beginning of a word. The letter *g* is silent in the word *design.* The *w* is silent in the word *sword.*

Read aloud each spelling word in the box. Then write the spelling words that have the matching silent letter spellings.

wrap	knot	wren	know	gnat
gnaws	write	knit	wring	wrists
wrote	wrong	sign	knee	knock

wr   **kn**   **gn**

1. _____   8. _____   13. _____

2. _____   9. _____   14. _____

3. _____   10. _____ 15. _____

4. _____   11. _____

5. _____   12. _____

6. _____

7. _____

 **Look back at the selections you read this week. Hunt for words with the silent letters *k, w,* and *g.* Read the words you find aloud, and record them in your writer's notebook.**

Name _____

A. Read aloud each spelling word in the box. Then write the spelling words that contain the matching spelling of the silent letters.

knock	wring	wristwatch	wrench	wrists
gnaws	writing	wrinkle	knead	wrote
wreck	knapsack	knitted	knight	gnome

wr	kn	gn
1. _____	9. _____	14. _____
2. _____	10. _____	15. _____
3. _____	11. _____	
4. _____	12. _____	
5. _____	13. _____	
6. _____		
7. _____		
8. _____		

B. Compare the words *knight* and *gnome*. How are the words alike? How are they different?

_____

_____

_____

 **Look back at the selections you read this week. Hunt for words with the silent letters *k, w,* and *g*. Read the words you find aloud, and record them in your writer's notebook.**

Name _____

wrap	gnaws	wreath	knight	gnome
sign	wring	knit	knock	wrists
wrote	knee	knife	write	wreck

A. Write the spelling words that match the clues below.

1. street marker _____

2. tap on a door _____

3. a ring of plants used for decoration _____

4. a sharp tool _____

5. cover a gift with paper _____

B. Write the spelling word that best completes each sentence.

6. The doctor checked both her _____ after she fell.

7. He _____ a letter to the mayor about the park.

8. I am learning to _____ a wool scarf.

9. A beaver _____ trees into logs.

10. My friend likes to _____ silly poems about animals.

11. My little sisters _____ my room when they come in.

12. My story is about a brave _____ who fights dragons.

13. I scraped my left _____ when I fell off my bike.

14. A _____ is small and usually wears a pointed hat.

15. We will _____ out the wet towels.

Name _____

There are six spelling mistakes in the paragraphs below. Underline each misspelled word. Then write the words correctly on the lines below.

When people run for office, they often nock on doors to ask people for votes. They have to rite speeches, too. They may make a sine for people to see.

I rote a funny story. It was about a mayor. He was a little green nome. Everybody voted for him. His best friend was a brave night who kept the town safe.

1. _____   4. _____

2. _____   5. _____

3. _____   6. _____

Writing Connection **Write about an election in your town. Use at least four spelling words in your writing.**

_____

_____

_____

_____

_____

_____

_____

_____

Name _____

Remember

Some words have silent letters, or letters that you do not pronounce. If a word begins with *wr*, the *w* is silent, as in the words *wrong* and *wreck*. If a word begins with *kn*, the *k* is silent, as in *knew* and *knot*. When a word is spelled with *gn*, the *g* is usually silent, as in *gnat* and *design*.

knee	gnaws	wreath	knight	wrote
wrists	wring	knit	knock	sign
gnome	write	knife	wrap	wreck

Write the missing letters to make a spelling word. Read each spelling word aloud, and then write the word on the line.

1. ____ ____ ife _____

2. ____ ____ ists _____

3. ____ ____ ome _____

4. ____ ____ eck _____

5. ____ ____ ing _____

6. ____ ____ ock _____

7. ____ ____ eath _____

8. ____ ____ it _____

9. ____ ____ ap _____

10. ____ ____ ight _____

11. ____ ____ ite _____

12. ____ ____ ee _____

13. ____ ____ ote _____

14. si ____ ____ _____

15. ____ ____ aws _____

Name _____

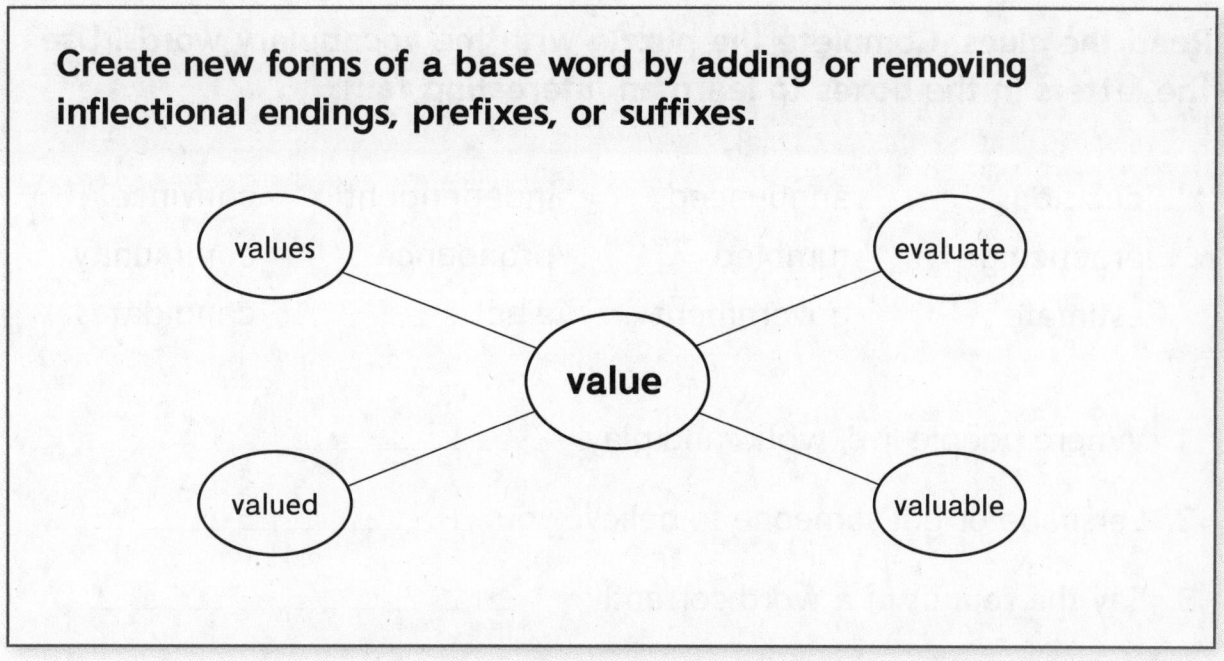

Create new forms of a base word by adding or removing inflectional endings, prefixes, or suffixes.

Use your notes from *The Castle on Hester Street*. Choose one word, and write it on the middle castle flag. Then fill in the remaining four flags with related words. Use a dictionary to help you.

Name _____

Read the clues. Complete the puzzle with the vocabulary words. Use the letters in the boxes to learn an interesting fact.

decisions	announced	independent	convince
practicing	tumbled	pronounce	community
estimate	government	elect	candidates

1. Where people live, work, and play _ _ _ _ _ _ _ _ _

2. Persuade or get someone to believe you _ _ _ _ _ _ _ _

3. Say the sounds of a word correctly _ _ _ _ _ _ _ _ _

4. Able to do things on your own _ _ _ _ _ _ _ _ _ _ _

5. Took a fall _ _ _ _ _ _ _

6. People running for office _ _ _ _ _ _ _ _ _ _

7. Repeating a task to get better _ _ _ _ _ _ _ _ _ _

8. Made known to a group of people _ _ _ _ _ _ _ _ _

9. Choose by voting _ _ _ _ _

10. Guess an amount of something _ _ _ _ _ _ _ _

11. The group in control of a country _ _ _ _ _ _ _ _ _ _

12. Choices you make _ _ _ _ _ _ _ _ _

This animal has many different names. In fact, it is listed in the dictionary under more names than any other animal. What is it?

Name _____

- **Combine sentences** by joining two nouns to form a compound subject.

- Use the word *and* to join the nouns. Leave out words that repeat. Make subjects and verbs agree.

- A combined sentence has a complete subject and predicate.

- The sentences *Apples grow on trees* and *Pears grow on trees* can be combined to read *Apples and pears grow on trees.*

Combine the sentences by joining the two nouns in the subject. Write the new sentence on the line.

1. Parents enjoyed the play. Children enjoyed the play.

_____

2. The grass swayed in the wind. The trees swayed in the wind.

_____

3. The story was really interesting. The pictures were really interesting.

_____

4. Carson helped clean up trash from the beach. Carson's friend helped clean up trash from the beach.

_____

5. The hawks fly high in the air. The eagles fly high in the air.

_____

 **In your writer's notebook, write about something fun you did with a friend. When you're done, check that you used the word *and* to form compound subjects, and make sure your subjects and verbs agree.**

Name _____

> • Sentences can be combined by joining two **predicate nouns**.
>
> • Use *and* to join the nouns. Leave out words that repeat.
>
> • A combined sentence has a complete subject and predicate.
>
> • The sentences *We built sandcastles* and *We built forts* can be combined to read *We built sandcastles and forts*.

A. Combine the sentences. Use the word *and* to join the underlined predicate nouns. Write the new sentences on the lines.

1. At the beach we saw <u>seagulls</u>. At the beach we saw <u>pelicans</u>.

   _____

2. The pelicans ate <u>fish</u>. The pelicans ate <u>crabs</u>.

   _____

3. Mom packed <u>sandwiches</u>. Mom packed <u>fruit</u>.

   _____

B. Read the excerpt from "Next Stop, America!" Combine the two underlined sentences. Write the new sentence on the lines below.

<u>The immigrants spoke many languages. They had different customs.</u> However, everyone shared one thing. They had all chosen to immigrate. They wanted to move to a new country. They wanted to be Americans.

_____

_____

Name _____

> - Use a comma between the day and year in a date: *May 5, 1991.*
> - Use a comma between a street address and a town or city and between a town or city and state: *25 Main Street, Denver, Colorado.*
> - Use commas to separate three or more items in a series. Do not use a comma after the last word: *I bought milk, eggs, and apples.*
> - Use a comma in direct address after the name of a person being spoken to and after words such as *yes* and *no* when beginning a sentence: *Ali, I like your tie! Yes, I will go to the beach with you.*

Rewrite each sentence. Add commas in the correct places.

1. Our new address is 24 Elm Street Madison Ohio.

   _____

2. I got books toys and a basketball for my birthday.

   _____

3. George Washington was born on February 22 1732.

   _____

4. Mr. Miller do you need someone to rake your leaves?

   _____

5. Yes I would be happy for you to help me today.

   _____

 **In your writer's notebook, list some of your favorite animals. Say why you like them. Check that you used commas to separate items in a series. Remember to write your thoughts legibly in cursive, and leave spaces between words.**

Name _____

> - Use a comma between the day and year in a date.
>
> - Use a comma between the names of a city or town and state and between a street address and the name of a town or city.
>
> - Use commas to separate three or more words in a series. Do not use a comma after the last word.
>
> - Use a comma after the name of a person being spoken to and after words such as *yes* and *no* when beginning a sentence.

Rewrite each sentence. Add commas in the correct places. Combine sentences that share the same subject nouns or predicate nouns.

1. Our teacher read the stories. Our teacher read the poems.

_____

_____

HANDWRITING CONNECTION

Be sure to write legibly. Use proper cursive and remember to leave spaces between words.

2. My grandmother moved to 68 Palm Court Sunnydale Florida.

_____

3. Mrs. Stamps thank you for visiting our school today.

_____

4. James likes to draw spaceships. Mark likes to draw spaceships.

_____

5. The first time our town had a parade was July 4 1892.

_____

Name _____

Read the student draft and look for revisions that need to be made.

(1) My aunt lives near the Great Smoky Mountains. (2) My uncle also lives near the Great Smoky Mountains. (3) They live in a town named Gatlinburg Tennessee. (4) I visited them last spring for my uncle's birthday. (5) "Carl happy birthday!" they said. (6) To celebrate, we baked lemon pie. (7) We baked cherry pie.

1. What is the best way to combine sentences 1 and 2?
   A My aunt lives near the Great Smoky Mountains and my uncle lives near the Great Smoky Mountains.
   B My aunt lives near the Great Smoky Mountains and my uncle lives near there.
   C My aunt and my uncle live near the Great Smoky Mountains.
   D My aunt lives near the Great Smoky Mountains and my uncle also.

2. What is the correct way to write sentence 3?
   F They live in a town named Gatlinburg, Tennessee.
   G They live, in a town named Gatlinburg Tennessee.
   H They live in a town named, Gatlinburg Tennessee.
   J No change needed in sentence 3.

3. What change should be made to sentence 5?
   A Carl happy birthday, they said.
   B "Carl, happy birthday!" they said.
   C Carl, "happy birthday!" they said.
   D No change needed in sentence 5.

4. What is the best way to combine sentences 6 and 7?
   F To celebrate, we baked lemon pie and we baked cherry pie.
   G To celebrate, we baked lemon pie and cherry pie.
   H To celebrate, we baked lemon pie and we celebrated with cherry pie.
   J We baked lemon pie to celebrate and we baked cherry pie to celebrate.

Name _____

Fold back the paper along the dotted line. Use the blanks to write each word as it is read aloud. When you finish the test, unfold the paper. Use the list at the right to correct any spelling mistakes.

1. _____
2. _____
3. _____
4. _____
5. _____
6. _____
7. _____
8. _____
9. _____
10. _____
11. _____
12. _____
13. _____
14. _____
15. _____

Review Words
16. _____
17. _____
18. _____

Challenge Words
19. _____
20. _____

1. scrubs
2. screams
3. scratch
4. scrape
5. screen
6. spread
7. splash
8. spray
9. streak
10. strength
11. strong
12. squeak
13. three
14. throw
15. thread
16. wrote
17. knife
18. sign
19. streamer
20. scribble

Name _____

> Three-letter blends are sounds made by three letters in a row. The letters *scr* make the sound at the beginning of the word *scrap*. Other three-letter blends are *str* as in *strap, spr* as in *spring, spl* as in *split, squ* as in *squid,* and *thr* as in *threw*.

Read aloud the spelling words in the box. Then write the spelling words that contain the three-letter blends below.

strength	scrape	squeak	screams	three
scrubs	throw	spray	strong	screen
splash	spread	streak	scratch	thread

scr

1. _____
2. _____
3. _____
4. _____
5. _____

spr

6. _____
7. _____

str

8. _____
9. _____
10. _____

thr

11. _____
12. _____
13. _____

squ

14. _____

spl

15. _____

Name _____

Three-letter blends are sounds made by three letters in a row. The letters *scr* make the sound at the beginning of the word *scrap*. Other three-letter blends are *str* as in *strap, spr* as in *spring, spl* as in *split, squ* as in *squid,* and *thr* as in *threw.*

DECODING WORDS

The three-letter blends *scr, spr, spl, str, squ,* and *thr* usually appear at the beginning of a word. If you see these letters in the middle of the word, they might not stand for one sound. For example, the letters *spl* in *display* are divided between two syllables: *dis/play.*

Read aloud the spelling words in the box. Then write the spelling words that contain the three-letter blends below.

split	squeak	splash	squint	three
throw	spray	straw	scrubs	screen
scrap	stream	thrill	strong	spree

scr

1. _____

2. _____

3. _____

spr

4. _____

5. _____

spl

6. _____

7. _____

str

8. _____

9. _____

10. _____

squ

11. _____

12. _____

thr

13. _____

14. _____

15. _____

Name _____

A. Read aloud the spelling words in the box. Then write the spelling words that contain the three-letter blends below.

scrubs	throne	sprinkle	strength	spray
threaten	scribble	throw	screams	scratch
scrape	spread	splinter	squeak	strong

	scr		spr		str
1. _____		6. _____		11. _____	
2. _____		7. _____		12. _____	
3. _____		8. _____			**thr**
4. _____			**spl**	13. _____	
5. _____		9. _____		14. _____	
			squ	15. _____	
		10. _____			

B. Compare the words *spray* and *strength*. How are they alike? How are they different?

_____

_____

 **Look at the selections you read this week, and look for words with the three-letter blends *scr, spr, spl, str, thr,* or *squ.* Read the words aloud, and record them in your writer's notebook.**

Name _____

streak	three	splash	strength	scrape
thread	screen	strong	spray	throw
scratch	spread	scrubs	squeak	screams

A. Write the spelling word that goes with the other two words.

1. washes, cleans, _____

2. powerful, mighty, _____

3. pitch, toss, _____

4. needle, scissors, _____

5. peep, squeal, _____

B. Write the spelling word that best completes each sentence.

6. The excited fan _____ when her team wins.

7. He had to teach his cat not to _____ the sofa.

8. I helped Dad _____ the old paint off the door.

9. Our tent flap has a _____ that keeps the bugs out.

10. I will _____ frosting on the cake.

11. We can use the water hose to _____ the sand off our feet.

12. The prize winner said that he had a _____ of good luck.

13. He used his _____ to lift the heavy box.

14. I will need _____ more dollars to buy that book.

15. When he stepped in the puddle, there was a huge _____!

Name _____

There are six spelling mistakes in the paragraphs below. Underline each misspelled word. Write the words correctly on the lines.

An eagle is a very shtrong bird. They spred their wings wide to fly high into the air. They fly so fast they look like a streek against the sky.

I saw theree whales on our island tour. I watched one blue whale shpray water into the air. Whales have a lot of srength to be able to swim so fast.

1. _____   4. _____

2. _____   5. _____

3. _____   6. _____

Writing Connection **Write an article about an animal that is very strong. Use at least four spelling words.**

_____
_____
_____
_____
_____
_____
_____
_____

Name _____

Remember

Three-letter blends are sounds created when three consonants are blended together. The letters *scr* create the three-letter blend in the word *scroll*. The letters *spr* create the blend in the words *sprint* and *spring*. Other common three-letter blends include *spl* as in *splat*, *str* as in *straw*, *squ* as in *squid*, and *thr* as in *throne*.

screen	throw	thread	strength	three
screams	scrubs	spray	strong	scrape
squeak	spread	streak	scratch	splash

Write the missing letters to make a spelling word. Read the spelling word aloud, and then write it on the line.

1. ___ ___ ___ ubs _____

2. ___ ___ ___ eams _____

3. ___ ___ ___ ow _____

4. ___ ___ ___ ape _____

5. ___ ___ ___ een _____

6. ___ ___ ___ ead _____

7. ___ ___ ___ ash _____

8. ___ ___ ___ ay _____

9. ___ ___ ___ eak _____

10. ___ ___ ___ ead _____

11. ___ ___ ___ ong _____

12. ___ ___ ___ eak _____

13. ___ ___ ___ ee _____

14. ___ ___ ___ atch _____

15. ___ ___ ___ ength _____

Name _____

> Like **homonyms, homographs** are words that have the same spelling but different meanings. For example, the word *bear* can refer to the large animal, or it can be a verb that means *to carry or support.*
>
> Unlike homonyms, even though homographs are spelled the same way, they are not always pronounced the same way. The *bow* or front of a ship rhymes with *how,* but the *bow* in someone's hair rhymes with *toe.*

Read the sentences below. Underline the context clues that help you understand the meaning of each homograph in bold. Then write the meaning of the homograph on the line.

1. When the wind died down I had to **row** my boat back to shore.

   _____

2. I lined up my tomato plants in a neat **row** in my backyard.

   _____

3. The carpenter cut through the tree trunk with a **saw**.

   _____

4. The bird was hard to spot, but I finally **saw** it hiding in the tree.

   _____

5. To **train** for a marathon, you must practice for months or even years.

   _____

6. I could hear a **train** traveling down the railroad far in the distance.

   _____

Name _____

A. Read the sentences. Write whether the sentence has a simile or hyperbole. Then write what the simile or hyperbole means on the line.

1. Lan was as white as a ghost.

   _____

2. Why, in no time at all, you'll be joining us.

   _____

3. The future was as open as the land.

   _____

B. Read the sentences below. Complete each simile or hyperbole by choosing the correct word from the box.

desert	million	mile	night

4. The glass broke into a _____ pieces.

5. With no rain, the landscape was as dry as a _____.

6. It was the middle of the day, but inside the forest it was as black as _____.

7. To Sara, it seemed that the door to the tower was a _____ high.

Name _____

> • A possessive noun is a noun that shows who or what owns or has something. In the sentence *I went to Kim's house* the possessive noun is *Kim's.*
>
> • Add an **apostrophe** (') and the letter *s* to make a singular noun possessive: *The dog's ball.*

A. Write the possessive form of each underlined noun on the line. The first one is done for you.

1. the tail of the pig   the __pig's__ tail

2. the ears of the rabbit   the _____ ears

3. the trunk of the elephant   the _____ trunk

4. the neck of the giraffe   the _____ neck

5. the whiskers of the cat   the _____ whiskers

6. the teeth of the shark   the _____ teeth

7. the feathers of the hawk   the _____ feathers

B. Read the excerpt from "Empanada Day." Find and circle the possessive noun. What belongs to the possessive noun you circled? Write your answer on the line below.

> One bite of Abuelita's empanadas
> And my mouth purrs like a cat.
>   "Teach me," I beg and bounce on my feet,
>   "Teach me to make this magical treat."

_____

Name _____

> • Adding an apostrophe to the end of a plural noun makes it possessive. For example, a nest that belongs to two birds is a *birds' nest*.
>
> • Adding an apostrophe and *s* forms a possessive of plural nouns not ending in *s*. These are called **irregular possessives**. Examples include *men's* and *women's*.
>
> • **Collective nouns** are a singular form of a word that refers to a group of things: *family, group, band, herd*.

Write the possessive form of each underlined plural noun.

1. the den of the <u>rabbits</u>   the _____ den

2. the cage of the <u>parrots</u>   the _____ cage

3. the pond of the <u>ducks</u>   the _____ pond

4. the home of the <u>family</u>   the _____ home

5. the lodge of the <u>beavers</u>   the _____ lodge

6. the nest of the <u>bluebirds</u>   the _____ nest

7. the burrow of the <u>chipmunks</u>   the _____ burrow

8. the cave of the <u>bears</u>   the _____ cave

9. the web of the <u>spiders</u>   the _____ web

10. the room of the <u>children</u>   the _____ room

 **In your writer's notebook, write three complete sentences using plural possessive nouns. You can select one of the nouns from the questions above or think of your own.**

Name _____

- Add an apostrophe and *s* to singular possessive nouns.
- Add an apostrophe at the end of plural possessive nouns that end in *s*: *The two swans' pond.*
- Add an apostrophe and *s* to the end of plural possessive nouns not ending in *s*: *The men's baseball team.*

Complete each sentence with the possessive form of the noun in parentheses.

1. The (moose) _____ antlers are large.

2. The (horse) _____ mane is soft and silky.

3. (Porcupines) _____ quills are sharp.

4. A (rabbit) _____ tail is like cotton.

5. The (owls) _____ eyes are round.

Connect to Community
Talk to a parent or another trusted adult about some of the animals that live around your community. What are some of their features? Why are they important?

_____

_____

_____

_____

_____

_____

Name _____

> • Add an apostrophe and *s* to singular possessive nouns.
>
> • Add an apostrophe to plural possessive nouns that end in *s*.
>
> • Add an apostrophe and *s* to the end of plural possessive nouns not ending in *s*.

Mark an X over any possessive noun that is not written correctly. Rewrite the sentence on the line using the correct form of each possessive noun.

1. The volunteer womens group at the hospital held a bake sale.

   _____

2. They raised money to help decorate the childrens's wing.

   _____

3. Now there is a beautiful mural showing animals homes.

   _____

4. My favorite part shows the Pacific Oceans's sea life.

   _____

5. I love the colors of the coral and fishes scales.

   _____

6. My sister likes the speckled pattern on the sea turtles's shells.

   _____

Name _____

A. Read the paragraph. Then answer the questions.

(1) There are many trees outside my bedroom window. (2) On summer mornings I wake up to the sound of the wind in the trees' leaves. (3) Today I heard something new. (4) When I woke up this morning, I heard chirping outside. (5) When I looked into the tree outside, I found a small bird's nest with two blue eggs.

1. Which word in sentence 2 is a plural possessive noun?
   A evenings
   B wind
   C trees'
   D leaves

2. Which word in sentence 5 is a singular possessive noun?
   F tree
   G bird's
   H nest
   J eggs

B. Read the student draft and look for revisions to be made.

(1) Today I found a small spider in the attic of my families home. (2) The spider was building a beautiful web in the shadows. (3) When the spiders web was finished, the spider walked to the edge of the web and sat very still. (4) Soon I heard the buzzing of a small fly. (5) Just like that, the fly was caught in the web.

3. What change, if any, should be made to sentence 1?
   A Change *families* to *families'*
   B Change *families* to *familys'*
   C Change *families* to *family's*
   D Make no change

4. What change, if any, should be made to sentence 3?
   F Change *spiders* to *spider's*
   G Change *spiders* to *spideres*
   H Change *spiders* to *spiders'*
   J Make no change

Name _____

Fold back the paper along the dotted line. Use the blanks to write each word as it is read aloud. When you finish the test, unfold the paper. Use the list at the right to correct any spelling mistakes.

1. _____
2. _____
3. _____
4. _____
5. _____
6. _____
7. _____
8. _____
9. _____
10. _____
11. _____
12. _____
13. _____
14. _____
15. _____

Review Words
16. _____
17. _____
18. _____

Challenge Words
19. _____
20. _____

1. chick
2. much
3. pitch
4. teacher
5. lunch
6. hatch
7. cheese
8. stretch
9. thick
10. truth
11. pathway
12. them
13. fish
14. whales
15. what
16. spray
17. streak
18. thread
19. sandwich
20. weather

Name _____

> Digraphs are two letters that form a new sound. The letters *th* form the sound at the start of *thunder*. The *tch* in *scratch* is a trigraph. Other digraphs are *ch* as in *couch,* *sh* as in *show,* and *wh* as in *where*.

> ## DECODING WORDS
>
> The first syllable in *bathtub* is spelled *bath*. The letter *b* stands for /b/ and *a* stands for /a/. The letters *th* form a digraph that stands for /th/. The second syllable is spelled *tub*. The letter *t* stands for /t/, *u* stands for /u/ and *b* stands for /b/. Blend the letters together and read the word aloud: *bath/tub*.

Read aloud the spelling words in the box. Then write the spelling words that contain the digraphs or trigraph below.

them	teacher	hatch	truth	pitch
thick	what	pathway	stretch	whales
fish	cheese	much	chick	lunch

ch

1. _____

2. _____

3. _____

4. _____

5. _____

th

6. _____

7. _____

8. _____

9. _____

sh

10. _____

tch

11. _____

12. _____

13. _____

wh

14. _____

15. _____

Name _____

Digraphs are two letters that form a new sound. The letters *th* form the sound at the start of *thunder*. The *tch* in *scratch* is a trigraph. Other digraphs are *ch* as in *couch,* *sh* as in *show,* and *wh* as in *where.*

DECODING WORDS

The first syllable in *bathtub* is spelled *bath*. The letter *b* stands for /b/ and *a* stands for /a/. The letters *th* form a digraph that stands for /th/. The second syllable is spelled *tub*. The letter *t* stands for /t/, *u* stands for /u/ and *b* stands for /b/. Blend the letters together and read the word aloud: *bath/tub.*

Read aloud the spelling words in the box. Then write the spelling words that contain the digraphs or trigraph below.

chick	truth	chair	shown	chin
wheel	cheese	sixth	thick	much
pitch	bench	fish	teacher	whales

ch

1. _____
2. _____
3. _____
4. _____
5. _____
6. _____
7. _____

tch

8. _____

th

9. _____
10. _____
11. _____

sh

12. _____
13. _____

wh

14. _____
15. _____

Copyright © McGraw Hill. Permission is granted to reproduce for classroom use.

Name _____

A. Read aloud the spelling words in the box. Then write the spelling words that contain the digraphs or trigraph below.

pitch	what	reach	shadow	thick
whales	stretch	chuckled	pathway	teacher
cheese	search	seashells	weather	crunch

ch	tch	sh
1. _____	7. _____	12. _____
2. _____	8. _____	13. _____
3. _____	**th**	**wh**
4. _____	9. _____	14. _____
5. _____	10. _____	15. _____
6. _____	11. _____	

B. Compare the words *crunch* and *pitch*. How are they alike? How are they different?

_____

_____

_____

 **Review the selections you read this week, and look for words with the digraphs *ch, th, sh,* and *wh* and trigraph *tch*. Read the words you find aloud, and record them in your writer's notebook.**

Name _____

chick	teacher	cheese	truth	fish
whales	lunch	stretch	pathway	much
pitch	hatch	thick	them	what

A. Write the spelling word that matches each definition below.

1. a baby bird _____

2. an honest story _____

3. a kind of dairy food _____

4. an afternoon meal _____

5. large sea animals _____

B. Write the spelling word that best completes each sentence.

6. We had so _____ snow that our schools closed.

7. I can _____ well, but I'm not a good catcher.

8. Our _____ asked us to open our books.

9. Did the turtle eggs _____ yet?

10. After the long test, we walked around to _____ our legs.

11. The ice on the pond is never _____ enough to walk on.

12. We walked down the curving _____ in the park.

13. Apples are my favorite fruit, but I like _____ peeled first.

14. We saw turtles on a log and _____ swimming in the pond.

15. Do you know _____ book we are supposed to read?

Name _____

There are six misspelled words in the paragraphs below. Underline each misspelled word. Write the words correctly on the lines.

Once there were three wales who were best friends. Every day they met for luntch. Then they played games in the wide open sea. One day, a small fisch swam nearby.

He asked if he could join theam. "Sure!" they said and asked him wat he liked to play. He said he liked to pich seashells. So the rest of the day the four friends played together.

1. _____   4. _____

2. _____   5. _____

3. _____   6. _____

Writing Connection **Write a story telling what you like to play with friends. Use at least four spelling words.**

_____
_____
_____
_____
_____
_____
_____
_____
_____

Name _____

Remember

Digraphs are two letters that create a new sound. The beginning sound in *thunder* can be formed only with the letters *th*. Other digraphs include *ch* as in *such,* *sh* as in *push,* and *wh* as in *wheel.* The letters *tch* in *switch* are a trigraph.

them	teacher	hatch	truth	pitch
thick	what	pathway	stretch	whales
fish	cheese	much	chick	lunch

Fill in the missing letters to make a spelling word. Then write the spelling word on the line. Use each word once.

1. ____ ____ ick _____

2. mu ____ ____ _____

3. pit ____ ____ _____

4. tea ____ ____ er _____

5. lun ____ ____ _____

6. hat ____ _____

7. ____ ____ eese _____

8. stret ____ ____ _____

9. ____ ____ ick _____

10. tru ____ ____ _____

11. pa ____ ____ way _____

12. ____ ____ em _____

13. fi ____ ____ _____

14. ____ ____ ales _____

15. ____ ____ at _____

Name

Create new forms of a base word by adding or removing inflectional endings, prefixes, or suffixes.

observes

observant

observe

observation

observing

Use your notes from "The Inventor Thinks Up Helicopters" and "Ornithopter." Choose one word, and write it on the blade of the helicopter's propeller. Fill in the remaining blades with related words.

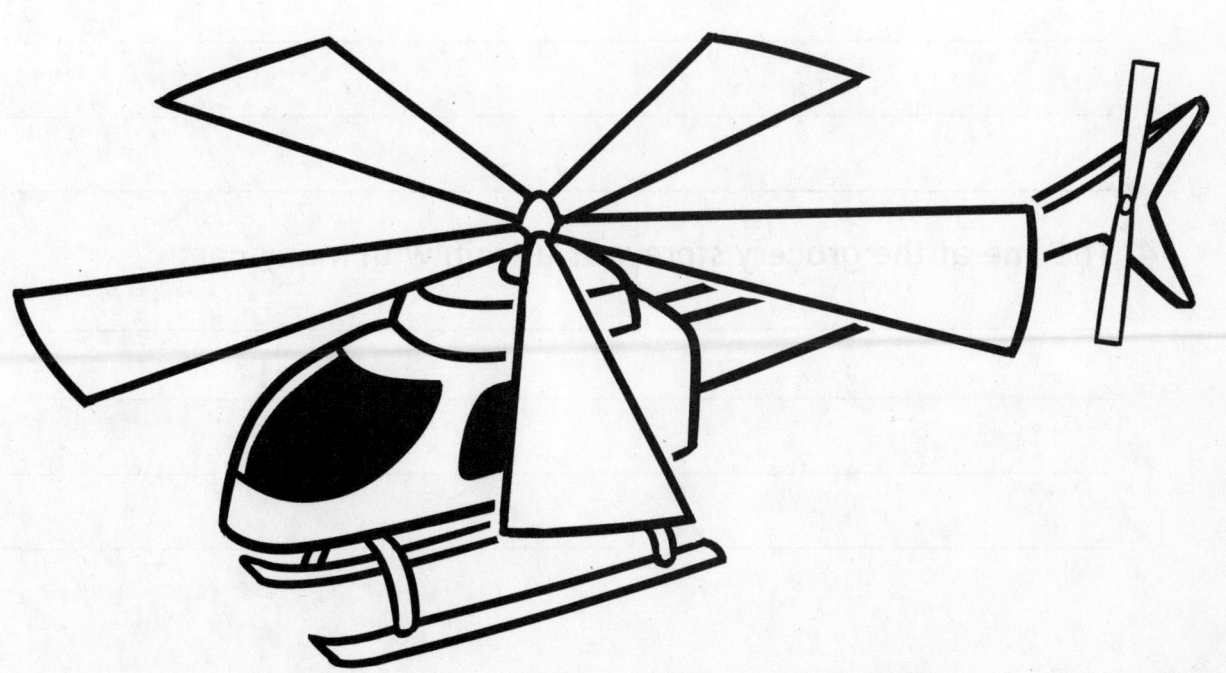

Name _____

**Read the sentences. Write the simile or metaphor on the line.
Then write the two things that are being compared.**

1. The letters stirred together
    like a thick, messy mush.

    _____

    _____

    _____

2. When I began reading,
    a book was like a bowl
    of letter soup.

    _____

    _____

    _____

3. Her voice was the song of a beautiful bird.

    _____

    _____

    _____

    _____

4. The line at the grocery store was a train with many cars.

    _____

    _____

    _____

Name _____

> - A complete **sentence** has a **subject** and a **predicate**.
> - The **subject** tells what or whom the sentence is about.
> - The **predicate** tells what the subject does and has a verb.
> - A **verb** is a word that tells what the subject **does** or **is**.
> - In the sentence *The monkey climbs the tree,* the subject is *The monkey* and the predicate is *climbs the tree*. The verb is *climbs*.

Draw a line under the verb in each sentence.

1. I read a book about birds.

2. I learned about their nests.

3. My neighbor is a bird watcher.

4. She writes about the birds in our town.

5. I saw a hummingbird in the flowers.

6. A hummingbird is very small.

Writing Connection **Write about some of the birds that you see in your community. Then reread your work. Make sure each sentence includes both a subject and predicate.**

_____

_____

_____

_____

_____

_____

Name _____

> • An **action verb** shows an action in the predicate part of a sentence. It tells what the subject does. Words like *read, climb, cry, ride,* and *speak* are action verbs.
>
> • Some action verbs tell about feelings and actions that cannot be seen. *Want, think, feel,* and *believe* are also action verbs.

A. Circle the action verb in each sentence.

1. Our class planned a picnic.

2. We put tablecloths on the picnic tables.

3. Everyone brought sandwiches.

4. Jon likes potato salad.

5. He cooked the potatoes.

B. Reread this paragraph from "Earth and Its Neighbors." Circle at least three action verbs. Then write them on the lines.

Galileo did not invent the telescope. However, 400 years ago he did build one that was strong enough to study the sky. When Galileo looked into space, he saw the rocky surface of the Moon. When he looked at the Sun, he discovered spots on its fiery surface.

_____

_____

Name _____

> • **Quotation marks** (") show that someone is speaking. Quotation marks come before and after a person's exact words. The end punctuation goes inside the quotation marks: *I asked, "What should we make for dinner?"*
>
> • Use a **colon** (:) between the hour and minutes when writing time. One o'clock is written as *1:00*. Two-thirty is written as *2:30*.

Rewrite each sentence. Add quotation marks before and after a speaker's exact words. Put a colon between the hour and minutes in times.

1. I'd like to see the new movie about penguins, said Mom.

   _____

2. I'll check the paper to see what time it starts, I told them.

   _____

3. Do you want to see the one at 230 or the one at 500? I asked.

   _____

4. Let's go see the show at 230, Mom said.

   _____

 **In your writer's notebook, write about a conversation you had this morning. When you're done, reread your work to make sure you used quotation marks and colons correctly.**

Name _____

> • Use **quotation marks** to show that someone is speaking. Quotation marks come at the beginning and end of a person's exact words. End punctuation goes inside the quotation mark.
>
> • Use a **colon** between the hour and minutes when writing time.

A. Proofread the paragraph. Draw a line under sentences that need quotation marks. Circle the times that need a colon.

A Surprise Party

Last week my sister said, Let's plan a birthday party for Dad. We decided to have the party on Saturday at 300. It will be fun to have the party in the park I told my sister and mom. I'll get some balloons and party hats Mom said. We went to the park at 230 to set up. Then we waited, but Dad did not come at 300. He did not come at 315. I think we forgot to tell Dad about the party! said Mom.

B. Rewrite the paragraph. Use quotation marks, commas, and colons where they belong.

_____
_____
_____
_____
_____
_____
_____
_____

Name _____

A. Read the paragraph. Then answer the questions.

(1) Every Thursday my parents and I go to my favorite restaurant for dinner. (2) I usually order the chicken. (3) The chef cooks it with lemon and garlic. (4) I can't wait to learn how to cook like that myself!

1. Which word is the action verb in sentence 1?
   A Thursday
   B go
   C dinner
   D favorite

2. What is the subject of sentence 3?
   F The chef
   G cooks
   H lemon
   J garlic

B. Read the student draft and look for revisions that need to be made. Then answer the questions.

(1) When are we going to dinner I asked. (2) We'll leave for the restaurant at 600, Dad replied. (3) "I am very hungry let's leave at 5:00 instead," Mom said.

3. What is the correct way to write sentence 1?
   A When are we going to dinner? I asked.
   B "When are we going to dinner? I asked."
   C "When are we going to dinner?" I asked.
   D No change needed in sentence 1.

4. What is the correct way to write sentence 2?
   F We'll leave for the restaurant at 6:00, Dad replied.
   G "We'll leave for the restaurant at 6:00," Dad replied.
   H "We'll leave for the restaurant at 600," Dad replied.
   J No change needed in sentence 2.

Name _____

Fold back the paper along the dotted line. Use the blanks to write each word as it is read aloud. When you finish the test, unfold the paper. Use the list at the right to correct any spelling mistakes.

1. _____
2. _____
3. _____
4. _____
5. _____
6. _____
7. _____
8. _____
9. _____
10. _____
11. _____
12. _____
13. _____
14. _____
15. _____

Review Words
16. _____
17. _____
18. _____

Challenge Words
19. _____
20. _____

1. whirl
2. third
3. girls
4. firm
5. fern
6. herds
7. stern
8. serve
9. hurt
10. nurse
11. turns
12. learn
13. pearl
14. word
15. world
16. stretch
17. thick
18. whales
19. perfect
20. Thursday

Name _____

> When a vowel is followed by the letter *r,* the *r* changes the vowel's sound. The /ûr/ *r*-controlled vowel sound is spelled *er* as in *her, ir* as in *bird, ur* as in *burn, or* as in *worthy,* and *ear* as in *earth.*

Read the spelling words aloud. Then write the spelling words that contain the matching *r*-controlled vowel sound spellings.

fern	hurt	stern	third	herds
nurse	whirl	serve	turns	learn
girls	pearl	firm	word	world

/ûr/ spelled *ir*

1. _____
2. _____
3. _____
4. _____

/ûr/ spelled *er*

7. _____
8. _____
9. _____
10. _____

/ûr/ spelled *ur*

13. _____
14. _____
15. _____

/ûr/ spelled *ear*

5. _____
6. _____

/ûr/ spelled *or*

11. _____
12. _____

Name _____

When a vowel is followed by the letter *r*, the *r* changes the vowel's sound. The /ûr/ r-controlled vowel sound is spelled *er* as in *her*, *ir* as in *bird*, *ur* as in *burn*, *or* as in *worthy*, and *ear* as in *earth*.

DECODING WORDS

The word *Thursday* has two syllables. Use your knowledge of digraphs and *r*-controlled vowels to blend the sounds of the first syllable: *thurs*. Now blend the sounds of the second syllable: *day*. Say the syllables together: *Thurs/day*.

Read the spelling words aloud. Then write the spelling words that contain the matching r-controlled vowel sound spellings.

whirl	word	serve	burn	nurse
pearl	herds	her	fern	third
firm	curve	earn	burst	birds

/ûr/ spelled *ir*

1. _____

2. _____

3. _____

4. _____

/ûr/ spelled *er*

7. _____

8. _____

9. _____

10. _____

/ûr/ spelled *ur*

12. _____

13. _____

14. _____

15. _____

/ûr/ spelled *ear*

5. _____

6. _____

/ûr/ spelled *or*

11. _____

Name _____

A. Read the spelling words aloud. Then write the spelling words that have the matching *r*-controlled vowel sound spellings.

third	stern	emerge	Thursday	preserve
worth	serve	word	nurse	whirl
firm	learn	suffered	worms	herder

/ûr/ spelled *ir*

1. _____

2. _____

3. _____

/ûr/ spelled *ur*

4. _____

5. _____

/ûr/ spelled *er*

6. _____

7. _____

8. _____

9. _____

10. _____

11. _____

/ûr/ spelled *or*

12. _____

13. _____

14. _____

/ûr/ spelled *ear*

15. _____

B. Compare the words *stern* and *learn*. How are the two words alike? How are they different?

_____

_____

 Look through your writer's notebook for words with *r*-controlled vowels spelled *ir, er, ur, ear,* and *or*. Read the words you find aloud. Then create a word sort for a partner.

Name _____

whirl	firm	stern	nurse	pearl
third	fern	serve	turns	word
girls	herds	hurt	learn	world

A. Write the spelling word that matches each definition below.

1. after second _____

2. short leafy plant _____

3. medical worker _____

4. hard or solid _____

5. all of Earth _____

B. Write the spelling word that best completes each sentence.

6. The wind blew and the dry leaves began to _____ around.

7. The boys lined up on the left and the _____ on the right.

8. The fisherman found a beautiful _____ inside the oyster.

9. The film showed _____ of grazing elephants.

10. Our principal is kind but can be _____ when she needs to be.

11. He will _____ as class president this year.

12. When I fell on the icy sidewalk, I _____ my elbow.

13. How many left _____ do we make to get to your house?

14. I want to _____ how to build a model spaceship.

15. Which _____ did you miss on the spelling test?

Name _____

There are six spelling mistakes in the paragraphs below. Underline the misspelled words. Write the words correctly on the lines.

Long ago there were three gurls who took a walk in the woods. They stopped to rest near a tree when a small fairy flew out from under a green furn. She was crying because she had hirt her wing.

The girls said they would nerse the fairy back to health. They took her home and put a bandage on her wing. When she was better, she told her new friends to close their eyes and count to three. On the theard count, they opened their eyes. Around each of their necks hung a beautiful purle necklace.

1. _____   4. _____

2. _____   5. _____

3. _____   6. _____

Writing Connection **Write a story about helping someone. Use at least four spelling words. Reread your work for errors.**

_____

_____

_____

_____

_____

_____

Name _____

Remember

When a word is spelled with a vowel and then the letter *r*, the *r* changes the vowel's sound. When *r* comes after *e*, it creates the vowel sound you hear in words like *verb* and *permit*. The same sound can be spelled with *ir* as in *girl* and *sir*, *ur* as in *burning* and *curb*, *or* as in *word*, and *ear* as in *earth*.

whirl	turns	learn	nurse	pearl
word	fern	serve	firm	third
girls	herds	hurt	stern	world

Write the missing letters to make a spelling word. Read the spelling word aloud and then write it on the line.

1. l ____ ____ ____ n   _____

2. f ____ ____ n   _____

3. wh ____ ____ l   _____

4. f ____ ____ m   _____

5. h ____ ____ t   _____

6. w ____ ____ d   _____

7. st ____ ____ n   _____

8. s ____ ____ ve   _____

9. th ____ ____ d   _____

10. n ____ ____ se   _____

11. w ____ ____ ld   _____

12. g ____ ____ ls   _____

13. p ____ ____ ____ l   _____

14. h ____ ____ ds   _____

15. t ____ ____ ns   _____

Name _____

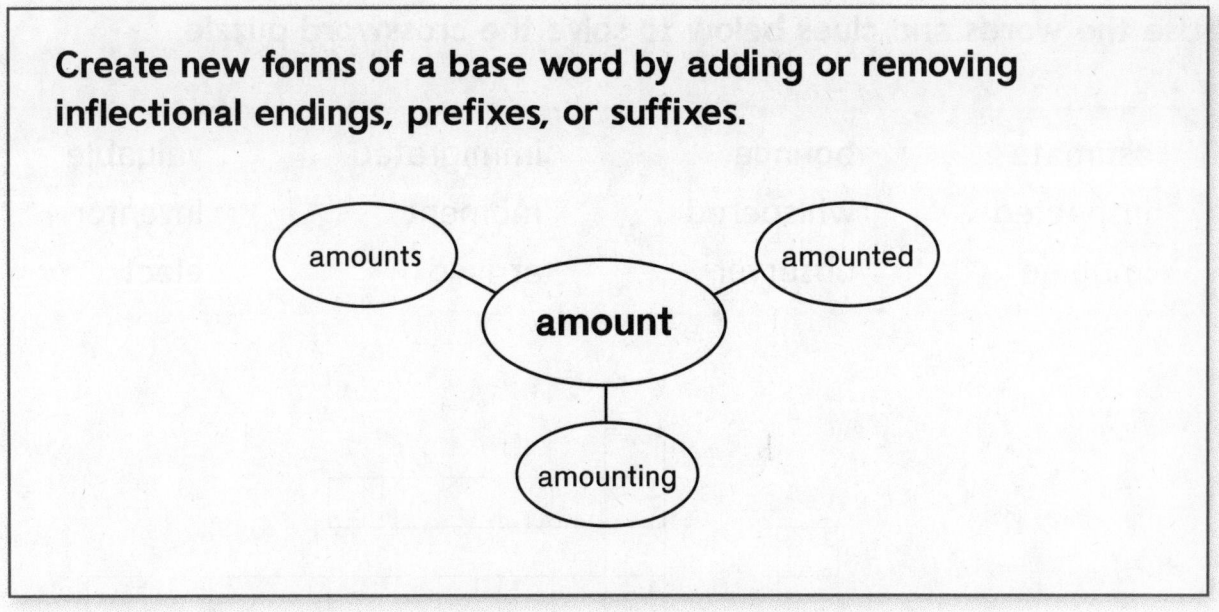

Create new forms of a base word by adding or removing inflectional endings, prefixes, or suffixes.

amounts

amount

amounted

amounting

Use your notes from *Earth*. Choose one word and write it inside the telescope. Then write related words in the planets that can be seen through the telescope. Use a dictionary for help.

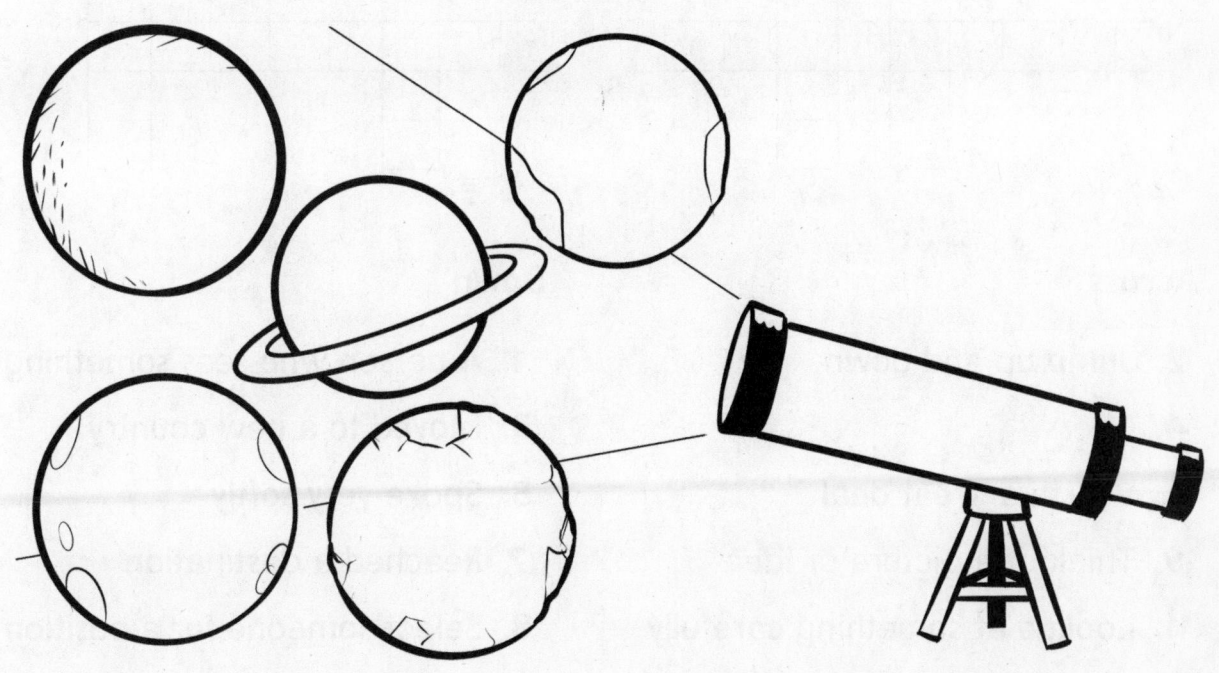

Name _____

Use the words and clues below to solve the crossword puzzle.

estimate	bounce	immigrated	valuable
inspected	whispered	moment	inventor
imagine	observer	arrived	elect

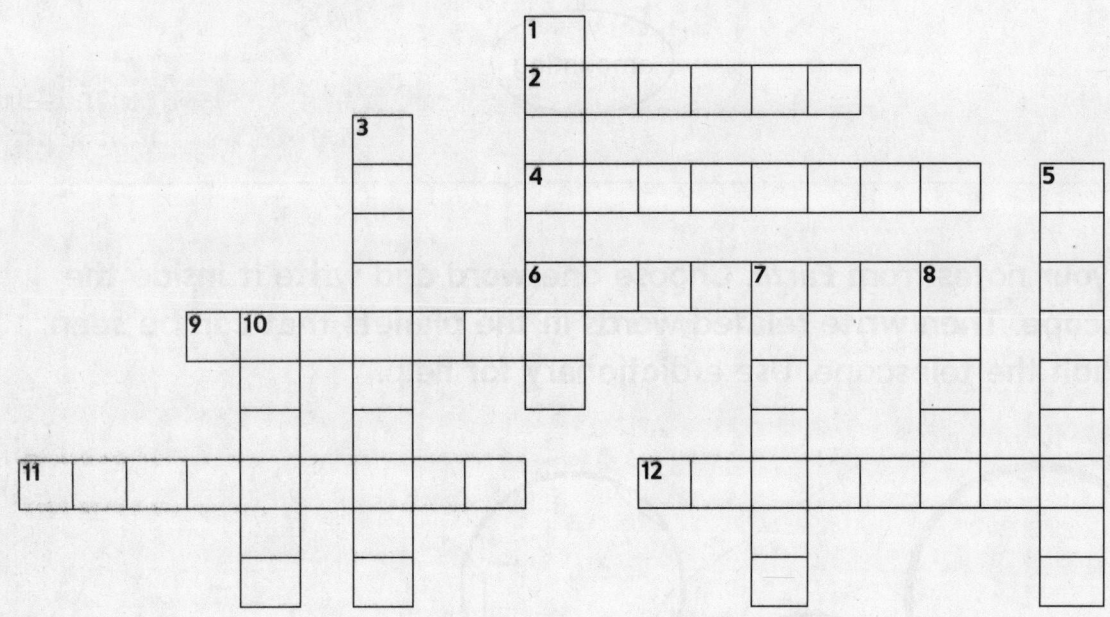

Across

2. Jump up and down

4. Guess

6. Worth a great deal

9. Think of a picture or idea

11. Looked at something carefully

12. Creator of a new machine or idea

Down

1. A person who sees something

3. Moved to a new country

5. Spoke very softly

7. Reached a destination

8. Select someone for a position

10. A very short period of time

Name _____

> • The **tense** of a verb tells when the action takes place. A verb in the **present tense** tells what happens now.
>
> • Add **-s** to most present-tense verbs with singular subjects. Do not add **-s** to present-tense verbs with plural subjects.
>
> • Remember that a simple sentence shows a complete thought and has a subject and predicate. A verb must agree in number with its subject in simple sentences.
>
> • In the sentence *The squirrel **climbs** the tree*, the present-tense verb *climbs* agrees with the singular subject *The squirrel.*
>
> • In the sentence *The squirrels **climb** the tree,* there is no *s* at the end of *climb* because *The squirrels* is a plural subject.

Choose the form of the verb that correctly agrees with the subject. Circle your answer and write it on the line.

1. Brandon _____ to make some money.   want   wants

2. He _____ of some ideas.   think   thinks

3. His parents _____ to him about his plans. talk   talks

4. They _____ him decide.   help   helps

5. Brandon _____ to walk dogs.   plan   plans

6. He _____ some flyers.   make   makes

 **In your writer's notebook, write about something you could do in your community to make money. Check your work when you're done to make sure your subjects and present-tense verbs agree.**

Name _____

> • A verb must agree in number with its subject.
>
> • When a present-tense verb with a singular subject ends in -sh, -ch, -ss, -zz, or x, add -es: *wishes, reaches, passes, buzzes, boxes*.
>
> • When a present-tense verb with a singular subject ends in a consonant and y, change the y to i and add -es: *try/tries, fry/fries*.

A. For each verb below, write the present-tense form that agrees with the subject given.

1. wash   Dan _____.

2. fix   Mom _____.

3. toss   They _____.

4. teach   Mr. Alvarez _____.

5. fly   Lana _____.

B. Reread this excerpt from "Seeing Red." Circle the first verb in the underlined sentence.

> These rovers sent images of Mars back to Earth. They let us know about the rocks and soil. These useful facts led to an answer. Scientists say Mars was once warm and wet like Earth is today.

If *Scientists* were changed to *A scientist*, how would you change the verb you circled to make the subject and verb agree? Rewrite the new sentence on the lines below.

_____

_____

Name _____

> • Add -*s* or -*es* to most present-tense verbs with singular subjects: *The fox* **runs** *across the field.*
>
> • Do not add -*s* or -*es* to a present-tense verb when the subject is plural: *The foxes* **run** *across the field.*
>
> • Do not add -*s* or -*es* when the subject is *I, you,* or a compound subject: *I* **cook** *dinner, and Charlie and Nora* **make** *a salad.*
>
> • Remember that a compound sentence is formed by two simple sentences joined by *and, or,* or *but.* Each subject must agree with the verb that comes after it in a compound sentence: *The* **dogs** **bark***, and the* **cat** **meows***.*

Choose the correct singular or plural form of the verb in each sentence below. Underline your answer.

1. The garden club members (meet, meets) at noon.

2. Jack and Shanda (lead, leads) the meeting.

3. Lisa (give, gives) a report on the flower sale.

4. She (tell, tells) us that we made fifty dollars.

5. Lisa (sit, sits) down, and I (stand, stands) up.

6. I (explain, explains) that we planted ten trees last week, and the members (cheer, cheers) loudly.

7. Jack and Shanda (end, ends) the meeting, and we all (walk, walks) home.

 **In your writer's notebook, write about some of the activities you would do if you started your own club. Use at least one compound sentence in your writing. When you're done, check your work to make sure your subjects and present-tense verbs agree.**

Name _____

A. Proofread the paragraph. Circle any verbs that do not agree with their subjects.

Mom and Dad tells us that they have a big surprise for us. We gets in the car. Dad drives for about an hour. We parks at the airport and go inside. We watches out the big window. Soon, a small plane land. Some time go by. I sees my grandparents waving to us from a distance. We hurries to the baggage claim to meet them. Everyone hugs! I carries their bags to the car.

> **HANDWRITING CONNECTION**
>
> Be sure to write legibly. Use proper cursive and remember to leave spaces between words.

B. Rewrite the paragraph. Write the verbs so that they agree with their subjects.

_____

_____

_____

_____

_____

_____

_____

_____

Name _____

A. Read the paragraph. Then answer the questions.

(1) Everyone is having a good time at the zoo. (2) A little girl jumps up and down as her brothers point at the elephants. (3) A boy sees a long snake. (4) People watch a lion and the lion stares back. (5) The polar bears take a dip in their pool.

1. Which word in sentence 2 is a singular verb?

   A girl
   B jumps
   C brothers
   D point

2. Which word in sentence 4 is a plural verb?

   F People
   G watch
   H lion
   J stares

B. Read the student draft and look for revisions that need to be made. Then answer the questions.

(1) Today my aunt, my brother, and I are at the zoo. (2) We visits the monkeys first. (3) A mother monkey carry her baby on her back. (4) We also see lions, elephants, and giraffes. (5) Soon it's time to leave. (6) I wish I could visit the zoo every day.

3. What is the correct way to write sentence 2?

   A We visit the monkeys first.
   B We visites the monkeys first.
   C We visit's the monkeys first.
   D No change needed in sentence 2.

4. What is the correct way to write sentence 3?

   F A mother monkey carrys her baby on her back.
   G A mother monkey carryes her baby on her back.
   H A mother monkey carries her baby on her back.
   J No change needed in sentence 3.

Name _____

Fold back the paper along the dotted line. Use the blanks to write each word as it is read aloud. When you finish the test, unfold the paper. Use the list at the right to correct any spelling mistakes.

1. _____
2. _____
3. _____
4. _____
5. _____
6. _____
7. _____
8. _____
9. _____
10. _____
11. _____
12. _____
13. _____
14. _____
15. _____

Review Words

16. _____
17. _____
18. _____

Challenge Words

19. _____
20. _____

1. sharp
2. yard
3. artist
4. carve
5. porch
6. storm
7. sport
8. story
9. chore
10. shore
11. sore
12. hoard
13. oars
14. pour
15. your
16. learn
17. word
18. turns
19. orchard
20. ignore

Name _____

> When the letter *r* follows the letter *a*, it creates the /är/ sound as in the word *star*. The /ôr/ sound in *wore* can be spelled *or* as in *torn*, *ore* as in *more*, *oar* as in *soar*, and *our* as in *four*.

DECODING WORDS

Words with a vowel, two consonants, and another vowel (VCCV) are usually divided into syllables between the two consonants (VC/CV). For example: *doc/tor*, *hor/net*.

Read the spelling words in the box aloud. Then write the spelling words that contain the matching sound spellings.

shore	chore	pour	sharp	yard
oars	your	story	sore	sport
artist	storm	carve	hoard	porch

/är/ spelled *ar*

1. _____
2. _____
3. _____
4. _____

/ôr/ spelled *or*

7. _____
8. _____
9. _____
10. _____

/ôr/ spelled *ore*

13. _____
14. _____
15. _____

/ôr/ spelled *oar*

5. _____
6. _____

/ôr/ spelled *our*

11. _____
12. _____

Name _____

> When the letter *r* follows the letter *a*, it creates the /är/ sound as in the word *star*. The /ôr/ sound in *wore* can be spelled *or* as in *torn*, *ore* as in *more*, *oar* as in *soar*, and *our* as in *four*.

DECODING WORDS

Words with a vowel, two consonants, and another vowel (VCCV) are usually divided into syllables between the two consonants (VC/CV). For example: *doc/tor, hor/net*.

Read the spelling words in the box aloud. Then write the spelling words that contain the matching sound spellings.

sport	story	porch	store	roar
soar	storm	card	sore	yard
sharks	hard	chore	more	your

/är/ spelled *ar*

1. _____

2. _____

3. _____

4. _____

/ôr/ spelled *or*

7. _____

8. _____

9. _____

10. _____

/ôr/ spelled *ore*

12. _____

13. _____

14. _____

15. _____

/ôr/ spelled *oar*

5. _____

6. _____

/ôr/ spelled *our*

11. _____

Name _____

A. Read the spelling words in the box aloud. Then write the spelling words that contain the matching sound spellings.

sharp	orchard	pour	shore	sore
your	porch	order	ignore	carve
artist	storm	uproar	soaring	tortilla

/är/ spelled ar   **/ôr/ spelled ore**   **/ôr/ spelled or**

1. _____   6. _____   11. _____

2. _____   7. _____   12. _____

3. _____   8. _____   13. _____

                                        14. _____

/ôr/ spelled oar   **/ôr/ spelled our**

4. _____   9. _____   15. _____

5. _____   10. _____

B. Compare the words *sore* and *pour*. How are they alike? How are they different?

_____

_____

 **Look back through the selections you read this week for words with *r*-controlled vowels. Read the words aloud and record them in your writer's notebook.**

Name _____

sharp	carve	sport	shore	oars
yard	porch	story	sore	pour
artist	storm	chore	hoard	your

A. Write the spelling word that matches each definition below.

1. strong wind and rain _____

2. edge of the sea _____

3. belonging to you _____

4. sculptor or painter _____

5. floor of a building _____

B. Write the spelling word that best completes each sentence.

6. Be careful, the pin is very _____.

7. I built a tree house in the back _____.

8. My dad likes to _____ the turkey for Thanksgiving dinner.

9. A _____ is usually built on the front of a house.

10. I think that basketball is my favorite _____ of all.

11. It is my _____ to take out the trash.

12. I hadn't played tennis in so long that my arms are now _____.

13. I read a story about a troll who liked to _____ gold.

14. We had to get new _____ for our row boat.

15. Would you like me to _____ you a glass of water?

Name _____

There are six spelling mistakes in the paragraphs below. Underline the misspelled words. Write the words correctly on the lines.

One day after lunch Caroline took a walk along the shoar. She saw a woman painting. Caroline stopped and asked, "Are you an airtist?" The woman said that she was. "My name is Mary Cassatt," she said. "And what is yore name?"

Caroline told the woman her name and then pointed toward the blue house with the wide yeard where she lived. Suddenly, the sky became dark. "I think it may stoarm!" said Caroline. "Come to my house until it's over." For the rest of the afternoon, Caroline and Mary sat on the pourch and talked about art.

1. _____   4. _____

2. _____   5. _____

3. _____   6. _____

Writing Connection **Write a story about meeting a famous artist. Use at least four spelling words in your story.**

_____
_____
_____
_____
_____
_____
_____
_____

Name _____

Remember

When a vowel is followed by the letter *r*, the *r* creates a new vowel sound.

- The /är/ sound is spelled *ar* as in *star, bar,* and *far.*
- The /ôr/ sound is spelled *or* as in *acorn, ore* as in *wore, oar* as in *roaring,* and *our* as in *fourteen.*

story	carve	sport	shore	oars
pour	porch	sharp	sore	yard
artist	storm	chore	hoard	your

Write the missing letters to make a spelling word. Read the spelling word aloud, then write it on the line.

1. ch ____ ____ e   _____

2. p ____ ____ ch   _____

3. ____ ____ tist   _____

4. p ____ ____ r   _____

5. y ____ ____ d   _____

6. st ____ ____ y   _____

7. sp ____ ____ t   _____

8. st ____ ____ m   _____

9. sh ____ ____ p   _____

10. y ____ ____ r   _____

11. ____ ____ ____ s   _____

12. h ____ ____ ____ d   _____

13. s ____ ____ e   _____

14. c ____ ____ ve   _____

15. sh ____ ____ e   _____

Name _____

> You can use a digital dictionary to look up unfamiliar words. Enter the word in the **search box**. Then click the **search icon**.
>
> When you search a word, you'll see it split into smaller parts. These are **syllables**. You'll also see symbols that show how the word is pronounced. The word *mountain* might look like this:
>
> **moun·tain | \ moun' tən **
>
> If you're still not sure of how to say a word, you can also listen to how a word is pronounced by clicking the **audio icon**.

Use the dictionary entry and context clues to figure out the meanings of the bold words. Write the meanings and part of speech on the line.

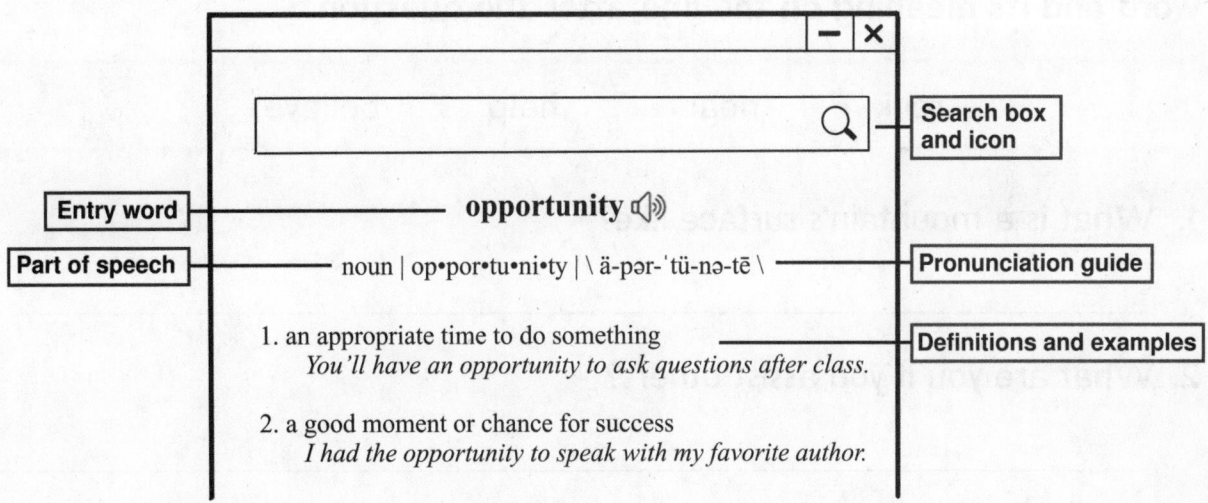

Search box and icon

Entry word — **opportunity**

Part of speech — noun | op•por•tu•ni•ty | \ ä-pər-ˈtü-nə-tē \ — Pronunciation guide

1. an appropriate time to do something — Definitions and examples
   You'll have an opportunity to ask questions after class.

2. a good moment or chance for success
   I had the opportunity to speak with my favorite author.

1. The book club gave us the **opportunity** to talk about the book.

_____

2. I have the **opportunity** to cook dinner for the family when Mom is away.

_____

Say the word in the dictionary entry out loud with a partner. How many syllables are in the word? How do you know?

Name _____

Suffixes are word parts that are added to the end of a word to create a new word with a different meaning.

- The suffix *-able* means *can be*. *Treatable* means *can be treated*.

- The suffix *-ful* means *full of*. The word *joyful* means *full of joy*.

- The suffix *-ly* means *like, or in a certain manner or way*. The word *quickly* means *in a fast or quick way*.

- The suffix *-y* means *having a lot of*. The word *spicy* means *having a lot of spice*.

Read each question below. Add the suffix *-able, -ful, -ly,* or *-y* to the word in the box that best answers each question. Then write the new word and its meaning on the line after the question.

rock	near	help	believe

1. What is a mountain's surface like?

   _____

2. What are you if you assist others?

   _____

3. What do you call a story that seems real?

   _____

4. How alike are two things that are almost the same?

   _____

Name _____

> • A **past-tense verb** shows an action that has already happened.
>
> • Add **-ed** to form the past tense of most verbs: *called, jumped.*
>
> • Drop the *e* and add *-ed* to verbs that end in *e*: *baked, smiled.*
>
> • The same form of a regular past-tense verb is used with both singular and plural subjects in simple and compound sentences.

Find the past-tense verb in each sentence. Write it on the line.

1. We walked to Ocean Park. _____

2. Mom looked for an empty bench. _____

3. She liked to watch us play. _____

4. I played with my little sister in the sand. _____

5. We packed sand into a bucket. _____

6. Then we formed a sand castle. _____

Connect to Community **Talk to a parent or another trusted adult about the parks in your community. Write about what people do there. Use past-tense verbs in your writing.**

_____

_____

_____

_____

_____

Name _____

- There are more special rules for making past-tense verbs.
- If a verb ends with a consonant and the letter *y*, change the *y* to *i* before adding *-ed*: *fry/fried, bury/buried.*
- Double the consonant and add *-ed* to verbs that end with one vowel and one consonant: *hug/hugged; stop/stopped.*

A. Choose the correct past-tense verb for each sentence. Circle the verb and write it on the line.

1. Dad and I _____ a movie about birds.   watchd   watched

2. The baby bird _____ for food.   cried   cryed

3. Eagles _____ through the air.   glideed   glided

4. Baby geese _____ to catch their mother.   hurryed   hurried

5. Tiny robins _____ for more worms.   begged   beged

6. Woodpeckers _____ to find insects in a tree.   tryed   tried

B. Reread this paragraph from "Anansi Learns a Lesson." Circle two past-tense verbs.

As soon as Anansi dropped the stones, he rocketed to the surface of the lake. Anansi sputtered furiously. "Fish and Turtle tricked me," he cried angrily.

What are the present-tense forms of the verbs you circled?

_____

_____

Name _____

> • An abbreviation is a shortened form of a word. It ends with a period. *Inches* is shortened to *in. Feet* is shortened *ft.*
>
> • Titles before a name are capitalized: *President Lincoln, Queen Elizabeth.* Some titles are abbreviated: *Mr.* for *Mister, Dr.* for *Doctor.*
>
> • Geographical names and places are capitalized: *Asia, Texas, the Rio Grande.* Some geographical names are abbreviated: *St.* for *Street, Ave.* for *Avenue, U.S.* for *United States.*
>
> • Don't sound out abbreviations like a regular word. Read the entire word that the abbreviation stands for.

A. Read each sentence aloud. Then rewrite the sentences with the correct spelling for titles and other abbreviations.

1. Last week, doctor Bennet spoke to our class about healthy eating.

_____

2. He bought them at ms. Baker's Fruit Market on Hill st in Maplewood.

_____

3. Our class wrote governor Rose to tell him what we learned.

_____

B. Read aloud and write the word that each abbreviation stands for. Look up abbreviations in a dictionary for help.

4. Ave. _____   **6.** Mt. _____   **8.** Dec. _____

5. in. _____   **7.** Dr. _____   **9.** Rd. _____

 In your writer's notebook, write a story about a king or queen of a faraway place. When you're done, check that you capitalized official titles of characters in your story. Also check that you capitalized geographical names and places.

Name _____

- To form the past tense of most verbs, add *-ed*. For verbs that end in the letter *e,* drop the *e* and add *-ed.*

- Change the *y* to *i* before adding *-ed* if the verb ends with a consonant and *y*. Double the consonant and add *-ed* to verbs that end with one vowel and one consonant.

- Capitalize abbreviations for geographical places and titles before a name: *St., Ave., Mrs., Dr.*

- When you read an abbreviation, say the entire word the abbreviation stands for.

A. Proofread the paragraph. Circle any past-tense verbs that are incorrect. Underline incorrect abbreviations and titles.

Last summer, I worked with my dad at the television station. I carryed some of my dad's equipment We talkd to people all over town. He recorded what they said. Mister Higgins, who lives on Lemon aven, said he once tryed to sail around the world. On Second str, mrs kemp said she skiped rope for fifteen hours to win a contest.

B. Rewrite the paragraph. Spell past-tense verbs, titles, and abbreviations correctly. Then read the paragraph out loud.

_____

_____

_____

_____

_____

_____

C. Work with a partner to read aloud the word that each of the following abbreviations stands for: ft., oz., Sept., TX. You can use a dictionary for help.

Name _____

A. Read the paragraph. Then answer the questions.

(1) I'm ready to go surfing today. (2) The sun and sand are hot, but the water is cool. (3) I carry my board into the water and paddle past the breaking waves. (4) I lie on my belly and listen to the ocean. (5) Soon a big wave comes. (6) I hop to my feet and ride it to shore.

1. How is the past-tense form of *carry* in sentence 3 spelled?
   A carryed
   B carryied
   C carried
   D caried

2. How is the past-tense form of *hop* in sentence 6 spelled?
   F hoped
   G hoppied
   H hops
   J hopped

B. Read the student draft and look for revisions that need to be made. Then answer the questions.

(1) My grandmother lives at 101 maple rd. (2) I visited her last summer. (3) Every morning, we baked pies for her neighbors. (4) I delivered the pies to mrs green and dr lopez. (5) In the afternoon, I played with my grandmother's dogs. (6) I had so much fun.

3. What is the correct way to write sentence 1?
   A My grandmother lives at 101 Maple road.
   B My grandmother lives at 101 maple Rd.
   C My grandmother lives at 101 Maple Rd.
   D No change needed in sentence 1.

4. What is the correct way to write sentence 4?
   F I delivered the pies to Mrs. Green and dr Lopez.
   G I delivered the pies to Mrs. Green and Dr. Lopez.
   H I delivered the pies to mrs Green and Dr. Lopez.
   J No change needed in sentence 4.

Name _____

Fold back the paper along the dotted line. Use the blanks to write each word as it is read aloud. When you finish the test, unfold the paper. Use the list at the right to correct any spelling mistakes.

1. _____
2. _____
3. _____
4. _____
5. _____
6. _____
7. _____
8. _____
9. _____
10. _____
11. _____
12. _____
13. _____
14. _____
15. _____

Review Words 16. _____

17. _____

18. _____

Challenge Words 19. _____

20. _____

1. careful
2. stared
3. shared
4. pair
5. stairs
6. wear
7. bear
8. where
9. there
10. dear
11. rear
12. gear
13. here
14. career
15. peer
16. shore
17. carve
18. storm
19. square
20. clearly

Name _____

The /âr/ sound in *hair* can be spelled *are* as in *bare, air* as in *repair, ear* as in *swear,* and *ere* as in *there*. The /îr/ sound in *near* can be spelled *ear* as in *fear, eer* as in *cheer,* and *ere* as in *sincere*.

SPELLING TIP

Sometimes the same letters can make different sounds. The words *swear* and *fear* have the letters *ear,* but *swear* rhymes with *hair,* while *fear* rhymes with *hear*. Confirm pronunciation in a dictionary.

Read the spelling words in the box aloud. Then write the spelling words with the matching *r*-controlled vowel spellings.

pair	gear	here	stared	wear
dear	stairs	career	rear	where
shared	bear	there	careful	peer

/âr/ spelled *are*

1. _____

2. _____

3. _____

/âr/ spelled *air*

4. _____

5. _____

/âr/ spelled *ear*

6. _____

7. _____

/âr/ spelled *ere*

8. _____

9. _____

/îr/ spelled *ere*

10. _____

/îr/ spelled *ear*

11. _____

12. _____

13. _____

/îr/ spelled *eer*

14. _____

15. _____

 **Look back at the selections you read this week and look for words that have *r*-controlled vowels. Read the words you find aloud and record them in your writer's notebook.**

Name _____

The /âr/ sound in *hair* can be spelled *are* as in *bare, air* as in *repair, ear* as in *swear,* and *ere* as in *there.* The /îr/ sound in *near* can be spelled *ear* as in *fear, eer* as in *cheer,* and *ere* as in *sincere.*

Read the spelling words in the box aloud. Then write the spelling words with the matching *r*-controlled vowel spellings.

care	stairs	pear	there	pair
near	deer	peer	dear	dare
lair	fair	wear	ear	bear

/âr/ spelled *are*

1. _____

2. _____

/âr/ spelled *air*

3. _____

4. _____

5. _____

6. _____

/âr/ spelled *ear*

7. _____

8. _____

9. _____

/âr/ spelled *ere*

10. _____

/îr/ spelled *ear*

11. _____

12. _____

13. _____

/îr/ spelled *eer*

14. _____

15. _____

 **Look back at the selections you read this week and look for words that have *r*-controlled vowels. Read the words you find aloud and record them in your writer's notebook.**

Name _____

A. Read the spelling words in the box aloud. Then write the words with the matching *r*-controlled vowel spellings.

shared	fairly	there	steer	gear
beard	where	stairs	nearly	square
careful	wear	career	weird	here

/âr/ spelled *are*

1. _____

2. _____

3. _____

/âr/ spelled *air*

4. _____

5. _____

/âr/ spelled *ere*

6. _____

7. _____

/âr/ spelled *ear*

8. _____

/îr/ spelled *eir*

9. _____

/îr/ spelled *ere*

10. _____

/îr/ spelled *ear*

11. _____

12. _____

13. _____

/îr/ spelled *eer*

14. _____

15. _____

B. Compare the words *wear* and *beard*. How are the two words alike? How are they different?

_____

_____

 **Look back at the selections you read this week and look for words that have *r*-controlled vowels. Read the words you find aloud and record them in your writer's notebook.**

Name _____

careful	pair	bear	dear	here
stared	stairs	where	rear	career
shared	wear	there	gear	peer

A. Write the spelling word that matches each definition below.

1. two of something _____

3. large mammal _____

2. back or end _____

4. job or occupation _____

B. Write the spelling word that best completes each sentence.

5. He and his brother _____ a sandwich together.

6. An acrobat must be _____ when walking the high wire.

7. The child _____ at the clown in the crazy costume.

8. Walking up and down _____ is good exercise.

9. I need to _____ my raincoat today.

10. Do you know _____ my book is?

11. I found it up _____ on the top shelf.

12. Be a _____ and help me sweep up.

13. What kind of camping _____ will we need this summer?

14. Do you want to come _____ for lunch?

15. After we wrote our stories, we had a _____ review.

Name _____

There are six spelling mistakes in the paragraphs below. Underline the misspelled words. Write the words correctly on the lines.

People often want to know whare to go to look at stars. Out in the country away from city lights is best. Be sure and go thair on a clear night. If it's cold, make sure to ware warm clothes.

Besides a telescope, make sure that a blanket is part of your geer. You can lie on it to look up at the sky. Some people have made a carear of studying stars. One scientist said, "I'd rather be heare looking at stars than anywhere else in the world."

1. _____   4. _____

2. _____   5. _____

3. _____   6. _____

| Writing Connection | **Write about a job that you would like to do. Use at least four spelling words.** |

_____

_____

_____

_____

_____

_____

_____

_____

_____

Name _____

Remember

When a vowel is followed by the letter *r*, the *r* creates a new vowel sound.

- The /âr/ sound is spelled *are* as in *bare* and *compare*, *air* as in *repair*, *ear* as in *swear*, and *ere* as in *there*.

- The /îr/ sound is spelled *ear* as in *fear*, *eer* as in *cheer*, and *ere* as in *sincere*.

careful	pair	bear	dear	here
stared	stairs	where	rear	career
shared	wear	there	gear	peer

Write the missing letters to make a spelling word. Read the spelling word aloud and then write it on the line.

1. r __ __ __   _____

2. w __ __ __   _____

3. h __ __ __   _____

4. p __ __ r   _____

5. th __ __ __   _____

6. st __ __ ed   _____

7. p __ __ __   _____

8. wh __ __ __   _____

9. st __ __ __ s   _____

10. d __ __ __   _____

11. c __ __ eful   _____

12. g __ __ __   _____

13. sh __ __ ed   _____

14. car __ __ __   _____

15. b __ __ __   _____

Name _____

Create new forms of a base word by adding or removing inflectional endings, prefixes, or suffixes.

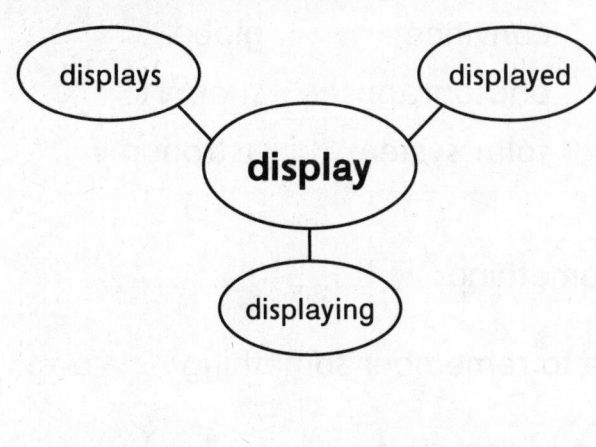

Use your notes from "Anansi Learns a Lesson." Choose one word and write it on the body of the spider. Then write as many related words as you can on the spider's legs. Use a dictionary to help you.

Name _____

Read the clues. Complete the puzzle with your vocabulary words. Put the letters in the boxes together to learn a fun fact at the end.

amount	convince	globe	courage
warmth	photographs	support	temperature
remind	solar system	astronomy	surface

1. A quantity of something _ _ ☐ _ _ _

2. Cause someone to remember something _ _ _ _ ☐ _

3. The outside part of something _ _ _ _ _ _ ☐

4. The world _ ☐ _ _ _

5. Cause someone to believe or do something _ _ _ _ ☐ _ _ _

6. Bravery _ _ _ _ _ ☐ _

7. Pictures taken with a camera _ ☐ _ _ _ _ _ _ _ _

8. Provide what someone or something needs _ _ _ _ _ _ ☐

9. Our sun and the planets around it _ _ _ _ _ _ ☐ _ _ _

10. A measurement of hot or cold _ ☐ _ _ _ _ _ _ _ _ _

11. The study of the stars and planets ☐ _ _ _ _ _ _ _

12. Heat _ _ ☐ _ _

This unit of distance is equal to 5.88 trillion miles.

☐ ☐ ☐ ☐ ☐ ☐ ☐ ☐ - ☐ ☐ ☐ ☐

Name _____

- Verbs can show actions that happen in the present, past, or future.
- A **future-tense verb** describes an action that is going to happen.
- Use the verb *will* to write about the future: *I will walk home soon.*
- Use consistent verb tenses across paragraphs.

A. Circle the verb in each sentence. Decide whether it is in the present or future tense. Write *present* or *future* on the line.

1. Carla waits in the car for her dad. _____

2. Dad will drop Carla off at school. _____

3. Dad gets in the car. _____

4. They will go down Elm Street. _____

5. Carla sees the school up ahead. _____

B. Read the following paragraph from "A Clever Crow." Circle the past-tense verb in the underlined sentence. Then rewrite the sentence with the future-tense form of the verb.

As she stared at the water in frustration, she noticed what looked like small clear stones in it. That gave her an idea. She started dropping stones inside the pitcher. After dropping several, she was sure the level of the water was rising. She kept dropping rocks until she could take a good long drink.

_____

_____

Name _____

> - A verb in the future tense tells about an action that will happen.
>
> - Use *will* with a verb to form the future tense.
>
> - A future-tense verb must agree with its subject.
>
> - The same future-tense verb is used for both singular and plural nouns: ***He will ride*** *his bike to the park.* ***His friends will come,*** *too.*

Change the underlined present-tense verbs to the future tense. Don't forget to use the word *will* with the verb. Write the new sentence.

1. We <u>plant</u> new flowers in the yard.

   _____

2. The rain <u>falls</u> into our new rain barrel.

   _____

3. We <u>water</u> the flowers with the water that we collect.

   _____

4. Dad <u>uses</u> the rain in the bird bath, too.

   _____

5. The birds <u>like</u> their new bird bath.

   _____

 **In your writer's notebook, write about what you will do for fun this weekend. Reread your work when you're done. Make sure you used future-tense verbs correctly.**

Name _____

> • The important words in a book or magazine title are always capitalized: *Adventures of Huckleberry Finn.*
>
> • The words *the, and, in, of,* and *a* are not capitalized in a title unless they are the first word: *Of Mice and Men.*
>
> • Underline all of the words in a book or magazine title if you are handwriting it. If you are using a computer, use italic type.

Rewrite each sentence. Write book and magazine titles correctly.

1. I checked out a book called the marching monkeys of Miami.

   _____

2. My friend's favorite book is We can sing a Song.

   _____

3. For my birthday, Gram gave me a magazine called good music.

   _____

 **Think of one of your favorite books. Write about what happens in the story. Tell why you like it. Reread your work to make sure you wrote the title correctly.**

_____

_____

_____

_____

Name _____

- A future-tense verb shows an action that is going to happen.
- Use the special verb *will* to write about the future.
- Capitalize the important words in a book or magazine title.
- Underline a book or magazine title if you are handwriting it. If you are using a computer, put the title in italic type.

A. Read the dialogue. Circle any verbs that are not written in the correct tense or do not agree with their subjects. Underline book titles that are not written correctly.

"I hoped you can come to my party," Tad said to Shanna.

"I will asked my mom," said Shanna. "I will tell you tomorrow."

"Great," said Tad. "Have you read the book frogs in a pond?"

"No," said Shanna. "I'm reading a Cricket asks A question."

"I will looked for that book at the library," said Tad.

"You will likes it," said Shanna. "It will makes you laugh."

B. Rewrite the dialogue. Write verbs correctly across the paragraphs. Correct the book titles and underline them.

_____

_____

_____

_____

_____

_____

Name _____

A. Read the paragraph. Then answer the questions.

(1) Tomorrow we will throw a big party to celebrate my sister's graduation. (2) Friends and family will be there. (3) Last week, my parents bought my sister a new bicycle for her graduation. (4) They will give it to her at the party. (5) She will be so happy!

1. What is the future-tense verb in sentence 1?
   A Tomorrow
   B will throw
   C party
   D celebrate

2. Which sentence does not contain a future-tense verb?
   F Sentence 1
   G Sentence 3
   H Sentence 4
   J Sentence 5

B. Read the student draft and look for revisions that need to be made. Then answer the questions.

(1) I love to read biographies. (2) One of my favorite books is the life and writings of mark twain. (3) Next week, my school will have a book fair. (4) I will look for the biography called The Story of Abraham Lincoln. (5) I hope I will find it.

3. What is the correct way to write sentence 2?
   A One of my favorite books is the Life and Writings of Mark Twain.
   B One of my favorite books is the life And writings Of mark twain.
   C One of my favorite books is The Life and Writings of Mark Twain.
   D No change needed in sentence 2.

4. What is the correct way to write sentence 3?
   F Next week, my school have a book fair.
   G Next week, a book fair my school will have.
   H Next week, my school had a book fair.
   J No change needed in sentence 3.

Name _____

Fold back the paper along the dotted line. Use the blanks to write each word as it is read aloud. When you finish the test, unfold the paper. Use the list at the right to correct any spelling mistakes.

1. _____
2. _____
3. _____
4. _____
5. _____
6. _____
7. _____
8. _____
9. _____
10. _____
11. _____
12. _____
13. _____
14. _____
15. _____

Review Words 16. _____
17. _____
18. _____

Challenge Words 19. _____
20. _____

1. misprint
2. misread
3. mistrust
4. misspell
5. mistreat
6. precut
7. preview
8. prepaid
9. preplan
10. preheat
11. distrust
12. discount
13. dishonest
14. discover
15. disable
16. stairs
17. rear
18. where
19. prejudge
20. disconnect

Name _____

> A **prefix** is a word part added to the beginning of a word. The prefix *dis-* means *not*. The word *disorder* means *not in order*. The prefix *mis-* means *bad* or *wrong*. *Misfortune* means *bad luck*. The prefix *pre-* means *before*. *Predate* means *to come before*.

DECODING WORDS

Prefixes often form the first syllable in a word. For example, the first syllable in the word *mislead* is the prefix *mis-*. The second syllable is the base word *lead*. Use the prefix to find the word's meaning. *Mislead* means *to lead the wrong way*.

Read the spelling words in the box aloud. Then write the spelling words that contain the prefixes below.

preplan	discount	preview	misread	dishonest
preheat	mistreat	disable	precut	discover
mistrust	distrust	misprint	misspell	prepaid

mis-

1. _____
2. _____
3. _____
4. _____
5. _____

pre-

6. _____
7. _____
8. _____
9. _____
10. _____

dis-

11. _____
12. _____
13. _____
14. _____
15. _____

 **Look back at the selections you read this week and look for words that have the prefixes *pre-*, *dis-*, and *mis-*. Read the words aloud and record them in your writer's notebook.**

Name _____

A **prefix** is a word part added to the beginning of a word. The prefix *dis-* means *not*. The word *disorder* means *not in order*. The prefix *mis-* means *bad* or *wrong*. *Misfortune* means *bad luck*. The prefix *pre-* means *before*. *Predate* means *to come before*.

DECODING WORDS

Prefixes often form the first syllable in a word. For example, the first syllable in the word *mislead* is the prefix *mis-*. The second syllable is the base word *lead*. Use the prefix to find the word's meaning. *Mislead* means *to lead the wrong way.*

Read the spelling words in the box aloud. Then write the spelling words that contain the prefixes below.

discount	mistreat	precut	preheat	preplan
disagree	prepay	distrust	misread	misuse
mistrust	mistake	mislead	discover	dismount

mis-

1. _____

2. _____

3. _____

4. _____

5. _____

6. _____

pre-

7. _____

8. _____

9. _____

10. _____

dis-

11. _____

12. _____

13. _____

14. _____

15. _____

Name _____

A. Read the spelling words in the box aloud. Then write the spelling words that contain the prefixes below.

misprint	preview	dishonest	presale	discover
disconnect	misspell	preplan	preheat	misread
mistreat	precut	miscount	dismounted	distrust

mis-	*pre-*	*dis-*
1. _____	6. _____	11. _____
2. _____	7. _____	12. _____
3. _____	8. _____	13. _____
4. _____	9. _____	14. _____
5. _____	10. _____	15. _____

B. Compare the words *misprint* and *misread*. How are the words alike? How are they different?

_____

_____

_____

 **Look back at the selections you read this week and look for words that have the prefixes *pre-, dis-,* and *mis-*. Read the words aloud and record them in your writer's notebook.**

Name _____

misprint	discount	preview	preheat	dishonest
discover	mistreat	mistrust	distrust	misread
prepaid	precut	preplan	misspell	disable

A. Write a spelling word that matches each meaning.

1. read incorrectly _____

2. paid before _____

3. not honest _____

4. to plan before _____

5. to treat badly _____

B. Write the spelling word that best completes each sentence.

6. The _____ in the newspaper listed my name incorrectly.

7. Do spelling bee winners ever _____ a word?

8. I helped the teacher _____ the paper for the first-graders.

9. After seeing the movie _____, I bought my tickets.

10. People _____ a salesperson who is not truthful.

11. We _____ the stove before putting in the cake.

12. I _____ that e-mail that tells me to send in $100.

13. The store gave us a _____ because we bought two bikes.

14. It would be exciting to _____ a new star or planet.

15. We had to _____ the car horn to make it stop.

Name _____

There are six spelling mistakes in the paragraphs below. Underline the misspelled words. Write the words correctly on the lines.

Every month, I get a magazine about nature. My mom got a descount on it. It tells about all the things you can disscover if you look closely. Once I mesread an article about stars and thought it was about movie stars!

Some articles tell you how to care for animals and not misstreat them. They also tell you to beware of disshonest ads that try to sell people wild animals. Wild animals are not pets. At the end of the magazine, there is a preaview of the next month's magazine.

1. _____   4. _____

2. _____   5. _____

3. _____   6. _____

Writing Connection **Write about one of your favorite things in nature. Use at least four spelling words.**

_____
_____
_____
_____
_____
_____
_____
_____

Name _____

Remember

A prefix is added to the beginning of a word or word part to make a new word with a different meaning.

- The prefix *pre-* means *before*. *Prehistory* means *before history*.
- The prefix *mis-* means *wrong*. *Misuse* means *to use wrongly*.
- The prefix *dis-* means *not*. It changes a word to the word's opposite meaning. The word *disorder* means *not in order*.

misprint	distrust	preview	preheat	dishonest
discover	mistreat	mistrust	misspell	misread
prepaid	precut	preplan	discount	disable

Write the missing letters to make a spelling word. Read the spelling word aloud, then write it on the line.

1. __ __ __ view _____

2. __ __ __ count _____

3. __ __ __ trust _____

4. __ __ __ spell _____

5. __ __ __ read _____

6. __ __ __ cut _____

7. __ __ __ print _____

8. __ __ __ able _____

9. __ __ __ plan _____

10. __ __ __ honest _____

11. __ __ __ trust _____

12. __ __ __ treat _____

13. __ __ __ heat _____

14. __ __ __ cover _____

15. __ __ __ paid _____

Name _____

> An **idiom** is a group of words that means something different from their literal meaning. The phrase *it slipped my mind* is an idiom. It means *I forgot*. If you come across an idiom you don't know, you can look for context clues in the same sentence or a nearby sentence to help you define the idiom.

A. Read the sentences below. Underline the context clues that help you understand each idiom in bold. Then write the meaning of the idiom on the lines below.

1. I knew the answer to every question on the math exam. That test was a **piece of cake**.

   _____

2. Johnny is **in hot water** because he is late to class every day.

   _____

3. Everyone started to leave the classroom when the teacher said, "**Hold your horses**. I still need to hand out the homework assignment."

   _____

4. They had to cancel their picnic because it was **raining cats and dogs**.

   _____

B. The idiom *under the weather* means *sick* or *unwell*. Write a sentence below using the idiom *under the weather*.

   _____

   _____

Name _____

Read each sentence below. Circle the synonym that helps you figure out the meaning of each word in bold. Then write the meaning of the bold word on the line.

1. Cara was **upset**. She was sad because her swim meet was canceled.

    _____

2. The girl giving the speech was young and **brave**. She was fearless even though she was speaking to a huge crowd.

    _____

3. The farmer couldn't work on the **barren** hill. Because it was empty, it was not a place to grow food and raise animals.

    _____

4. The cheetah was **swift**. He used his quickness to catch the antelope.

    _____

5. The runner wasn't **injured**, but his pride was hurt. He knew he had lost the race.

    _____

Writing Connection | **Think of something cold. Write about it on the lines below. In your writing, use a synonym for the word *cold*, like *cool, frigid,* or *frosty*.**

_____

_____

_____

_____

_____

Name _____

> • Join two sentences with the same subject by combining the predicates. Combine the predicates by using the word *and*.
>
> • The sentences *The wolves run in the field* and *The wolves howl in the field* can be combined: *The wolves run and howl in the field.*

The pairs of sentences below share the same subject. Combine the sentences by using the word *and* to join the verbs. Then write the new sentence on the line.

1. The dancer slides. The dancer leaps.

   _____

2. The musicians smile. The musicians play.

   _____

3. More dancers appear. More dancers twirl.

   _____

4. People stand. People cheer.

   _____

5. The dancers smile. The dancers wave.

   _____

 **In your writer's notebook, write two simple sentences describing what you did for fun this weekend. Use two different verbs. Then combine the two simple sentences into one sentence. Use the above sentences as a model.**

Name _____

> • Subjects and verbs must agree. If a subject is singular, its verb must be singular. If a subject is plural, its verb must be plural.
>
> • In the sentence *The owl hop along a branch*, the subject and verb do not agree. You could correct this sentence by making the subject plural (*The owls*) or by making the verb singular (*hops*).
>
> • If a clause or phrase intervenes, or comes between, the subject and the verb, the subject and the verb must still agree.

A. Circle the correct verbs below. Then rewrite each sentence.

1. The mayor (listen, listens) to people and (help, helps) them.

_____

2. Librarians (read, reads) to children and (tell, tells) them about books.

_____

3. A baseball player (hit, hits) the ball and (run, runs) to first base.

_____

B. Circle the verb that agrees with the underlined noun.

4. The <u>children</u> who didn't go to the play left after recess.

5. <u>Angel,</u> the first boy to bake a cake for our sale, is a talented artist.

6. The <u>fox,</u> a sly gray animal, hid behind the trees.

Name _____

- Place a comma between the day and year in a date: *July 4, 1776*
- Place a comma between a street address and a city and between a town and a state in a location: *350 5th Avenue, New York, NY*
- Place a colon after the greeting of a formal letter: *Dear Mr. Lowry:*
- Place a comma after the closing of a letter: *Sincerely,*

Rewrite the letter on the lines below. Correct any missing punctuation.

808 Maple Street
Lake City FL 35678
June 15 2014

Dear Ms. Alvarez

    I ordered a Sparkle Yo-Yo from your company on May 20 2014. The yo-yo came in the mail yesterday, on June 14 2014. It looks as if you sent the Rocket Yo-Yo by mistake. I am returning the Rocket Yo-Yo. Please send the Sparkle Yo-Yo that I ordered.

Sincerely

_____

_____

_____

_____

_____

_____

_____

_____

Name _____

> • Subjects and verbs must agree with one another in number. If a subject is singular, its verb must also be singular. If a subject is plural, its verb must also be plural.
>
> • Place a comma between the day and year in a date. Place a comma between a street address and a city and between a town and a state in a location.
>
> • Place a colon after the greeting of a formal letter. Place a comma after the closing of a letter.

Rewrite each sentence on the lines below. Make sure that the verbs agree in number with the subject. Correct any mistakes in punctuation.

1. Bears eats a lot of berries and then hibernates during the winter.

_____

2. The new school in Daleville Ohio will open on September 4 2015.

_____

3. The athlete jog ten miles each day and swim twenty laps.

_____

4. Each day, I folds the newspapers and delivers them to my customers.

_____

5. The students writes the letters and sends them to Albany New York.

_____

Name _____

A. Read the paragraph. Then answer the questions.

(1) I enjoy playing baseball. (2) I enjoy playing soccer. (3) I like to be the pitcher when I play baseball. (4) My teammates say I have a good arm. (5) When I play soccer, I like to be the goalie.

1. What is the best way to combine sentences 1 and 2?
   A I enjoy playing baseball and I enjoy playing soccer.
   B I enjoy playing baseball and soccer.
   C I enjoy playing baseball and playing soccer too.
   D I enjoys playing baseball and soccer.

2. What are the subject and verb in sentence 4?
   F teammates; say
   G teammates; have
   H arm; say
   J arm; have

B. Read the student draft and look for revisions that need to be made. Then answer the questions.

(1) I wrote a letter to my cousin on April 20 2017. (2) She lives in Santa Fe New Mexico. (3) I told her that I can't wait to visit her next summer. (4) We're planning to hike through the desert!

3. What is the correct way to write sentence 1?
   A I wrote a letter to my cousin on April, 20, 2017.
   B I wrote a letter to my cousin on April, 20 2017.
   C I wrote a letter to my cousin on April 20, 2017.
   D No change needed in sentence 1.

4. What is the correct way to write sentence 2?
   F She lives in Santa Fe, New Mexico.
   G She lives in Santa Fe: New Mexico.
   H She lives in Santa Fe. New Mexico.
   J No change needed in sentence 2.

Name _____

Fold back the
paper along
the dotted line.
Use the blanks
to write each
word as it is
read aloud.
When you finish
the test, unfold
the paper. Use
the list at the
right to correct
any spelling
mistakes.

1. _____
2. _____
3. _____
4. _____
5. _____
6. _____
7. _____
8. _____
9. _____
10. _____
11. _____
12. _____
13. _____
14. _____
15. _____

Review Words
16. _____
17. _____
18. _____

Challenge Words
19. _____
20. _____

1. foil
2. coins
3. noise
4. point
5. enjoy
6. joyful
7. down
8. owl
9. crowd
10. plow
11. round
12. couch
13. proud
14. bounce
15. loudly
16. misprint
17. prepaid
18. discount
19. choice
20. snowplow

Name _____

> **Diphthongs** are sounds created when two vowels make one syllable. The /oi/ sound in *boy* can be spelled *oy* as in *toy* and *oi* as in *join*. The /ou/ sound in *cow* can be spelled *ow* as in *brown* and *ou* as in *cloud*.

DECODING WORDS

Look for word parts you know in the word *enjoyable,* such as the suffix *able.* Now look at the base word left over: *enjoy.* Divide the base word into syllables: *en/joy.* Blend the syllables together: *en/joy/a/ble.*

Read the spelling words in the box aloud. Then write the spelling words with the matching sound spellings below.

plow	bounce	couch	foil	proud
enjoy	point	owl	round	coins
noise	crowd	joyful	loudly	down

oi	*ow*	*ou*
1. _____	7. _____	11. _____
2. _____	8. _____	12. _____
3. _____	9. _____	13. _____
4. _____	10. _____	14. _____
oy		15. _____
5. _____		
6. _____		

Name _____

Diphthongs are sounds created when two vowels make one syllable. The /oi/ sound in *boy* can be spelled *oy* as in *toy* and *oi* as in *join*. The /ou/ sound in *cow* can be spelled *ow* as in *brown* and *ou* as in *cloud*.

Look for word parts you know in the word *enjoyable*, such as the suffix *able*. Now look at the base word left over: *enjoy*. Divide the base word into syllables: *en/joy*. Blend the syllables together: *en/joy/a/ble*.

Read the spelling words in the box aloud. Then write the spelling words with the matching sound spellings below.

plow	point	town	crowd	coins
house	proud	owl	shout	foil
boil	joy	oil	round	sound

oi

1. _____
2. _____
3. _____
4. _____
5. _____

oy

6. _____

ow

7. _____
8. _____
9. _____
10. _____

ou

11. _____
12. _____
13. _____
14. _____
15. _____

Name _____

A. Read the spelling words in the box aloud. Then write the spelling words with the matching sound spellings below.

voice	prowling	joyful	proud	snowplow
crowd	loyal	couch	royally	coins
noise	louder	bowed	bounce	foil

oi	*ow*	*ou*
1. _____	8. _____	12. _____
2. _____	9. _____	13. _____
3. _____	10. _____	14. _____
4. _____	11. _____	15. _____

oy

5. _____

6. _____

7. _____

B. Compare the words *crowd* and *proud*. How are the words alike? How are they different?

_____

_____

 **Look through the selections you read this week. Look for words with diphthongs spelled *oi, oy, ow,* and *ou*. Read the words you find aloud and write them in your writer's notebook.**

Name _____

foil	point	down	plow	enjoy
bounce	proud	loudly	round	coins
noise	joyful	crowd	couch	owl

A. Write the spelling word that belongs with each word group.

1. hawk, crow, _____   4. circle, ball, _____

2. sofa, chair, _____   5. lower, below, _____

3. delighted, cheerful, _____

B. Write the spelling word that best completes each sentence.

6. Mom wrapped my sandwich in _____.

7. He put three _____ in the snack machine.

8. It made a lot of _____ when she dropped the pans.

9. Can you _____ to the correct spelling?

10. We always _____ being with our good friends.

11. A huge _____ of people lined up to see the movie.

12. The farmer uses a _____ to break up the hard soil.

13. Dad was _____ of me when I won the math prize.

14. The basketball needs more air for it to _____ properly.

15. We cheered _____ when our team won the game.

Name _____

There are six misspelled words in the paragraphs below. Underline each misspelled word. Write the words correctly on the lines.

I read a book about a family who moved west. They were tired of all the noyse in the big city. There was always a croud of people on the busy streets. People shouted lowdly all the time.

They knew they would enjoi the peace and quiet of the country. They settled in a place with lots of farms. They used a plouw to break up the hard earth so they could plant wheat. At night they would poynt to all the stars they could see in the sky. They were so happy to be on their new farm.

1. _____   4. _____

2. _____   5. _____

3. _____   6. _____

Writing Connection **Write to tell some reasons that people move to new places. Use at least four spelling words.**

_____

_____

_____

_____

_____

_____

_____

_____

Name _____

Remember

A diphthong is created when two vowels make one syllable. Sometimes the same diphthong can be spelled in different ways.

- The /oi/ sound that you hear in *boy* can be spelled *oi* as in *soil* and *join*. It can also be spelled *oy* as in *toy* and *annoy*.

- The /ou/ sound that you hear in *cow* can be spelled *ou* as in *cloud* and *out*. It can also be spelled *ow* as in *brown* and *town*.

crowd	point	down	plow	proud
bounce	couch	owl	round	coins
noise	joyful	foil	enjoy	loudly

Write the missing letters to make a spelling word. Read the spelling word aloud and then write it on the line.

1. enj ____ ____   _____   9. cr _____ d   _____

2. c ____ ____ ns   _____   10. j ____ ____ ful   _____

3. l ____ ____ dly   _____   11. d ____ ____ n   _____

4. pr ____ ____ d   _____   12. c ____ ____ ch   _____

5. f ____ ____ l   _____   13. p ____ ____ nt   _____

6. pl ____ ____   _____   14. b ____ ____ nce   _____

7. r ____ ____ nd   _____   15. n ____ ____ se   _____

8. ____ ____ l   _____

Name _____

> **Content words** are specific to a field of study. The words *national* and *government* are social studies content words.
>
> You can figure out what a content word means by using context clues. You can also use a dictionary.

 **Go on a word hunt with a partner. Find content words related to unique events in our history, such as the creation of our national anthem. Write them on the stripes of the flag below.**

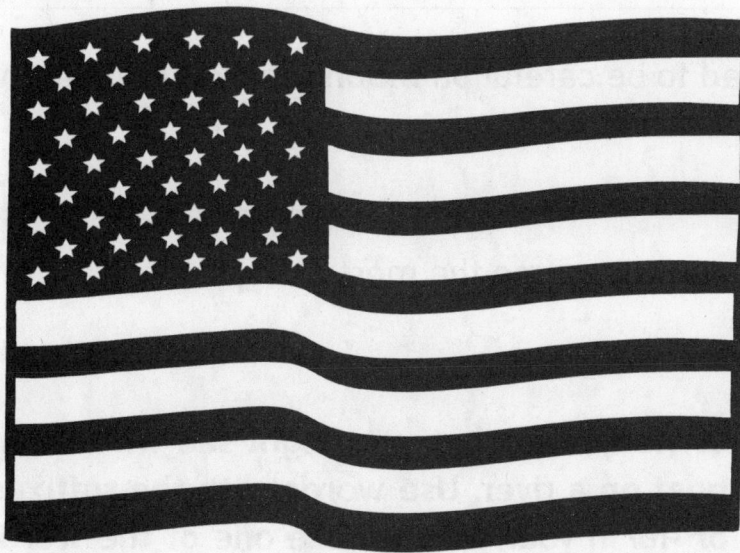

Pick two words that you were able to figure out the meaning of by using context clues. Write the words and what they mean on the lines.

_____

_____

Name _____

Read the sentences from "Mississippi Steamboats." Read each word in bold aloud. Then underline the suffix of the word in bold and write the meaning of the word on the line.

1. Captains steered the steamboats from a little house on the roof of the cabin. They had to be **watchful** of objects in the river.

   _____

2. John Fitch made the first **successful** American steamboat, but it could only float in deep water.

   _____

3. The Mississippi was not deep. However, this problem was **fixable**.

   _____

4. Captains had to be careful on **moonless** nights when it was hard to see.

   _____

5. As a result, trains became the most **acceptable** way to travel.

   _____

Writing Connection **Write about what you might see while traveling on a boat on a river. Use words with the suffixes *-ly, -able,* or *-ful* in your writing. Use one of the words above or think of your own.**

   _____
   _____
   _____
   _____
   _____

Name _____

> • An **action verb** tells what the subject does.
>
> • A **linking verb** does not show action. It connects the subject to the predicate. It describes the subject. In the sentence *The wolf is gray*, the linking verb is the word *is*.
>
> • The verb *to be* is the most common linking verb. It has special forms in the present tense: *am, is, are*.

Circle the verb in each sentence. Decide whether it is an action verb or a linking verb. Write *action* or *linking* on the line.

1. Lee is my older brother. _____

2. He plays baseball for the Comets. _____

3. My family goes to see every game. _____

4. We are so proud of him. _____

5. Lee is one of the best athletes on the team. _____

6. My dad was a football quarterback in college. _____

7. Now he coaches football for a local team. _____

8. Mom is an amazing tennis player. _____

9. I am a pretty good swimmer. _____

10. We are a very active family. _____

 **In your writer's notebook, write about a sport or game that you like to play. Reread your work when you're done to make sure you used action verbs and linking verbs correctly.**

Name _____

> • The verb *to be* is the most common linking verb. Its past tense
>   forms are *was* and *were*: He **was** a writer. They **were** readers.
>
> • Use the linking verbs *am, is,* and *was* when the subject is singular.

A. Write *am, is,* or *was* to finish each sentence.

1. I _____ in the school play that opens today.

2. My friend, Jason, _____ also in the play.

3. I _____ an astronaut who gets lost in space.

4. The play _____ funny and exciting.

5. Jason _____ silly and forgetful during yesterday's rehearsal.

6. Yesterday I _____ nervous about going on stage.

7. But today I _____ excited!

**B. Reread this paragraph from "The Impossible Pet Show." Circle the
linking verb in the underlined sentence.**

> When the show began, I gulped and announced
> the first pet. It was a parakeet named Butter whose
> talent was walking back and forth on a wire.

 **Think of a time you were nervous. In your writer's notebook,
write about what you did and how you felt. Reread your work
to make sure you used linking verbs and action verbs correctly.**

Name _____

> • Statements and commands end with periods.
>
> • A question ends with a question mark.
>
> • An exclamation ends with an exclamation point.
>
> • A complete sentence has a subject and predicate. A complete sentence must show a complete thought.

Rewrite each of the sentences below. Make sure you use correct end punctuation and capitalization.

1. a new restaurant opened in town

_____

2. what is your favorite food

_____

3. go to the new Oakville Café on Saturday

_____

4. wow, they have the best cherry pies

_____

5. have you tried the apple pies yet

_____

 **In your writer's notebook, write about your favorite food. Reread your work when you're done to make sure you used end punctuation correctly.**

Name _____

> • Statements and commands end with periods. Questions end with
>   question marks. Exclamations end with exclamation points.
>
> • The verb *to be* is the most common linking verb. Its past tense
>   forms are *was* and *were*. Use the linking verbs *am, is,* and *was*
>   when the subject is singular. Use *are* and *were* for plural subjects.
>
> • A complete sentence has a subject and a predicate and shows a
>   complete thought.

**A. Rewrite each of the sentences below. Correct the incorrect linking
verbs and any other mistakes you find.**

1. what time are the train leave the station

   _____

2. the train to Hartford are always on time

   _____

3. wow, I is going to be late if I don't hurry

   _____

4. we am at the station

   _____

**B. Add a subject or predicate to the group of words below to form a
complete sentence. Write the new sentence on the line.**

5. My grandparents are

   _____

Name _____

A. Read the paragraph. Then answer the questions.

(1) I am ten years old. (2) My older sister, Amanda, is twelve. (3) We are good friends and do a lot of things together. (4) Yesterday we were in the pool. (5) Today we are tired from swimming so much.

1. Which sentence contains a linking verb in the past tense?
   A Sentence 1
   B Sentence 2
   C Sentence 3
   D Sentence 4

2. What is the linking verb in sentence 5?
   F we
   G are
   H tired
   J swimming

B. Read the student draft and look for revisions that need to be made. Then answer the questions.

(1) My father are a great baker. (2) Yesterday he made an apple pie. (3) The filling was bubbling up through the golden crust. (4) It smelled so delicious. (5) I is so excited to try a piece!

3. What is the correct way to write sentence 1?
   A My father were a great baker.
   B My father am a great baker.
   C My father is a great baker.
   D No change needed in sentence 1.

4. What is the correct way to write sentence 5?
   F I am so excited to try a piece!
   G I are so excited to try a piece!
   H I were so excited to try a piece!
   J No change needed in sentence 5.

Name _____

Fold back the
paper along
the dotted line.
Use the blanks
to write each
word as it is
read aloud.
When you finish
the test, unfold
the paper. Use
the list at the
right to correct
any spelling
mistakes.

1. _____
2. _____
3. _____
4. _____
5. _____
6. _____
7. _____
8. _____
9. _____
10. _____
11. _____
12. _____
13. _____
14. _____
15. _____

Review Words
16. _____
17. _____
18. _____

Challenge Words
19. _____
20. _____

1. spoon
2. goose
3. booth
4. gloom
5. rude
6. tube
7. due
8. clues
9. true
10. chew
11. July
12. look
13. shook
14. notebook
15. could
16. coins
17. joyful
18. round
19. classroom
20. childhood

Name _____

> The vowel sound in the word *blue* can be spelled *oo* as in *room*, *u_e* as in *cube*, *ue* as in *cue*, *ew* as in *few*, or *u* as in *truly*. The vowel sound in the word *book* can be spelled *oo* as in *took* or *ou* as in *would*.

DECODING WORDS

The word *untrue* has two syllables that divide after the prefix *un-*, or between the consonants *n* and *t*. Blend the sounds in the syllables together: *un/true*.

Read aloud the spelling words in the box. Then write the spelling words that contain the matching sound spellings.

could	July	goose	true	rude
due	shook	clues	spoon	notebook
booth	look	chew	tube	gloom

oo as in *broom*

1. _____
2. _____
3. _____
4. _____

ew as in *few*

5. _____

u_e as in *tune*

6. _____
7. _____

ue as in *cue*

8. _____
9. _____
10. _____

oo as in *cook*

11. _____
12. _____
13. _____

ou as in *would*

14. _____

u as in *truly*

15. _____

Name _____

> The vowel sound in the word *blue* can be spelled *oo* as in *room*, *u_e* as in *cube*, *ue* as in *cue*, *ew* as in *few*, or *u* as in *truly*. The vowel sound in the word *book* can be spelled *oo* as in *took* or *ou* as in *would*.

DECODING WORDS

The word *untrue* has two syllables that divide after the prefix *un-*, or between the consonants *n* and *t*. Blend the sounds in the syllables together: *un/true*.

Read aloud the spelling words in the box. Then write the spelling words that contain the matching sound spellings.

loop	hoop	grew	true	rude
look	chew	group	soup	spoon
gloom	tube	glue	due	shook

oo as in broom

1. _____

2. _____

3. _____

4. _____

ew as in few

5. _____

6. _____

u_e as in tune

7. _____

8. _____

ue as in cue

9. _____

10. _____

11. _____

ou as in you

12. _____

13. _____

oo as in cook

14. _____

15. _____

Name _____

A. Read aloud the spelling words in the box. Then write the spelling words with the matching sound spellings.

spoon	classroom	clues	chew	booth
groups	tube	through	renew	notebook
childhood	include	could	shook	gloom

oo as in *broom*	*u_e* as in *tune*	*ew* as in *few*
1. _____	6. _____	11. _____
2. _____	7. _____	12. _____
3. _____	*oo* as in *cook*	*ou* as in *would*
4. _____	8. _____	13. _____
ue as in *cue*	9. _____	*ou* as in *you*
5. _____	10. _____	14. _____
		15. _____

B. How are the words *could* and *groups* alike? How are they different?

_____

_____

_____

Name _____

spoon	gloom	due	clues	shook
could	rude	chew	July	notebook
booth	tube	true	look	goose

Read the clues. Then use the spelling words to complete the sentences.

1
2
3
4
5   6
7
8
9
10   11
12
13

Across

3. The opposite of false

4. A hollow cylinder or pipe

6. Something to eat soup with

7. Where you buy tickets

9. The past tense of *can*

11. Hints

12. Use your eyes

13. Expected at a certain time

Down

1. Where you write things down

2. The month after June

5. A bird that lives near water

6. The past tense of *shake*

8. Darkness

10. The opposite of polite

11. Move your teeth up and down

Name _____

There are six misspelled words in the paragraphs below. Underline each misspelled word. Write the words correctly on the lines.

Once there was a gouse named Sam who didn't know how to fly. Some of the ducks on the pond were roode to Sam and teased him unkindly. One day a kind duck walked up to Sam and said, "Is it trew that you don't know how to fly?"

"I cood teach you how, if you want," said the kind duck. Duck showed Sam what to do. He said, "Lok at me fly and then do what I do." Soon, Sam was flying just like Duck. He was so happy that he shoulk with joy!

1. _____   4. _____

2. _____   5. _____

3. _____   6. _____

Writing Connection **Write a story about a character who learns something new. Use at least four spelling words in your writing.**

_____

_____

_____

_____

_____

_____

_____

Name _____

Remember

Words with the long *u* sound as in *blue* can be spelled in several ways: *oo* as in *room*, *u_e* as in *cube*, *ue* as in *cue*, *ew* as in *few*, and *u* as in *truly*. The vowel sound you hear in the word *book* can be spelled *oo* as in *took* and *ou* as in *would*.

spoon	gloom	due	chew	shook
goose	rude	clues	July	notebook
booth	tube	true	look	could

Write the missing letters to make a spelling word. Read the spelling word aloud, and then write it on the line.

1. sh ___ ___ k _____

2. sp ___ ___ n _____

3. cl ___ ___ s _____

4. r ___ d ___ _____

5. c ___ ___ ld _____

6. b ___ ___ th _____

7. ch ___ ___ _____

8. gl ___ ___ m _____

9. d ___ ___ _____

10. noteb ___ ___ k _____

11. tr ___ ___ _____

12. J ___ ___ y _____

13. l ___ ___ k _____

14. t ___ b ___ _____

15. g ___ ___ se _____

Name _____

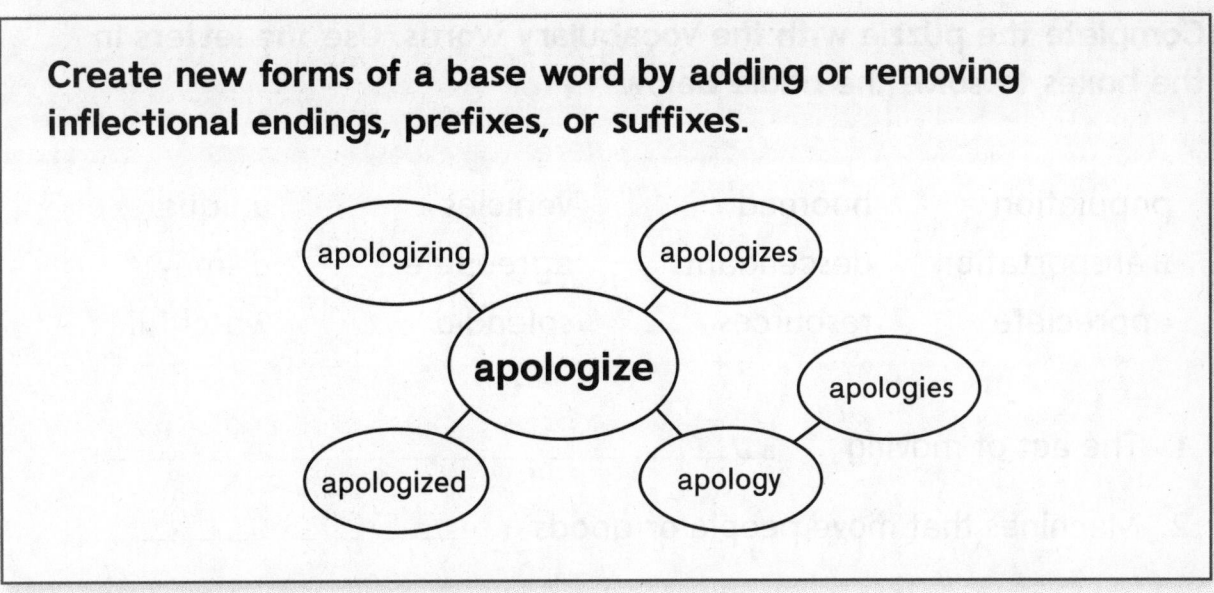

Create new forms of a base word by adding or removing inflectional endings, prefixes, or suffixes.

apologizing

apologizes

apologize

apologies

apologized

apology

Use your notes from *The Talented Clementine*. Choose one word and write it on the movie clapper board below. Then write as many related words as you can on the lines. Use a dictionary to help you.

DIRECTOR

Name _____

Complete the puzzle with the vocabulary words. Use the letters in the boxes to solve the riddle below.

population	boomed	vehicles	unique
transportation	descendants	agreeable	dismay
appreciate	resources	splendid	watchful

1. The act of moving ☐ _ _ _ _ _ _ _ _ _ _ _ _ _

2. Machines that move people or goods _ _ ☐ _ _ _ _ _

3. One of a kind _ _ _ _ _ ☐

4. Wonderful ☐ _ _ _ _ _ _ _

5. Number of people in one place _ ☐ _ _ _ _ _ _ _ _

6. Nice or pleasant _ _ _ _ _ _ _ ☐ _

7. Being careful to look out for something _ ☐ _ _ _ _ _ _

8. Be grateful for something _ _ _ ☐ _ _ _ _ _

9. Grew or expanded in a short period of time ☐ _ _ _ _ _ _

10. People after earlier generations _ ☐ _ _ _ _ _ _ _ _ _

11. Shock and surprise _ _ _ _ ☐ _

12. Materials used to perform a task _ _ _ _ _ _ ☐ _ _ _

This land animal can swim up to 100 miles at a time. What is it?

☐ ☐ ☐ ☐ ☐ ☐ ☐ ☐ ☐ ☐ ☐ ☐

Name _____

- A **contraction** is a shortened form of two words.

- An **apostrophe** (') takes the place of one or more letters in a contraction.

- Common contractions are *isn't* for *is not*, *wasn't* for *was not*, *hasn't* for *has not*, and *won't* for *will not*.

- Some contractions are formed with forms of the verbs *be, do, have* and the word *not*: *isn't, wasn't, aren't, hasn't, haven't.*

- A contraction usually changes the sound of one or both of the words being combined. For example, the short *o* in *not* is dropped in the word *isn't*. A contraction may also have a different number of syllables than the two words being combined. For example, *will not* is two syllables, but *won't* is one.

Circle the contraction in each sentence. Write the words that form the contraction.

1. Tim's book isn't on the bookshelf. _____

2. He hasn't finished reading it yet. _____

3. He won't stop looking until he finds it. _____

4. I looked in my room but it wasn't there. _____

5. The book isn't on the table. _____

6. Tim hasn't looked under the chair. _____

7. It isn't on top of Dad's bookshelf. _____

 **In your writer's notebook, write about a time when you lost something. Describe where you looked for it. Did you find it? Check for errors in contractions when you're done.**

Name _____

> • A contraction is a shortened form of two words. An apostrophe takes the place of one or more letters in a contraction.
>
> • Some more important contractions are *can't* for *can not*, *doesn't* for *does not*, *aren't* for *are not*, and *didn't* for *did not*.

A. Rewrite each sentence using a contraction with *not* in place of the underlined verb.

1. I <u>did</u> see the parade last Saturday.

_____

2. The marching band <u>does</u> practice every day.

_____

3. The big floats <u>are</u> made with lots of flowers.

_____

B. Reread this paragraph from "Painting From Memory." Circle one contraction. Write the two words that the contraction combines.

> New York was not easy at first because I knew no one and spoke imperfect English. Yet I didn't feel homesick when I looked at my paintings of home. I soon found friends at school, too. Like me, they're artists, and we now paint together after school.

_____

 **In your writer's notebook, write about something that you're lucky to have. Reread your work to check for errors.**

Name _____

> - Do not confuse contractions with **possessive nouns**. An apostrophe is used with a noun to show ownership: *The **girl's** toy*.
> - The words *don't, won't,* and *haven't* are contractions. The apostrophe shows where letters are left out.

Read each sentence. Write *C* if the underlined word is a contraction. Write *P* if it is a possessive noun.

1. I <u>don't</u> know what time the train leaves. _____

2. <u>Dave's</u> bag is already packed. _____

3. We <u>won't</u> need heavy coats in Florida. _____

4. We <u>haven't</u> decided which beach to visit first. _____

5. My <u>aunt's</u> house is near Sunrise Beach. _____

 **Write about a trip you have taken or would like to take in the future. Reread your work to make sure you used apostrophes in contractions and possessive nouns.**

_____

_____

_____

_____

_____

_____

Name _____

> • A contraction is a shortened form of two words. An apostrophe shows where letters have been left out.

A. Proofread this passage. Circle any contractions that are not correctly written.

Just a few years ago I didnt know how to tie my shoes. My Uncle Jeff said he would teach me. "It isnt' hard to do," he said. "It wont take me more than five minutes to show you how."

He showed me the steps and then I tried. But it didnt work. I ended up tying a big knot in my shoelace. "I know this is'nt how to do it," I said. Uncle Jeff showed me again. "We arent going to give up!" he told me. I tried to tie my shoe but it just wasnt working. My loops were either too big or too small. But Uncle Jeff didnt give up. Finally, I tied my shoe! "That wasnt so hard, was it?" he asked. I just laughed.

B. Rewrite the passage. Write the contractions correctly.

_____

_____

_____

_____

_____

_____

_____

_____

_____

Name _____

A. Read the paragraph. Then answer the questions.

(1) My cat's name is Max. (2) He is very independent. (3) He doesn't come when I call him. (4) He will not sit on my lap. (5) But yesterday when he was playing in the backyard, I called, "Max, Max, come inside." (6) He actually listened!

1. Which sentence uses an apostrophe that shows possession?
   A Sentence 1
   B Sentence 2
   C Sentence 3
   D Sentence 4

2. What is the correct way to write sentence 4 with a contraction for *will not*?
   F He willn't sit on my lap.
   G He won't sit on my lap.
   H He w'ont sit on my lap.
   J He wasn't sit on my lap.

B. Read the student draft and look for revisions that need to be made. Then answer the questions.

(1) My friend is a great guitar player. (2) I cant' play guitar. (3) One day, my friend said he would teach me how to play. (4) He said I could borrow his brother guitar. (5) It was so fun to learn something new.

3. What is the correct way to write sentence 2?
   A I cant play guitar.
   B I ca'nt play guitar.
   C I can't play guitar.
   D No change needed in sentence 2.

4. What is the correct way to write sentence 4?
   F He said I could borrow his brothers guitar.
   G He said I could borrow his brother's guitar.
   H He said I could borrow his brotheres' guitar.
   J No change needed in sentence 4.

Name _____

Fold back the paper along the dotted line. Use the blanks to write each word as it is read aloud. When you finish the test, unfold the paper. Use the list at the right to correct any spelling mistakes.

1. _____
2. _____
3. _____
4. _____
5. _____
6. _____
7. _____
8. _____
9. _____
10. _____
11. _____
12. _____
13. _____
14. _____
15. _____

Review Words

16. _____
17. _____
18. _____

Challenge Words

19. _____
20. _____

1. years
2. twins
3. trays
4. states
5. ashes
6. foxes
7. inches
8. flies
9. cities
10. ponies
11. bunches
12. alleys
13. lunches
14. cherries
15. daisies
16. spoon
17. clues
18. shook
19. heroes
20. libraries

Name _____

To form plural nouns, add -s to most singular nouns: *cars, books.* Add *-es* if a noun ends in *-s, -ss, -sh, -ch,* or *-x*: *buses, dresses, dishes, couches, boxes.* If a noun ends in a consonant and the letter *y,* change the *y* to an *i* and add *-es*: *stories, babies, bodies.*

DECODING WORDS

An **abbreviation** is a shortened form of a word. You don't usually sound out an abbreviation like a normal word. Instead, you pronounce the entire word that the abbreviation stands for. For example, for *in.* you read *inches.*

Read aloud the spelling words in the box. Then write the spelling words that have the plural endings listed below.

years	lunches	inches	twins	foxes
ponies	cities	flies	bunches	cherries
daisies	states	ashes	alleys	trays

add -s	add -es	change *y* to *i* and add -es
1. _____	6. _____	11. _____
2. _____	7. _____	12. _____
3. _____	8. _____	13. _____
4. _____	9. _____	14. _____
5. _____	10. _____	15. _____

Name _____

To form plural nouns, add -s to most singular nouns: *cars, books*. Add -*es* if a noun ends in -*s*, -*ss*, -*sh*, -*ch*, or -*x*: *buses, dresses, dishes, couches, boxes*. If a noun ends in a consonant and the letter *y*, change the *y* to an *i* and add -*es*: *stories, babies, bodies*.

SPELLING TIP

An **abbreviation** is a shortened form of a word. You don't usually sound out an abbreviation like a normal word. Instead, you pronounce the entire word that the abbreviation stands for. For example, for *in.* you read *inches*.

Read aloud the spelling words in the box. Then write the spelling words that have the plural endings listed below.

years	states	inches	lunches	ashes
bodies	skies	boxes	horses	twins
trays	foxes	cities	ties	flies

add -*s*

1. _____

2. _____

3. _____

4. _____

5. _____

6. _____

add -*es*

7. _____

8. _____

9. _____

10. _____

11. _____

change *y* to *i* and add -*es*

12. _____

13. _____

14. _____

15. _____

Name _____

A. Read aloud the spelling words in the box. Then write the spelling words that have the plural endings listed below.

trays	inches	alleys	heroes	cherries
journeys	ponies	eyelashes	libraries	ashes
foxes	bunches	daisies	chimneys	scratches

add -s

1. _____
2. _____
3. _____
4. _____

add -es

5. _____
6. _____
7. _____
8. _____
9. _____
10. _____
11. _____

change _y_ to _i_ and add -es

12. _____
13. _____
14. _____
15. _____

B. How are the words _alleys_ and _ponies_ alike? How are they different?

_____

_____

_____

 **Look back through the reading selections you read this week for plural nouns. Read the words you find aloud. Then create a word sort for a partner.**

Name _____

years	states	inches	ponies	lunches
twins	ashes	flies	bunches	cherries
trays	foxes	cities	alleys	daisies

A. Write a spelling word that goes with the other two words.

1. apples, grapes, _____
4. puppies, calves, _____

2. towns, villages, _____
5. days, months, _____

3. bears, wolves, _____
6. roses, tulips, _____

B. Write the spelling word that best completes each sentence.

7. Small streets behind buildings are called _____.

8. The waiters brought our food to us on large _____.

9. There are fifty _____ in the United States.

10. Tiny insects called _____ can buzz through the air.

11. After the campfire is out, we pour water on the _____.

12. Students may buy their _____ at school or bring them from home.

13. Groups of something are often called _____.

14. This ruler shows that there are 12 _____ in one foot.

15. A brother and sister who are _____ are alike in many ways.

Name _____

There are six spelling mistakes in the paragraphs below. Underline the misspelled words. Write the words correctly on the lines.

Pam and Tam are eight yeares old. They are also twines who look exactly alike. But Pam and Tam like different things. Pam's favorite fruit is cherrys, but Tam likes apples the best.

Pam likes insects, such as bees, flys, and moths. She also likes birds, especially the big crows that make such noise. Tam likes working in her flower garden. She grows roses, lilies, and daisys. She doesn't like the crows that fly down and nip at her colorful flowers. One day, Pam had a good idea. She made a scarecrow. It was thirty inchs tall. She placed him on a pole in the garden. The crows never bothered Tam's flowers again!

1. _____ 4. _____

2. _____ 5. _____

3. _____ 6. _____

Writing Connection **Write a story about a character who solves a problem. Use at least four spelling words in your story.**

_____

_____

_____

_____

_____

_____

Name _____

Remember

Add *-s* to most singular nouns to create plural nouns. Add *-es* if a singular noun ends in *-s, -ss, -sh, -ch,* or *-x*. If a singular noun ends in a consonant and *y*, change the *y* to an *i* and add *-es*.

years	states	inches	ponies	lunches
twins	ashes	flies	bunches	cherries
trays	foxes	cities	alleys	daisies

Write the missing letters to make a spelling word. Read the spelling word aloud and then write it on the line.

1. fl __ __ __   _____

2. bunch __ __   _____

3. twin __   _____

4. fox __ __   _____

5. cherr __ __ __   _____

6. lunch __ __   _____

7. dais __ __ __   _____

8. tray __   _____

9. pon __ __ __   _____

10. all __ __ __   _____

11. inch __ __   _____

12. cit __ __ __   _____

13. ash __ __   _____

14. year __   _____

15. stat __ __   _____

Name _____

> A **base word** is the simplest form of a word. It has no prefixes, suffixes, or inflectional endings added to it. For example, *success* is the base word of *successful*.
>
> You can use base words to figure out the meaning of an unfamiliar word. You might know that *success* means a result that you hoped for. You know that the suffix *-ful* means *full of.* So the word *successful* must mean *full of success*.

How many words can you make with the base word *perfect*? Write the words on the tree branches below. Use a dictionary and your knowledge of prefixes, suffixes, and inflectional endings to help you.

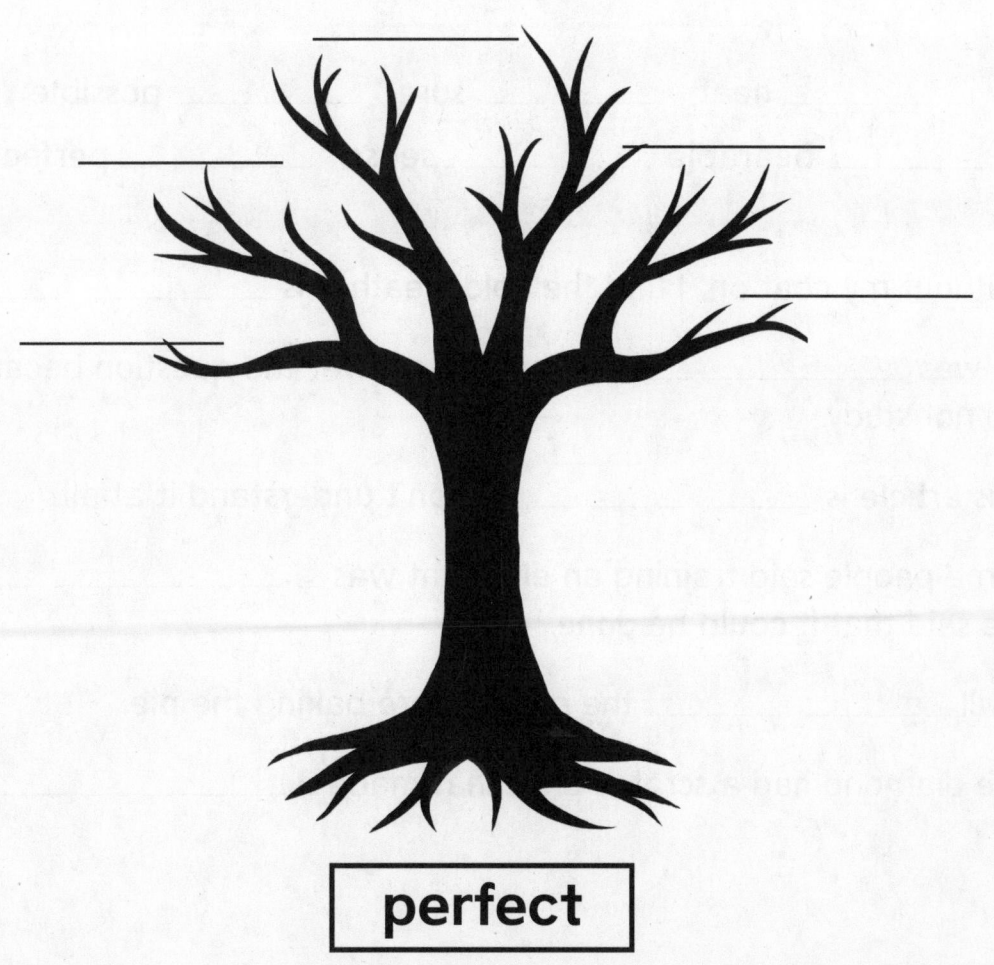

perfect

Name _____

A **prefix** is a word part added to the beginning of a word. A prefix changes the meaning of the word it is added to. You can use prefixes to help you figure out the meaning of unfamiliar words.

- The prefix *pre-* means *before.* For example, the word *preview* means to *view or see before.*

- The prefixes *un-, im-,* and *non-* mean *not* or *opposite of.* The word *uncomfortable* means *not comfortable, impolite* means *not polite,* and *nonfiction* means *the opposite of fiction.*

Add the prefix *pre-, un-, im-,* or *non-* to the words in the box below. Then complete the sentences with the new words.

_____ heat   _____ sure   _____ possible
_____ bearable   _____ sense   _____ perfect

1. Without my coat on, I find the cold weather is _____.

2. He was _____ of how to answer the question because he did not study.

3. This article is _____! I don't understand it at all.

4. Some people said training an elephant was _____, but she said that it could be done.

5. I will _____ the oven before baking the pie.

6. The diamond had a scratch on it that made it _____.

Name _____

> • A verb may be more than one word. The **main verb** tells what the subject is or does. The **helping verb** helps the main verb show action: *has baked; have climbed; had seen.*
>
> • The words *have, has,* and *had* can be helping verbs in simple and compound sentences: *Mom and I have baked a cake. She had baked a pie, and Dad had baked bread.*
>
> • The words *can, could, should* and *must* are special helping verbs. They tell whether something is possible or a duty: *I can sing. I must study.*

Read each sentence. Underline the main verb. Circle the helping verb.

1. Jenna has read a book about recycling.

2. Mr. Hart's class had started recycling last year.

3. We have decided that we want to help his class.

Read each sentence. Underline the special helping verb. Circle the main verb. Tell whether it says something is possible or a duty.

4. We must learn how to recycle our bottles and papers. _____

5. Ali can tell us how to recycle a milk carton. _____

6. I should share my ideas about recycling with our class. _____

7. We could write about how we recycle. _____

Name _____

> • Perfect tenses use the past participle of the verb being helped: *He has walked two miles today.*
>
> • Progressive tenses use the *-ing* form of the verb being helped with the present, past, or future tense of the verb *to be. We are leaving early tomorrow.*
>
> • The verb forms of *to be* can also act as helping verbs. *Is, are, am, was, were,* and *will* can be helping verbs: *I **am thinking** about it.* So can the verb *to have: have, has, had, will have. I will have eaten by 1:00.*
>
> • The helping verb must agree with the subject of the sentence.

A. Complete each sentence with the correct helping verb.

1. Next week my family _____ visit Mount Rushmore.   will   are

2. We _____ planning to leave Tuesday.   am   are

3. I _____ reading a book about the monument.   is   am

4. My dad _____ telling us about his first trip there.   was   will

5. The car trip _____ take ten hours.   is   will

B. Add helping verbs and circle the main verbs.

6. We _____ learned how to swim by the end of summer.

7. Amir _____ gone to school by 8:00 a.m.

8. She _____ reading her book when the lights went out.

9. They _____ waiting for the bus yesterday in the rain.

10. He _____ written a long report.

Name _____

> • Quotation marks show that someone is speaking. They come at the beginning and end of the speaker's exact words: *"Let's go swimming," I said.* Punctuation appears inside quotation marks.
>
> • If the end of a quotation comes at the end of a sentence, end the sentence with a period, question mark, or exclamation mark.
>
> • If the sentence continues after a quotation, close the quotation with a comma, question mark, or exclamation mark.

Rewrite each line of dialogue below. Use quotation marks and commas correctly.

1. We had lots of snow last night said Mom.

_____

2. Do you think the schools will be closed today I asked.

_____

3. Mom said, Let's turn on the TV to see if there is an announcement.

_____

4. School officials just told us that Baker City Schools will be closed today said the announcer.

_____

_____

 **In your writer's notebook, write about a conversation you had with a friend or family member. Check your work to make sure you used quotation marks to show a speaker's exact words.**

Name _____

> • Use quotation marks at the beginning and end of a speaker's exact words. Commas and periods always appear inside quotation marks.
>
> • The helping verb must agree with the subject of the sentence in simple and compound sentences.

A. Proofread this passage. Circle any incorrect helping verbs. Underline any dialogue that is not written correctly.

I are helping my neighbor with his vegetable garden. He am planting lettuce and tomatoes. I said Mr. Jackson where do you want me to plant these cucumber seeds. He said Let's put them in the next row. Mr. Jackson and I was working hard all afternoon. Look at that dark cloud I told him. I hope the rain are wait until we finish he said. "Me, too, I said."

> **HANDWRITING CONNECTION**
>
> Be sure to write legibly. Use proper cursive and remember to leave spaces between words.

B. Rewrite the passage. Write helping verbs correctly. Use commas and quotation marks correctly.

_____

_____

_____

_____

_____

_____

Name _____

A. Read the paragraph. Then answer the questions about the progressive tense.

(1) Yesterday I was painting a picture of our garden when my friend Samantha stopped by. (2) "Today my Mom and I are driving up to the mountains for a picnic," Samantha said. (3) "Do you want to come along?" she asked. (4) "Absolutely!" I exclaimed. (5) "You can paint a picture of the mountains," Samantha said.

1. What is the helping verb in sentence 1?

A was

B painting

C picture

D stopped

2. What is the main verb in sentence 2?

F are

G driving

H mountains

J picnic

B. Read the student draft and look for revisions that need to be made. Then answer the questions about the progressive and perfect tenses.

(1) Katie has an amazing singing voice. (2) She have taken singing lessons for three years. (3) I am planning a party for all my students, her singing teacher said. (4) "Will you sing at the party?" she asked. (5) "Sure!" Katie said.

3. What is the correct way to write sentence 2?

A She is taken singing lessons for three years.

B She taken singing lessons for three years.

C She has taken singing lessons for three years.

D No change needed in sentence 2.

4. What is the correct way to write sentence 3?

F "I am planning a party for all my students." Her singing teacher said.

G "I am planning a party for all my students," her singing teacher said.

H "I am planning a party for all my students, her singing teacher said."

J No change needed in sentence 3.

Name _____

Fold back the paper along the dotted line. Use the blanks to write each word as it is read aloud. When you finish the test, unfold the paper. Use the list at the right to correct any spelling mistakes.	
	1. _____
	2. _____
	3. _____
	4. _____
	5. _____
	6. _____
	7. _____
	8. _____
	9. _____
	10. _____
	11. _____
	12. _____
	13. _____
	14. _____
	15. _____
Review Words	16. _____
	17. _____
	18. _____
Challenge Words	19. _____
	20. _____

1. taught
2. hauls
3. caused
4. paused
5. squawk
6. drawing
7. crawl
8. flawless
9. lawn
10. salt
11. talked
12. halls
13. water
14. bought
15. thoughtless
16. inches
17. cities
18. cherries
19. walrus
20. autumn

Name _____

> The vowel sound in the word *straw* can be spelled *au* as in *autumn*, *aw* as in *dawn*, *a* as in *tall*, and *ough* as in *thought*.

DECODING WORDS

The word *thoughtless* has two syllables that divide between the base word *thought* and the suffix *-less*. Blend the syllables: *thought/less*. **Note:** The letters *ough* also form long *o* as in *though*, *off* as in *cough*, and *uff* as in *tough*.

Read aloud the spelling words in the box. Then write the spelling words that contain the matching spelling patterns.

salt	paused	halls	hauls	drawing
taught	squawk	flawless	lawn	caused
bought	water	talked	crawl	thoughtless

/ô/ spelled *au*

1. _____

2. _____

3. _____

4. _____

/ô/ spelled *aw*

5. _____

6. _____

7. _____

8. _____

9. _____

/ô/ spelled *a*

10. _____

11. _____

12. _____

13. _____

/ô/ spelled *ough*

14. _____

15. _____

Look through the selections you read this week for words with the vowel sound spellings *au*, *aw*, *a*, and *ough*. Read the words you find aloud and record them in your writer's notebook.

Name _____

The vowel sound in the word *straw* can be spelled *au* as in *autumn, aw* as in *dawn, a* as in *tall,* and *ough* as in *thought*.

DECODING WORDS

The word *thoughtless* has two syllables that divide between the base word *thought* and the suffix *-less*. Blend the syllables together: *thought/less*. **Note:** The letters *ough* can also form long *o* as in *though*, *off* as in *cough*, and *uff* as in *tough*.

Write the spelling words that contain the matching spelling patterns.

crawl	salt	draw	raw	walk
water	halt	ball	taught	hauls
caused	halls	lawn	small	bought

/ô/ spelled *au*

1. _____

2. _____

3. _____

/ô/ spelled *ough*

4. _____

/ô/ spelled *a*

5. _____

6. _____

7. _____

8. _____

9. _____

10. _____

11. _____

/ô/ spelled *aw*

12. _____

13. _____

14. _____

15. _____

 Look through the selections you read this week for words with the vowel sound spellings *au, aw, a,* and *ough*. Read the words you find aloud and record them in your writer's notebook.

Name _____

A. Read aloud the spelling words in the box. Then write the spelling words that have the matching spelling patterns.

taught	paused	squawk	crawl	walrus
thoughtless	fault	halted	sought	hauls
stalk	salt	smallness	scrawny	flawless

/ô/ spelled *au*

1. _____

2. _____

3. _____

4. _____

/ô/ spelled *a*

5. _____

6. _____

7. _____

8. _____

9. _____

/ô/ spelled *aw*

10. _____

11. _____

12. _____

13. _____

/ô/ spelled *ough*

14. _____

15. _____

B. Compare the words *taught* and *sought*. How are they alike? How are they different?

_____

_____

_____

 **Look through the selections you read this week for words with the vowel sound spellings *au*, *aw*, *a*, and *ough*. Read the words you find aloud and record them in your writer's notebook.**

Name _____

taught	paused	crawl	salt	flawless
bought	halls	water	talked	hauls
caused	drawing	lawn	squawk	thoughtless

A. Write the spelling word with the opposite meaning of each word written below.

1. learned _____

3. thoughtful _____

2. sold _____

4. listened _____

B. Write the spelling word that best completes each sentence.

5. That truck _____ loads of dirt and rock.

6. The ice storm _____ many trees to break.

7. Please get a glass of _____ for the speaker.

8. The students hung artwork in the _____ of our school.

9. A diamond that is perfect is called _____.

10. Some birds make pleasing sounds, but other birds only _____.

11. If it doesn't rain soon, Dad will have to water the _____.

12. I made a _____ of our school using charcoal pencils.

13. Babies learn to _____ before they walk.

14. Our principal _____ before he continued speaking.

15. This popcorn has too much _____ and butter.

Name _____

There are six misspelled words in the paragraphs below. Underline the misspelled words. Write the words correctly on the lines.

I heard a loud squauk sound outside my window. I saw a bird sitting in the bird bath in the middle of our laun. The bird splashed in the wawter and made a lot of noise.

I made a drauing of the bird so I would remember it. The next day I showed it to my teacher. She looked at it and then pawsed. "I think it might be a blue jay," she said. Together, we found a book about birds in the library. She tawt me how to identify the bird by finding it in the book. "Yes, that's it!" I said when I saw the blue jay's picture.

1. _____ 4. _____

2. _____ 5. _____

3. _____ 6. _____

Writing Connection **Write about a bird that you have seen. Tell what it looks and sounds like. Use at least four spelling words.**

_____
_____
_____
_____
_____
_____
_____
_____
_____
_____

Name _____

Remember

The vowel sound that you hear in the word *straw* can be spelled in different ways: *au* as in *autumn*, *aw* as in *dawn*, *a* as in *tall*, and *ough* as in *thought*.

taught	paused	crawl	salt	water
hauls	squawk	flawless	talked	bought
caused	drawing	lawn	halls	thoughtless

Write the missing letters to make a spelling word. Read the spelling word aloud and then write it on the line.

1. s ___ ___ t   _____

2. h ___ ___ ls   _____

3. squ ___ ___ k   _____

4. c ___ ___ sed   _____

5. dr ___ ___ ing   _____

6. b ___ ___ ght   _____

7. w ___ ter   _____

8. t ___ ___ ght   _____

9. p ___ ___ sed   _____

10. h ___ lls   _____

11. cr ___ ___ l   _____

12. l ___ ___ n   _____

13. fl ___ ___ less   _____

14. t ___ ___ ked   _____

15. th ___ ___ ghtless   _____

Name _____

Content words are specific to a field of study. The word *desert* is a science content word.

Authors use content words to explain a concept or idea. You can figure out what a content word means by using context clues or a dictionary.

CONNECT TO CONTENT

Amazing Wildlife of the Mojave is an informational text that gives facts about the Mojave Desert and the animals that live there. The author uses science content words such as *adapted* to help you understand how mammals, birds, reptiles, and insects survive in the hot, dry desert.

 Go on a word hunt with a partner. Find content words related to deserts and wildlife. Write them on the hawk's wings.

Pick two words you could figure out the meaning of using context clues. Write the words and what they mean on the lines.

_____

_____

Name _____

Use the words in the box and the clues to solve the crossword puzzle.

apologized	confidence	talents	disbelief
attention	embarrassed	achievement	fabulous
audience	realized	offered	features

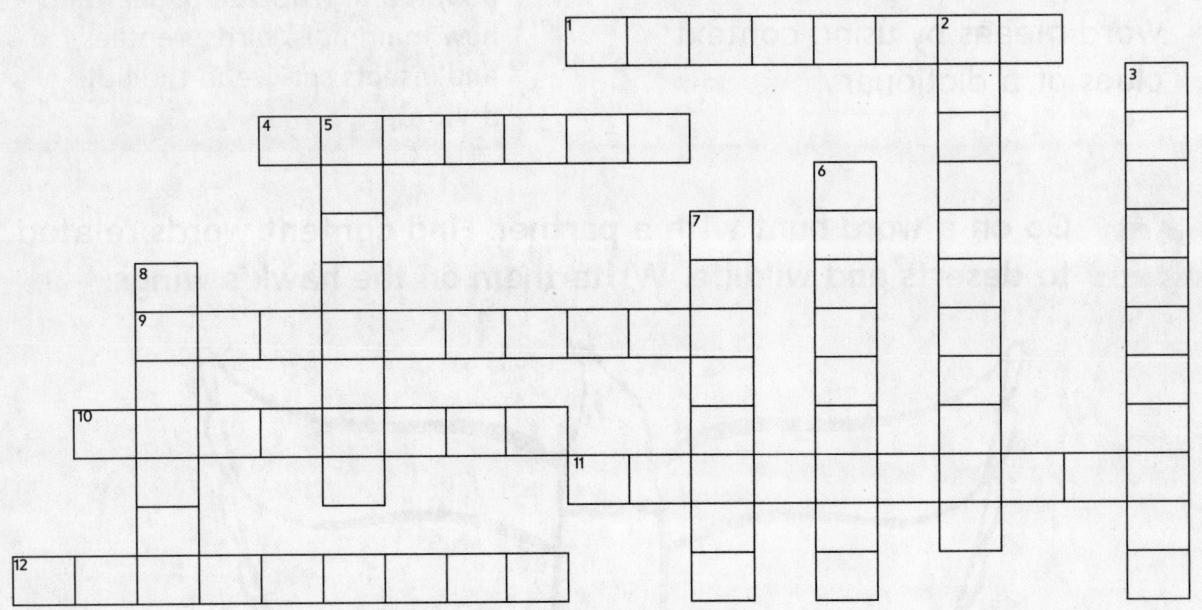

Across

1. Understood or became aware of something

4. Presented help for someone to accept or turn down

9. Said sorry

10. Traits or qualities of something

11. Belief or trust in yourself

12. Lack of faith or trust in something

Down

2. Uncomfortable or ashamed

3. The result of hard work

5. Excellent

6. Careful watching or listening

7. A group of people watching a performance

8. Natural abilities or skills

Name _____

- A **clause** is a group of words that has a subject and a verb.

- An **independent, or main, clause** can stand alone as a sentence: *He was tired.* A **dependent, or subordinate, clause** cannot stand alone as a sentence: *Because he went for a hike.*

- A verb must agree with the subject, even when a clause separates them. *Jane and Lee, who is from China, visit us often.*

- A **simple sentence** has one independent clause.

- A **compound sentence** has two or more independent clauses.

A. Read each clause. Write *yes* if the clause is independent. Write *no* if it is not an independent clause.

1. My dad works at a pet store. _____

2. Takes care of the fish and reptiles. _____

3. He tells people how to care for their new pets. _____

4. Mom likes dogs, but I like cats. _____

5. People who want to buy pets. _____

B. Circle the verb that agrees with the underlined noun.

6. The <u>dog</u> that my friend watches ran fast.

7. <u>Bert,</u> who I met at school, won the spelling bee.

Name _____

> • Dependent, or subordinate, clauses cannot stand alone as a sentence and are introduced by **subordinating conjunctions**: *When I get older . . .*
> • Some examples of subordinating conjunctions are *after, because, if, unless, while, until, when,* and *before.*

A. Read each sentence. Circle the dependent clause. Write the subordinating conjunction on the line.

1. After my dad gets home, we will go to the game. _____

2. While Mom makes dinner, I'll do my homework. _____

3. I think the game will be called off because it is raining. _____

4. I won't know the score until they make an announcement. _____

5. If the game isn't played today, it will be held next Saturday. _____

B. Reread the paragraph from "Gray Wolf! Red Fox!" Underline the dependent clause in the last sentence. Circle the subordinating conjunction.

Did you ever see a photograph of a gray wolf or a red fox? Don't they look a lot like dogs? Aren't they fantastic-looking animals? Well, dogs, foxes, and wolves are all related. They are all members of the same family. And while gray wolves and red foxes might look alike, they are different in many ways.

 **In your writer's notebook, write about some other animals that look alike, like cheetahs and tigers or horses and zebras. Reread your work to make sure you used complete sentences.**

Name _____

> • When an independent, or main, clause begins a sentence, it is not usually followed by a comma: *We'll eat lunch after we go swimming.*
>
> • When a dependent, or subordinate, clause begins a sentence, it is usually followed by a comma: *After we go swimming, we'll eat lunch.*
>
> • A **complex sentence** includes an independent, or main, clause and one dependent, or subordinate, clause introduced by a subordinating conjunction.

Combine the clauses, using a comma when needed.

1. Our school day ends. When the bell sounds at 3:30.

_____

2. Unless I have soccer practice. I go home and do my homework.

_____

3. My dad picks me up. When my mom has to work late.

_____

4. If school is closed early. My neighbor, Mrs. Carter, picks me up.

_____

 **In your writer's notebook, write about what you do when you get home from school. Use the sentences above as a model. Check that you used commas correctly.**

Name _____

> • An independent, or main, clause can stand alone as a sentence. A dependent, or subordinate, clause cannot stand alone as a sentence.
>
> • A simple sentence has one independent clause. A compound sentence has two or more independent clauses. A complex sentence includes an independent and dependent clause.
>
> • When an independent clause begins a sentence, it usually is not followed by a comma. When a dependent clause begins a sentence, it usually is followed by a comma.

A. Rewrite the sentences below. Use commas correctly as needed.

1. When vacation starts I am going to visit my aunt in California.

_____

2. My aunt lives in Malibu and she, has a house on the beach.

_____

3. Mom, plans to go there, after her job ends in June.

_____

4. If my aunt will let me I hope, to learn how to surf.

_____

B. Combine the following dependent and independent clauses. Write the sentence correctly on the line.

5. Because my aunt is a professional surfer. She can give me lessons.

_____

Name _____

A. Read the paragraph. Then answer the questions.

(1) Today my family and I are going to the amusement park. (2) We'll go on the roller coaster first. (3) After we ride the roller coaster, we'll go on the Ferris wheel. (4) It'll be a lot of fun!

1. Which sentence begins with a dependent clause?
   A Sentence 1
   B Sentence 2
   C Sentence 3
   D Sentence 4

2. What is the subordinating conjunction in sentence 3?
   F After
   G we
   H the
   J on

B. Read the student draft and look for revisions that need to be made. Then answer the questions.

(1) My mother is teaching my older brother how to drive a car. (2) Because there is little traffic they practice in the morning. (3) My brother must pass the driving test, before he gets his license. (4) When he has his license, he can drive me to school.

3. What is the correct way to write sentence 2?
   A Because, there is little traffic they practice in the morning.
   B Because there is little traffic they, practice, in the morning.
   C Because there is little traffic, they practice in the morning.
   D No change needed in sentence 2.

4. What is the correct way to write sentence 3?
   F My brother must pass the driving test before he gets his license.
   G My brother must pass the driving test before, he gets his license.
   H My brother must pass, the driving test before he gets his license.
   J No change needed in sentence 3.

Name _____

Fold back the
paper along
the dotted line.
Use the blanks
to write each
word as it is
read aloud.
When you finish
the test, unfold
the paper. Use
the list at the
right to correct
any spelling
mistakes.

1. _____
2. _____
3. _____
4. _____
5. _____
6. _____
7. _____
8. _____
9. _____
10. _____
11. _____
12. _____
13. _____
14. _____
15. _____

Review Words 16. _____
17. _____
18. _____

Challenge Words 19. _____
20. _____

1. sale
2. sail
3. beet
4. beat
5. rode
6. road
7. rowed
8. its
9. it's
10. your
11. you're
12. their
13. they're
14. peace
15. piece
16. taught
17. talked
18. bought
19. seen
20. scene

Name _____

> **Homophones** are words that sound alike but have different meanings and spellings. For example, the words *blue* and *blew* sound the same, but *blue* refers to the color and *blew* is the past tense of the verb *blow*.

> **DECODING WORDS**
>
> A **contraction** is formed when two words combine into one word. A contraction usually changes or drops a sound from one or both of the words being combined. For example, in the word *doesn't* the short *o* in *not* is dropped.

Write the spelling words that are homophones of the words below.

sale	its	rowed	your	they're
peace	rode	beat	beet	sail
you're	road	it's	their	piece

1. piece _____
2. you're _____
3. beet _____
4. it's _____

5. sale _____
6. rode _____
   _____
7. they're _____

Which spelling words are contractions?

8. _____   9. _____   10. _____

Write the spelling words with long *e* as in *tree*.

11. _____
12. _____

13. _____
14. _____

 Look through the selections you read this week and search for homophones. Read the words you find aloud. Then record them in your writer's notebook.

Name _____

Homophones are words that sound alike but have different meanings and spellings. For example, the words *blue* and *blew* sound the same, but *blue* refers to the color and *blew* is the past tense of the verb *blow*.

DECODING WORDS

A **contraction** is formed when two words combine into one word. A contraction usually changes or drops a sound from one or both of the words being combined. For example, in the word *doesn't* the short *o* in *not* is dropped.

Write the spelling words that are homophones of the words below.

road	your	it's	sea	you're
see	rode	beet	two	sail
to	sale	too	beat	its

1. see _____

2. you're _____

3. beet _____

4. it's _____

5. sale _____

6. to _____

_____

7. rode _____

Which spelling words are contractions?

8. _____

9. _____

Write the spelling words with long *e* as in *tree*.

10. _____

11. _____

12. _____

13. _____

 **Look through the selections you read this week and search for homophones. Read the words you find aloud. Then record them in your writer's notebook.**

Name _____

A. Read aloud the spelling words in the box. Then write the spelling words that are homophones of the words below.

its	you're	their	seen	flee
weight	flea	scene	peace	it's
piece	they're	your	there	wait

1. piece _____
2. you're _____
3. seen _____
4. it's _____

5. flea _____
6. there _____
7. wait _____

Which spelling words are contractions?

8. _____ 9. _____ 10. _____

Write the spelling words with long *e* as in *tree*.

11. _____ 13. _____ 15. _____
12. _____ 14. _____ 16. _____

B. Compare the words *wait* and *weight*. How are they alike? How are they different?

_____

_____

_____

Look through the selections you read this week and search for homophones. Read the words you find aloud. Then record them in your writer's notebook.

Name _____

sale	beat	rowed	your	they're
sail	rode	its	you're	peace
beet	road	it's	their	piece

A. Write the spelling word that matches each meaning.

1. cloth to catch wind _____ 4. part of something _____

2. red vegetable _____ 5. path for vehicles _____

3. opposite of *my* _____

B. Write the spelling word that best completes each sentence.

6. Alex used both oars and _____ the canoe to the island.

7. Sean said to me, "_____ going to love summer camp."

8. After the loud concert, I will need _____ and quiet.

9. Our scout troop _____ on a big float in the parade.

10. I finally _____ my big brother at chess.

11. This is a good time to buy a bike because they are on _____.

12. The campers lost _____ map on the first day.

13. Do you think _____ too early to show up?

14. Dad pointed to the firefighters and said, "_____ the real heroes."

15. The cat licked _____ sore paw.

Name _____

There are six mistakes in the use of homophones in the paragraphs below. Circle the incorrectly used homophones. Write the correct homophones on the lines.

Come visit Lakeview Cottages on you're next vacation. You can sale on Lake Emerald and picnic on Jasper Island. Their are lots of things to see and do in the area.

If your looking for piece and quiet, then this is the place to come. We are just up the rode on Saddleback Highway, about ten miles from Dover. Hope to see you soon!

1. _____   4. _____

2. _____   5. _____

3. _____   6. _____

Writing Connection **Write a vacation booklet about a place you want to see. Use at least four spelling words or other homophones in your writing.**

_____

_____

_____

_____

_____

_____

_____

_____

Name _____

Homophones are words that sound the same but have different spellings and meanings. A pair or group of homophones often use different vowel spellings, such as the words *blue* and *blew, ate* and *eight,* and *meat* and *meet.*

sale	beat	their	your	they're
peace	it's	its	you're	sail
beet	road	rode	rowed	piece

Write the missing letters to make a spelling word. Read the spelling word aloud, then write it on the line.

1. r __ d __ _____
2. r __ __ d _____
3. r __ __ ed _____
4. pea __ __ _____
5. pie __ __ _____
6. th __ __ r _____
7. th __ __ 're _____
8. s __ l __ _____

9. s __ __ l _____
10. y __ __ r _____
11. y __ __ 're _____
12. i __ s _____
13. i __ 's _____
14. b __ __ t _____
15. b __ e __ _____

Name _____

Many words have roots from Greek and Latin. You can use your knowledge of Greek and Latin roots to figure out the meaning of an unfamiliar word.

The Latin root *aud* means to hear. This can help you understand that the word *audible* means *can be heard*.

The Greek root *graph* means *written,* and the root *bio* means *life*. This helps me see that a *biography* is a written work about someone's life.

The Greek root *tele-* means *far away*. How many words can you make with *tele-*? Write a word in each column. Use a dictionary for help.

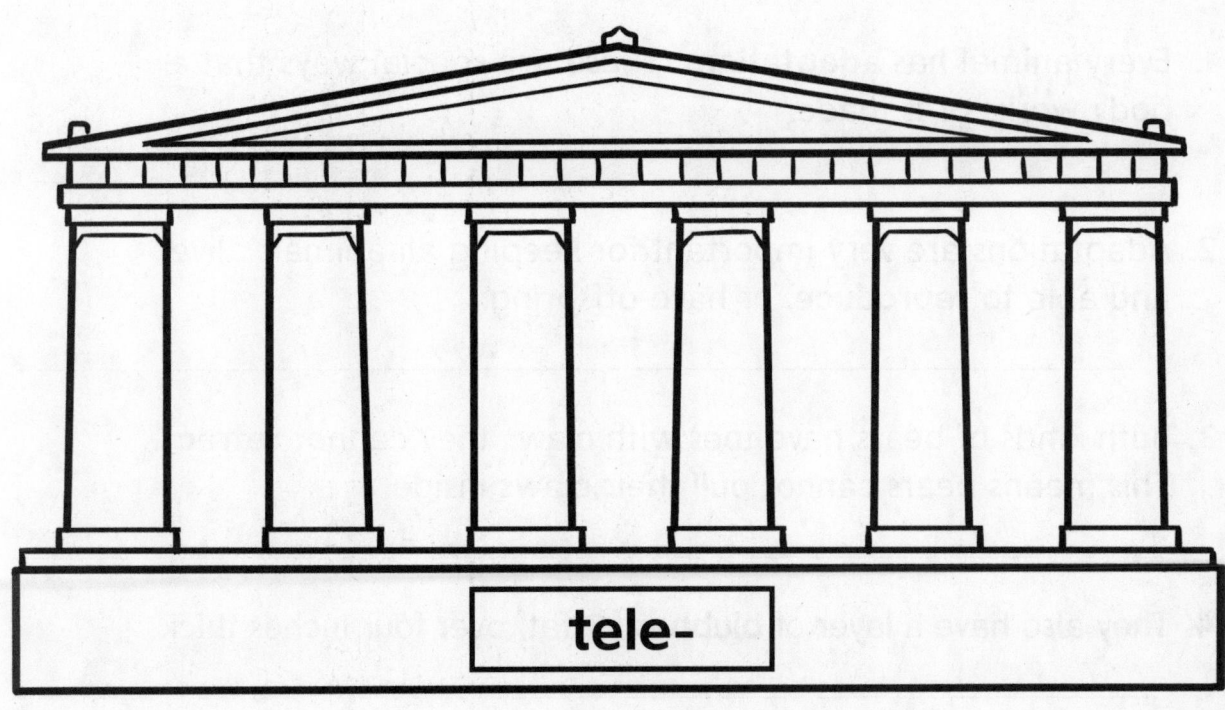

tele-

Name _____

> When you come across a new word, you can look for clues in the sentence or a nearby sentence to figure out the word's meaning. Also use your background knowledge, or what you know already.
>
> *Most bats are nocturnal. They sleep during the daytime and look for food at night.*
>
> To find the meaning of *nocturnal* in the first sentence, look at the second sentence for a clue. If bats sleep during the day and eat at night, then *nocturnal* must mean *active during the nighttime.*

Read the following sentences from "Adaptations: Grizzly and Polar Bears." Underline the sentence clues that help you figure out the meaning of each word in bold. Write the word's meaning on the line.

1. Every animal has **adaptations**. These are special ways that a body works or is made.

   _____

2. Adaptations are very important for keeping all animals alive and able to **reproduce**, or have offspring.

   _____

3. Both kinds of bears have toes with claws they cannot **retract**. This means bears cannot pull their claws inside.

   _____

4. They also have a layer of **blubber**, or fat, over four inches thick.

   _____

5. This helps them blend in with the trees and rocks in their **environment**, or where they live.

   _____

Name _____

> • Not all verbs add -*ed* to form the past tense.
>
> • An **irregular verb** has a special spelling for the past tense. Some irregular verbs are: *come/came, do/did, say/said, go/went, eat/ate,* and *sing/sang.*
>
> • A simple sentence has one independent clause.
>
> • A compound sentence has two or more independent clauses.

Write the correct past-tense form of the verb to finish the sentence.

1. come   An author _____ to our school yesterday.

2. sing   I _____ a song for our school talent show.

3. do   Cam _____ the same juggling act as last year.

4. eat   We _____ our lunch outside today.

5. go   My friend _____ camping last week.

6. say   Our teacher _____ that everyone did a great job.

7. run   My sister _____ a marathon last year.

8. give   We _____ a box of canned goods to the shelter.

9. begin   The play _____ at noon.

10. bring   Sam _____ his pet hamster to school.

 **In your writer's notebook, write about what you did last weekend. Reread your work when you're done to check that you used the correct past tense forms of irregular verbs.**

Name _____

> • Some irregular verbs have a special spelling when used with helping verbs: *sing/sang/had sung, eat/ate/had eaten.*
> • Subjects and helping verbs must always agree.

A. Rewrite the sentences. Write the underlined verbs correctly.

1. My family has <u>goed</u> to the seashore often during the summer.

   _____

2. My teacher has <u>gived</u> a speech at the White House.

   _____

3. The puppy has <u>growed</u> a lot this past year.

   _____

4. The birds had <u>singed</u> all morning.

   _____

B. Reread the lines from "Why I Run." Write the present tense of the underlined verb in the first line. Then write how the verb should be spelled if you add the helping verb *had*.

> The first marathon I ever <u>saw</u>
> was years ago with my grandma.
> We stood out on our city's streets
> and marveled at the number of feet
> and marveled at the number of feet.

_____

Name _____

> • Irregular verbs have a special spelling to show that an action happened in the past: *build/built, find/found, run/ran, fly/flew.*
>
> • Some verbs have a special spelling when used with helping verbs: *fly/flew/had flown, swim/swam/had swum.*

Rewrite the sentences using the correct past tense form of the verb in parentheses.

1. Have you ever (go) to a national park?

   _____

2. At Yellowstone National Park, my family (see) lots of wildlife.

   _____

3. Dad had (bring) his best camera to get lots of pictures.

   _____

4. My friend Andi had (came) with us, too.

   _____

5. I (give) Andi the seat next to the window.

   _____

 **In your writer's notebook, write about a park or landmark that you have seen or would like to see. You can use a dictionary to make sure you used the correct verb forms.**

Name _____

- Irregular verbs have a special spelling to show that an action happened in the past.
- Some verbs have a special spelling when used with helping verbs like *have, has,* and *had.*

A. Proofread this passage. Circle any incorrect irregular verbs.

   Last week my mom comed to our school and gived a speech about being a volunteer. She has always sayed how important it is for people to help others. She has gave many hours of her time helping out at the animal shelter. I have seed her go out many times to rescue an animal. At the shelter she has sitted with several sick animals until they has eated a meal. I am proud to say that my mom has winned the Volunteer of the Year Award.

B. Rewrite the passage. Write irregular verbs correctly.

_____

_____

_____

_____

_____

_____

_____

_____

Name _____

A. Read the paragraph. Then answer the questions.

(1) Yesterday my uncle and I went to the movies. (2) We bought some popcorn. (3) Then we found great seats. (4) We sat in our seats and ate the popcorn. (5) We enjoyed the movie because it told an exciting story about brave heroes.

1. Which sentence contains two irregular verbs?
   A Sentence 1
   B Sentence 3
   C Sentence 4
   D Sentence 5

2. Which is the irregular verb in sentence 5?
   F enjoyed
   G told
   H exciting
   J movie

B. Read the student draft and look for revisions that need to be made. Then answer the questions.

(1) Last year, my family moved to a new town. (2) At first, I feel sad. (3) I missed my friends. (4) But when I gone to my new school, I meet a lot of nice kids. (5) Now I am happy we moved.

3. What is the correct way to write sentence 2?
   A At first, I have feel sad.
   B At first, I felt sad.
   C At first, I feeled sad.
   D No change needed in sentence 2.

4. What is the correct way to write sentence 4?
   F But when I went to my new school, I meeted a lot of nice kids.
   G But when I have went to my new school, I have met a lot of nice kids.
   H But when I went to my new school, I met a lot of nice kids.
   J No change needed in sentence 4.

Name _____

Fold back the paper along the dotted line. Use the blanks to write each word as it is read aloud. When you finish the test, unfold the paper. Use the list at the right to correct any spelling mistakes.

1. _____
2. _____
3. _____
4. _____
5. _____
6. _____
7. _____
8. _____
9. _____
10. _____
11. _____
12. _____
13. _____
14. _____
15. _____

Review Words 16. _____

17. _____

18. _____

Challenge Words 19. _____

20. _____

1. pounce
2. placed
3. dice
4. cents
5. price
6. space
7. mice
8. office
9. wage
10. age
11. gyms
12. giant
13. changes
14. message
15. pages
16. your
17. road
18. peace
19. giraffe
20. peaceful

Name _____

> The letters *c* and *g* can have a hard or soft sound. The letter *c* has a hard /k/ sound in *cat*, but a soft /s/ sound in *center*. The letter *g* has a hard /g/ sound in *garden*, but a soft /j/ sound in *gem*.

DECODING WORDS

When the letter *c* comes before the letters *i* or *e*, it usually has a soft /s/ sound: *circle, center*. When *g* comes before the letters *i* or *e*, it usually has a soft /j/ sound: *age, gigantic*.

Write the spelling words that contain the matching soft *c* and soft *g* spellings. Read the words aloud to hear the soft *c* and *g* sounds.

pounce	pages	wage	mice	changes
age	giant	office	gyms	message
dice	space	placed	price	cents

soft *c* spelled *ce*

1. _____
2. _____
3. _____
4. _____
5. _____
6. _____
7. _____
8. _____

ending in -*ge* or -*ges*

9. _____
10. _____
11. _____
12. _____
13. _____

beginning with *g*-

14. _____
15. _____

Name _____

The letters *c* and *g* can have a hard or soft sound. The letter *c* has a hard /k/ sound in *cat,* but a soft /s/ sound in *center.* The letter *g* has a hard /g/ sound in *garden,* but a soft /j/ sound in *gem.*

DECODING WORDS

When the letter *c* comes before the letters *i* or *e,* it usually has a soft /s/ sound: *circle, center.* When *g* comes before the letters *i* or *e,* it usually has a soft /j/ sound: *age, gigantic.*

Write the spelling words that contain the matching soft *c* and soft *g* spellings. Read the words aloud to hear the soft *c* and *g* sounds.

cell	price	mice	age	pages
village	giant	cents	since	placed
gyms	space	gems	slice	large

soft *c* spelled *ce*

1. _____
2. _____
3. _____
4. _____
5. _____
6. _____
7. _____
8. _____

ending in -*ge* or -*ges*

9. _____
10. _____
11. _____
12. _____

beginning with *g-*

13. _____
14. _____
15. _____

Name _____

A. **Read the words aloud and then write the spelling words that contain the matching soft c and soft g spellings.**

peaceful	message	officer	changes	garage
cabbage	cents	citizen	gently	pounce
office	Egypt	pages	placed	giant

soft c spelled ce	soft c spelled ci	ending in -ge or -ges
1. _____	7. _____	10. _____
2. _____	**beginning with g-**	11. _____
3. _____	8. _____	12. _____
4. _____	9. _____	13. _____
5. _____		14. _____
6. _____		

15. Which word has an unusual soft g spelling? _____

B. **Say the word garage aloud. What do you notice about the sounds each letter g makes?**

_____

_____

 **Look back through your writer's notebook for words with the soft c or g. Read the words you find aloud. Then create a word sort for a partner.**

Name _____

pounce	cents	mice	age	changes
placed	price	office	gyms	message
dice	space	wage	giant	pages

A. Write the spelling word that matches each definition below.

1. parts of books _____

2. cost of something _____

3. numbered cubes _____

4. coins or change _____

5. small rodents_____

B. Write the spelling word that best completes each sentence.

6. My kitten likes to _____ on her squeaky toy.

7. I called and left a _____ for Coach Stanton.

8 Mom _____ my birthday cake on the table.

9. New technology _____ the way people communicate.

10. The vastness of _____ is hard to imagine.

11. Mr. Helton is very lively for a man of his _____.

12. The book is about a _____ who is taller than a skyscraper.

13. My mom works in a big _____ building in the city.

14. All the school _____ will get new basketball nets.

15. Do astronauts earn a big _____ for the work they do?

Name _____

There are six misspelled words in the paragraphs below. Underline each misspelled word. Write the words correctly on the lines.

Once there were three mise named Pip, Kip, and Flip who lived in a school. They had lots of spase to play when school was over for the day. They liked to play in the principal's offisce because there was always a lot of paper to chew there.

One night the principal came back to school to do some work. He brought his cat with him. The big cat tried to pounse on poor Pip! Pip had never seen a cat before and thought it was a terrible jiant! "We don't like all these chanjes!" said Kip. He and his brothers left the school to look for a safer place to live.

1. _____   4. _____

2. _____   5. _____

3. _____   6. _____

Writing Connection **Write a story about where the mice might go next. Use at least four spelling words in your story.**

_____
_____
_____
_____
_____
_____

Name _____

Remember

> The letters *c* and *g* can make hard or soft sounds. When *c* is followed by an *e* or *i*, it usually makes the soft /s/ sound that you hear in words like *center*. When the letter *g* is followed by an *e* or *i*, it usually makes the soft /j/ sound that you hear in *gentle*.

pounce	cents	mice	age	changes
placed	price	office	gyms	message
dice	space	wage	giant	pages

Fill in the missing letters to make a spelling word. Read the spelling word aloud, then write it on the line.

1. off ___ ___ e _____

2. pri ___ ___ _____

3. ___ yms _____

4. mess ___ ___ e _____

5. pla ___ ___ d _____

6. chan ___ ___ s _____

7. d ___ ___ e _____

8. p ___ ___ es _____

9. poun ___ ___ _____

10. ___ ___ ant _____

11. ___ ___ nts _____

12. wa ___ e _____

13. sp ___ ___ e _____

14. a ___ e _____

15. m ___ ___ e _____

Name _____

Create new forms of a base word by adding or removing inflectional endings, prefixes, or suffixes.

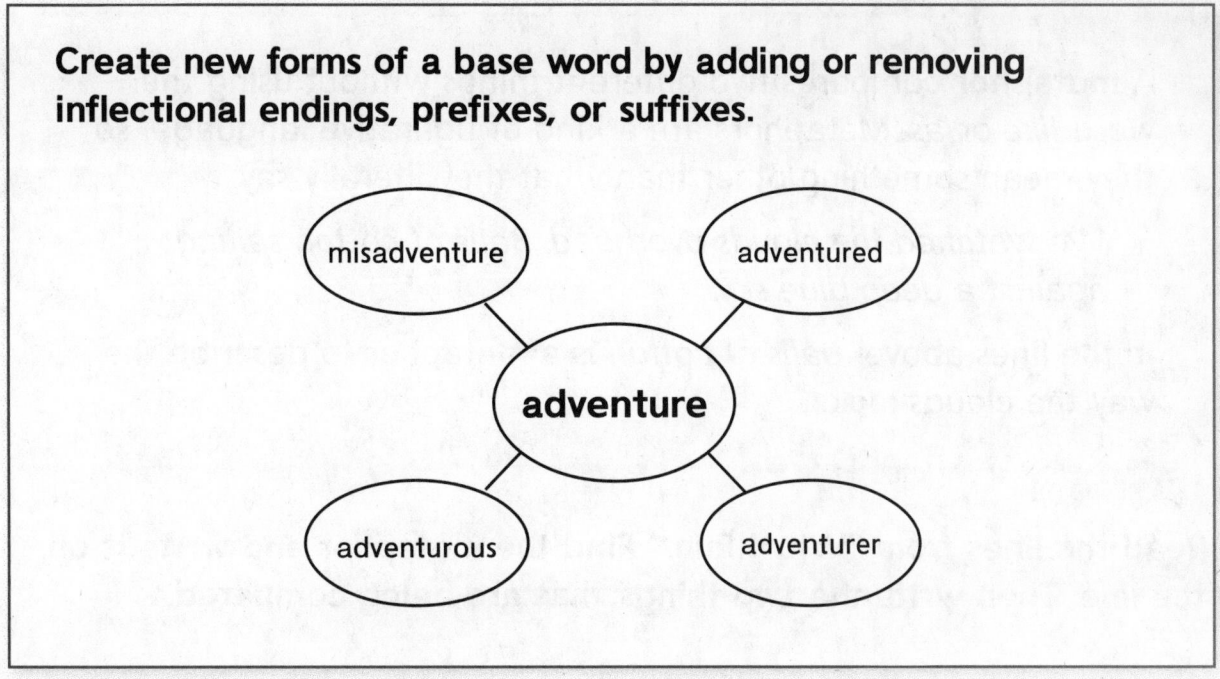

misadventure

adventured

adventure

adventurous

adventurer

Use your notes from "The Winningest Woman of the Iditarod Dog Sled Race." Choose one word and write it on the sled below. Then write related words on the dogs. Use a dictionary for help.

Name _____

> A **metaphor** compares two different things without using the word *like* or *as*. Metaphors are a kind of figurative language, so they mean something other than what they literally say.
>
> *We watched the clouds overhead. Balls of cotton sailing against a deep blue sky.*
>
> In the lines above, *balls of cotton* is a metaphor to describe the way the clouds look.

Read the lines from "Why I Run." Find the metaphor and write it on the line. Then write the two things that are being compared.

1. The runners were a rumbling herd,
    except for a few—

    _____

    _____

2. Motorboats speeding over gray water,
    these runners would inspire anyone's daughter.

    _____

    _____

3. I went home that day and laced up my shoes
    and although my feet started out as one big bruise

    _____

    _____

Name _____

> • A **singular pronoun** replaces a singular noun.
>
> • A **plural pronoun** replaces a plural noun or more than one noun.
>
> • A **personal pronoun** replaces a noun that refers to a person or thing. It can be singular or plural. Personal pronouns include *I, me, you, we, us, he, she, it,* and *they.*

Rewrite each sentence below. Use the correct singular or plural pronoun to replace the underlined noun or nouns.

1. <u>Carlos</u> is reading a book about African lions.

   _____

2. <u>Marcus and Ana</u> are interested in Bengal tigers.

   _____

3. Jonas said, "<u>Jonas</u> saw a movie about wildlife in Costa Rica."

   _____

4. <u>The library</u> closes at noon today.

   _____

5. Carmen said, "<u>Thalia and Carmen</u> are planning a report on reptiles."

   _____

6. <u>Jenna</u> wants to write about sea turtles.

   _____

 **In your writer's notebook, write about an animal you would like to learn more about. Reread your work when you're done. Make sure you used pronouns correctly.**

Name _____

> - A plural pronoun must match the word or words it replaces: **My friends and I** saw **the jugglers** perform. **We** saw **them** perform.
> - A pronoun must agree with the word or pronoun it replaces in both number and gender: **Tess** lost **her** notebook.

A. Circle the correct pronoun to replace the underlined noun. Write the sentence on the line using the correct pronoun.

1. <u>Cam and Tara</u> helped out at the bake sale.   He   They

_____

2. Our principal let us put <u>a table</u> up outside.   it   he

_____

3. <u>David</u> made lots of posters for the bake sale.   She   He

_____

B. Circle the proper noun in the underlined sentence in this passage from "Hiram Revels—The First African American Senator." Rewrite the sentence and replace the proper noun with a pronoun.

> <u>Hiram Revels helped many people throughout his life.</u> He helped people learn. As a senator, he helped the country progress. He was truly a good citizen!

_____

_____

Name _____

> • Pronouns must match a noun's number and gender.
>
> • If the sentence is not clear as to what noun or nouns the pronoun refers to, avoid using a pronoun.
>
> • Proper nouns begin with a capital letter and name specific people, places, and things. They include names, titles, holidays, and geographical names: *Jim, Doctor Garcia, Labor Day, Boston.*

Rewrite each sentence using correct capitalization.

1. My friend sam and i both have pen pals in other countries.

_____

2. Sam's pen pal is named amit and he lives in india.

_____

3. My pen pal's name is belinda and she lives in australia.

_____

4. When i see a letter from melbourne, i get really excited.

_____

Writing Connection **Write about a country you want to learn more about. When you're done, check your writing for correct capitalization and pronoun agreement.**

_____
_____
_____
_____
_____

Name _____

> • A pronoun must agree with the word or noun it replaces in both number and gender.
>
> • A proper noun begins with a capital letter. The pronoun *I* is always capitalized.

A. Proofread the paragraph. Circle any incorrect pronouns and words that should be capitalized.

   Last summer my mom and i went to seattle, washington. Us had a great time there seeing all the sights. We went to the seattle aquarium and learned all about sea otters and salmon. Mom took lots of pictures, and he plans to make a scrapbook of our trip. My favorite place to eat was mike and mary's pizza on jackson street. We even got to meet Mike and Mary. them have been making pizzas for over twenty years! Mom and i had such a great time that us plan to go back next july.

B. Rewrite the paragraph with the correct pronouns. Make sure all proper nouns and *I* are capitalized.

_____

_____

_____

_____

_____

_____

Name _____

A. Read the paragraph. Then answer the questions.

    (1) My brother Ben and I are interested in astronomy. (2) After dark, we look at the planets through telescopes. (3) Ben's telescope is stronger than mine. (4) When I look through it, I can see Jupiter and Saturn. (5) It's exciting to study astronomy.

1. What is the plural pronoun in sentence 2?
   A we
   B look
   C and
   D through

2. What does "it" refer to in sentence 4?
   F Ben
   G the telescope
   H Jupiter
   J Saturn

B. Read the student draft and look for revisions that need to be made. Then answer the questions.

    (1) My friend susie and me want to be astronauts when we grow up. (2) Us like to read about famous astronauts such as john glenn. (3) Someday we want to travel to the International Space Station. (4) How amazing to see Earth from space!

3. What is the correct way to write sentence 1?
   A My friend Susie and i want to be astronauts when we grow up.
   B My friend Susie and I want to be astronauts when we grow up.
   C My friend Susie and me want to be astronauts when we grow up.
   D No change needed in sentence 1.

4. What is the correct way to write sentence 2?
   F We like to read about famous astronauts such as john glenn.
   G Us like to read about famous astronauts such as John Glenn.
   H We like to read about famous astronauts such as John Glenn.
   J No change needed in sentence 2.

Name _____

Fold back the paper along the dotted line. Use the blanks to write each word as it is read aloud. When you finish the test, unfold the paper. Use the list at the right to correct any spelling mistakes.

1. _____
2. _____
3. _____
4. _____
5. _____
6. _____
7. _____
8. _____
9. _____
10. _____
11. _____
12. _____
13. _____
14. _____
15. _____

Review Words 16. _____
17. _____
18. _____

Challenge Words 19. _____
20. _____

1. airplane
2. daytime
3. birthday
4. daylight
5. hairdo
6. somebody
7. birdhouse
8. barefoot
9. headlight
10. sometime
11. someone
12. newspaper
13. sidewalks
14. basketball
15. stagecoach
16. placed
17. office
18. giant
19. handwriting
20. windshield

Name _____

A **compound word** is formed by two shorter words. Use the shorter words to figure out the meaning of the compound word. For example, break *waterfall* into the words *water* and *fall* to see that a *waterfall* is made by water falling over the edge of a cliff.

Read aloud the spelling words in the box. Then write the spelling words that include the words written below.

airplane	daylight	birdhouse	sometime	sidewalks
daytime	hairdo	barefoot	someone	basketball
birthday	somebody	headlight	newspaper	stagecoach

1. day _____

_____

2. some _____

_____

3. time _____

_____

4. foot _____

5. light _____

6. basket _____

7. news _____

8. walk _____

9. do _____

10. house _____

11. coach _____

12. ball _____

Name _____

A **compound word** is formed by two shorter words. Use the shorter words to figure out the meaning of the compound word. For example, break *waterfall* into the words *water* and *fall* to see that a *waterfall* is made by water falling over the edge of a cliff.

DECODING WORDS

You should also divide a compound word into its smaller words to sound it out. Read these examples aloud: *horse/back, book/store, water/melon, grass/hopper, sun/shine.*

Read aloud the spelling words in the box. Then write the spelling words that include the words written below.

airplane	daylight	birdhouse	sometime	sidewalks
daytime	sunset	railroad	birthday	doghouse
someone	notebooks	headlight	newspaper	stoplight

1. day _____

_____

_____

2. some _____

_____

3. sun _____

4. light _____

_____

5. time _____

_____

6. road _____

7. news _____

8. walk _____

9. air _____

10. house _____

12. books _____

Name _____

A. Read aloud the spelling words in the box. Then write the spelling words that include the words written below.

homemade	hairdo	barefoot	someone	basketball
windowpane	stagecoach	headlight	newspaper	birthday
thumbnail	whoever	windshield	throughout	handwriting

1. day _____

2. some _____

3. home _____

4. who _____

5. through _____

6. thumb _____

7. window _____

8. shield _____

9. light _____

10. hand _____

11. news _____

12. foot _____

13. do _____

14. coach _____

15. ball _____

B. Compare the words *daytime* and *birthday*. How are they alike? How are they different?

_____

_____

_____

 **Look for compound words in the selections you read this week. Read the words you find aloud. Then use the words to make a word sort for a partner.**

Name _____

airplane	daylight	birdhouse	sometime	sidewalks
daytime	hairdo	barefoot	someone	basketball
birthday	somebody	headlight	newspaper	stagecoach

A. Join two words from the riddle to make a compound word.

1. Time during the day _____

2. A house for a bird _____

3. A ball thrown in a basket _____

4. Places for walks on the side of a street _____

5. The day of your birth _____

6. The light of the day _____

7. A foot that is bare _____

8. A paper containing news _____

B. Write the spelling word that best completes each sentence.

9. Mom went to the salon and asked for a new _____.

10. I saw a really old _____ at the Transportation Museum.

11. A bulb burned out of our car's left _____.

12. We flew on an _____ to get across the ocean.

13. Come to my house _____ on Saturday to watch a movie.

14. Dad asked if _____ would help him with the dishes.

15. Did _____ lose a red wool scarf at the game?

Name_____

There are six misspelled words in the story below. Underline each misspelled word. Write the words correctly on the lines.

Princess Anna was having a birtday party. It was such an important day that she decided to get a new hairdoo. Later, she arrived at the party in a stagecoch that was made of pure gold.

The princess danced until her feet began to hurt! She tossed off her shoes and danced bearfoot. When daylite came, the happy but tired princess went home. The next day there was a picture in the newzpaper showing the laughing princess at her party.

1. _____ 4. _____

2. _____ 5. _____

3. _____ 6. _____

Writing Connection **Write a story about your birthday or another special day. Use at least four spelling words.**

_____
_____
_____
_____
_____
_____
_____
_____

Name _____

Remember

Compound words are formed when two shorter words are put together, as in the words *bookstore, backpack,* and *underground.* Sound out a compound word by dividing it into its two shorter words. Look for familiar spelling patterns in the shorter words. For example, divide the word *lifetime* into the words *life* and *time.* Note how each of the shorter words has a VCe spelling pattern and long *i* vowel sound. Read the entire word aloud: *life/time.*

Dividing a compound word into shorter words can also help you figure out a compound word's meaning. *Lifetime* refers to the amount of time in one life.

airplane	daylight	birdhouse	sometime	sidewalks
daytime	hairdo	barefoot	someone	basketball
birthday	somebody	headlight	newspaper	stagecoach

Write the missing word to complete each compound spelling word. Read the spelling word aloud. Then write it on the line.

1. _____ plane _____

2. head _____ _____

3. day _____ _____

   day _____ _____

4. hair _____ _____

5. _____ body _____

   some _____ _____

   some _____ _____

6. news _____ _____

7. bare _____ _____

8. _____ house _____

9. birth _____ _____

10. side _____ _____

11. _____ coach _____

12. _____ ball _____

Name _____

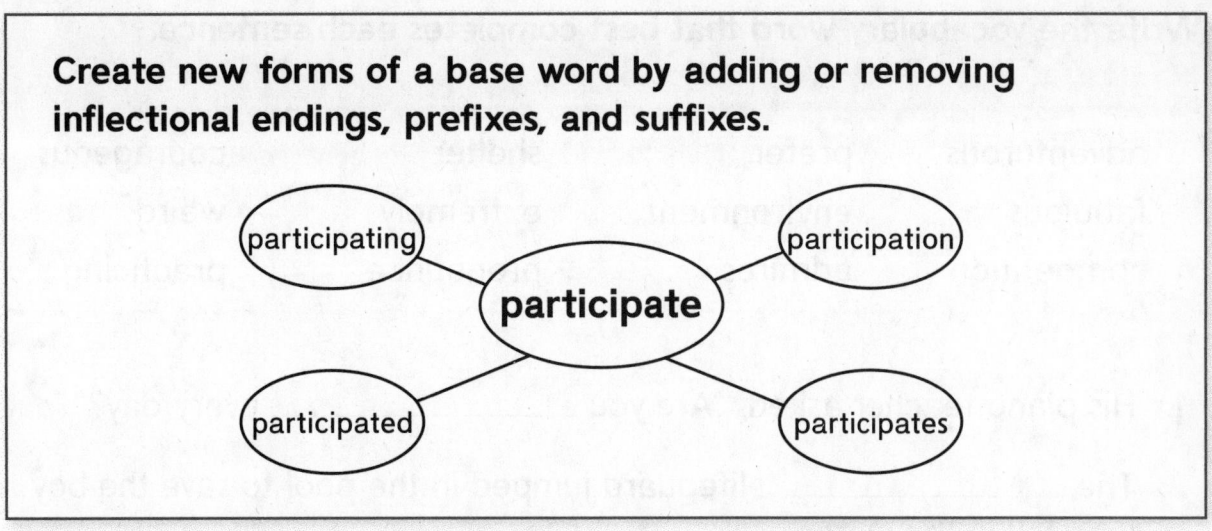

Create new forms of a base word by adding or removing inflectional endings, prefixes, and suffixes.

participating

participate

participation

participated

participates

Review your notes on _Elizabeth Leads the Way_. Choose one word from your notes or the selection and write it on the bottom book. Then write related words on the other books. Use a dictionary for help.

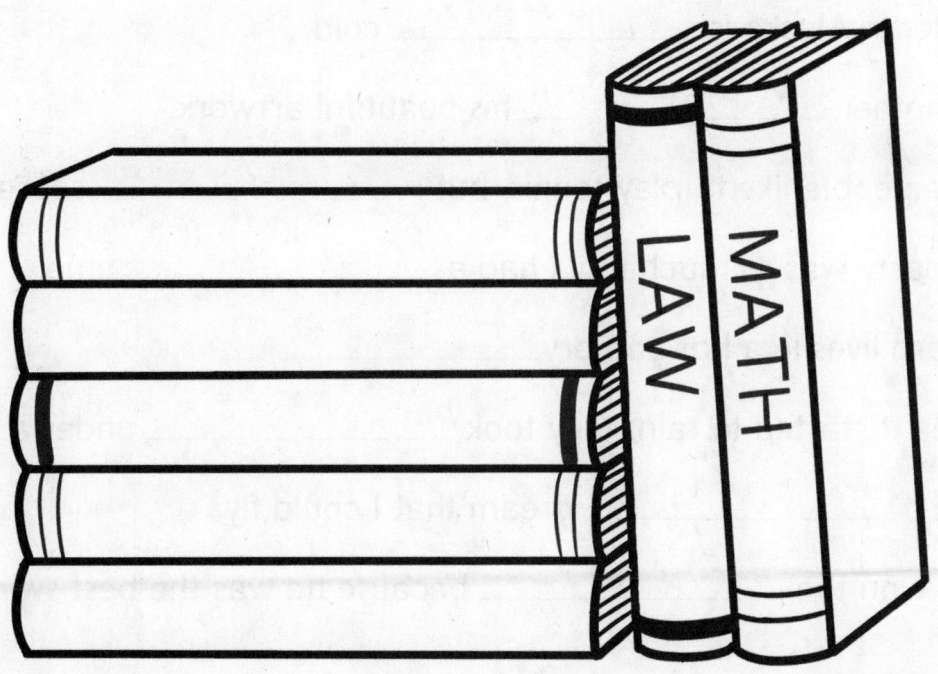

Name _____

Write the vocabulary word that best completes each sentence.

adventurous	prefer	shelter	courageous
fabulous	environment	extremely	weird
competition	admires	pronounce	practicing

1. His piano teacher asked, "Are you _____ every day?"

2. The _____ lifeguard jumped in the pool to save the boy who fell in the water.

3. Her French teacher taught her how to _____ new words.

4. A mountain climber is an example of an _____ person.

5. Winter in Alaska is _____ cold.

6. His mother _____ his beautiful artwork.

7. Some people like to play tennis, but I _____ soccer.

8. The party was so much fun. I had a _____ time.

9. A lizard lives in a hot and dry _____.

10. When it started to rain, they took _____ under a tree.

11. I had a _____ dream that I could fly.

12. Andy won the _____ because he was the best swimmer.

Name _____

> • A **subject pronoun** is used as the subject of a sentence.
>
> • Singular subject pronouns are *I, you, he, she,* and *it*: *I drive the car.* ***He** plays football.*
>
> • Plural subject pronouns are *we, you,* and *they*: ***We** go swimming.* ***They** eat dinner.*

Read the sentences. Choose the correct pronoun in parentheses to complete each sentence. Write the pronoun.

1. My friend Ted and _____ started a lawn service. (me, I)

2. _____ made a list of all the services we will offer. (We, Us)

3. _____ am good at raking and cleaning up. (Me, I)

4. _____ is good at planting and weeding. (He, Him)

5. We asked the Smiths, "Would _____ like our help?" (you, them)

6. _____ signed up for a one month trial. (Them, They)

7. Dad said that _____ is very proud of us. (him, he)

8. _____ is a good way to make money this summer. (It, You)

9. _____ hope to have at least five customers. (Us, We)

10. Ted and _____ plan to work hard. (me, I)

 **In your writer's notebook, write about a way you could earn money during the summer. Then reread your work. Make sure you used subject pronouns correctly.**

Name _____

> • An **object pronoun** can take the place of an object noun: Mark invited *Kim*. Mark invited *her*.
> • Singular object pronouns are *me, you, him, her,* and *it*.
> • Plural object pronouns are *us, you,* and *them*.

A. Read the sentences. Choose the correct pronoun in parentheses to complete each sentence. Write the pronoun.

1. Dad helped _____ build a tree house.   (we, us)

2. I hope _____ can come see it.   (you, us)

3. I asked _____ to help me clean up.   (she, her)

4. We can help _____ put away the tools.   (he, him)

5. Mom saw _____ reading a book.   (them, they)

B. Reread this paragraph from "Susan B. Anthony Takes Action." Circle the object pronouns in the underlined sentence.

> When Susan went to school, she saw that boys and girls were not treated the same way. One of her teachers refused to teach Susan long division. She said that girls did not have any reason to know math. As a result, Susan's family took her out of school and taught her at home.

In your writer's notebook, write about your favorite school subject. Check your work when you are done to make sure you used object pronouns correctly.

Name _____

> • Use the subject pronouns *I, you, he, she, it, we,* and *they* to replace subject nouns: *I throw the ball to Jack.*
>
> • Use the object pronouns *me, you, him, her, it, us,* and *them* to replace object nouns: *I throw the ball to **him**.*
>
> • A present-tense verb must agree with its subject pronoun.
>
> • Add *-s* or *-es* to most present-tense action verbs when using the singular pronouns *he, she,* and *it*. Do not add *-s* or *-es* to a present-tense action verb when using the plural pronouns *we, you,* and *they*: *He **eats** dinner. They **eat** dinner.*

Replace each underlined word or group of words with the correct subject or object pronoun. Write the new sentences.

1. <u>My grandmother</u> took <u>my brother and me</u> to Washington, D.C.

   _____

2. <u>The Smithsonian</u> is an amazing place to spend the day.

   _____

3. <u>My grandmother, brother, and I</u> got to tour the White House.

   _____

4. <u>My brother</u> asked <u>my grandmother</u> if she had ever been there before.

   _____

 **In your writer's notebook, write about what you would see on a trip to Washington, D.C. Reread your work to make sure your pronouns agree with your verbs.**

Name _____

> • Use the subject pronouns *I, you, he, she, it, we,* and *they* as the subject of a sentence or to replace subject nouns.
>
> • Use the object pronouns *me, you, him, her, it, us,* and *them* to replace object nouns.
>
> • A present-tense verb must agree with its subject pronoun.

A. Proofread the paragraph below. Circle any pronouns that are used incorrectly.

My classmates and I have been learning about space. Us got to visit a planetarium last week. Zach and me made a big mural that shows planets, moons, and constellations. We invited other classes to come and see our mural. Them were amazed at what they saw. Our teacher, Ms. Alba, asked our principal to come see it. We asked he if he would like to hang it in his office. Mr. Costas gave we a big compliment. Him said he would be honored to have it on his wall.

B. Rewrite the paragraph with the correct pronouns.

_____

_____

_____

_____

_____

_____

_____

Name _____

A. Read the paragraph. Then answer the questions.

(1) David's mother is a doctor. (2) She takes care of many people and helps them get well. (3) Her patients like her very much because she is caring and kind. (4) David is proud of his mother. (5) He wants to be a doctor like his mom.

1. What is the object pronoun in sentence 2?
   A She
   B takes
   C people
   D them

2. What is the subject pronoun in sentence 5?
   F He
   G wants
   H his
   J mom

B. Read the student draft and look for revisions that need to be made. Then answer the questions.

(1) I love my new puppy. (2) My sister and me named she Scout. (3) Scout enjoys playing in the backyard. (4) Sometimes she chases birds, but she can't catch they.

3. What is the correct way to write sentence 2?
   A My sister and I named she Scout.
   B My sister and me named her Scout.
   C My sister and I named her Scout.
   D No change needed in sentence 2.

4. What is the correct way to write sentence 4?
   F Sometimes her chases birds, but her can't catch them.
   G Sometimes she chases birds, but she can't catch them.
   H Sometimes she chases birds, but her can't catch they.
   J No change needed in sentence 4.

Name _____

Fold back the paper along the dotted line. Use the blanks to write each word as it is read aloud. When you finish the test, unfold the paper. Use the list at the right to correct any spelling mistakes.

1. _____
2. _____
3. _____
4. _____
5. _____
6. _____
7. _____
8. _____
9. _____
10. _____
11. _____
12. _____
13. _____
14. _____
15. _____

Review Words 16. _____
17. _____
18. _____

Challenge Words 19. _____
20. _____

1. names
2. named
3. naming
4. hopes
5. hoped
6. hoping
7. dances
8. danced
9. dancing
10. drops
11. dropped
12. dropping
13. wraps
14. wrapped
15. wrapping
16. basketball
17. airplane
18. birthday
19. driving
20. traded

Name _____

> **Inflectional endings** are letters added to the end of a word to change the word's meaning. The letter *-s* is used to form plural nouns and some present verbs. The letters *-ed* are added to regular verbs to show that an action happened in the past. The letters *-ing* show that an action is happening now.

RULE REVIEW

If a word ends in silent *e,* drop the *e* before adding *-ed* or *-ing*: *type/typed/typing.* If a word ends in a vowel and consonant, double the final consonant before adding *-ed* or *-ing*: *stop/stopped/stopping.*

Read the spelling words aloud. Then write the spelling words that contain the matching spelling pattern.

wrapped	dropped	named	drops	hoping
dances	hoped	danced	hopes	names
naming	wraps	wrapping	dropping	dancing

drop *e* and add *-ed*
1. _____
2. _____
3. _____

double consonant and add *-ed*
4. _____
5. _____

drop *e* and add *-ing*
6. _____
7. _____
8. _____

double consonant and add *-ing*
9. _____
10. _____

add *-s*
11. _____
12. _____
13. _____
14. _____
15. _____

Name _____

Inflectional endings are letters added to the end of a word to change the word's meaning. The letter *-s* is used to form plural nouns and some present verbs. The letters *-ed* are added to regular verbs to show that an action happened in the past. The letters *-ing* show that an action is happening now.

Read aloud the spelling words in the box. Then write the spelling words that contain the matching spelling pattern.

hoped	hopes	naming	racing	hugs
hugged	names	raced	hugging	named
races	hoping	drops	dropping	dropped

drop *e* and add *-ed*

1. _____
2. _____
3. _____

double consonant and add *-ed*

4. _____
5. _____

drop *e* and add *-ing*

6. _____
7. _____
8. _____

double consonant and add *-ing*

9. _____
10. _____

add *-s*

11. _____
12. _____
13. _____
14. _____
15. _____

Name _____

A. Read aloud the spelling words in the box. Then write the spelling words with the matching spelling pattern.

arrived	hopes	achieves	dropped	danced
noticed	dropping	wrapping	hoped	driving
offering	traded	dancing	wrapped	hoping

drop *e* and add *-ed*

1. _____

2. _____

3. _____

4. _____

5. _____

double consonant and add *-ed*

6. _____

7. _____

drop *e* and add *-ing*

8. _____

9. _____

10. _____

double consonant and add *-ing*

11. _____

12. _____

add *-s*

13. _____

14. _____

add *-ing*

15. _____

B. Compare the words *hoped* and *dropped*. How are they alike? How are they different?

_____

_____

_____

_____

Name _____

hoped	hopes	dances	drops	danced
wrapped	names	wraps	hoping	named
naming	dropped	dancing	dropping	wrapping

A. Write the spelling word that best completes each sentence.

1. Last week I _____ in a musical play at school.

2. Mom is _____ my birthday present in the other room.

3. I am _____ that we will have a snow day soon.

4. We _____ our three puppies Spot, Dot, and Not.

5. I had _____ the rain would stop before the big game.

6. The people were _____ and singing on stage.

7. Our school will be _____ our team's mascot this week.

8. My apple rolled across the floor when I _____ it.

9. The girls _____ sandwiches for the picnic.

10. We are _____ my sister off at soccer practice first.

B. Write the spelling words that mean the same thing as the words below.

11. give a name to _____

12. want to be true _____

13. move to music _____

14. to fall _____

15. cover _____

Name _____

There are six misspelled words in the story below. Underline each misspelled word. Write the words correctly on the lines.

Dave was always looking for ways to help others. He hopeed to travel around the world helping people in need. One day he was droping off some canned goods at the soup kitchen when he learned some bad news. The soup kitchen would close because there wasn't enough money. He droped the cans into the bin and went home, hopeing to get an idea to save the soup kitchen.

At home, his mom was watching a dance contest on TV. "People just love danceing," she said to Dave. And that's how Dave got the idea for a fundraiser. He charged five dollars per person and asked everyone to bring three cans of soup. People danceed all evening and had fun helping the soup kitchen.

1. _____   4. _____

2. _____   5. _____

3. _____   6. _____

Writing Connection **Write a story about someone who helps others. Use at least four spelling words in your story.**

_____

_____

_____

_____

_____

_____

_____

Name _____

Remember

An inflectional ending is added to a base word to create a new word. The letter *-s* is added to form most plural nouns and some present-tense verbs. The ending *-ed* shows that an action already happened. The ending *-ing* shows that an action is still happening.

Drop the final *e* in words that end in *e* before adding the ending *-ed* or *-ing*. Double the final consonant in words that end in a vowel and consonant before adding *-ed* or *-ing*.

names	dropping	dances	danced	wraps
wrapped	hoped	drops	dropped	named
hoping	naming	dancing	hopes	wrapping

Join each word with the ending to form a spelling word. Read the spelling word aloud and then write it on the line.

1. name + ed _____

2. dance + ed _____

3. name + ing _____

4. hope + s _____

5. wrap + ed _____

6. dance + ing _____

7. drop + s _____

8. wrap + s _____

9. wrap + ing _____

10. name + s _____

11. drop + ed _____

12. hope + ing _____

13. dance + s _____

14. hope + ed _____

15. drop + ing _____

Name _____

> **Antonyms** are two words that have opposite meanings. For example: *old* and *new, hot* and *cold, early* and *late, large* and *small, easy* and *difficult, open* and *closed.*
>
> When you come across a word you don't know, look for a nearby antonym to help you figure out the word's meaning.

Read the sentences below. Underline the antonym in the second sentence that has the opposite meaning of the word in bold in the first sentence. Write the meaning of the bold word on the line.

1. Your hands are **filthy** from playing in the dirt. Make sure they are clean before you eat dinner.

   _____

2. The monkey moved **swiftly** from tree to tree. The snake crawled slowly on the ground below.

   _____

3. They saw **enormous** redwood trees when they visited California. The redwood trees made the tall oak trees in their hometown look tiny.

   _____

4. I was **amused** when the movie began. But by the time it was over, I felt bored.

   _____

5. The **frigid** weather was very uncomfortable. She was finally able to warm up when she got inside.

   _____

Name _____

Prefixes and suffixes are word parts that are added to a base word to create a new word with a new meaning. Prefixes are added to the beginning of a word. Suffixes are added to the end of a word.

The prefixes *un-* and *dis-* mean *not* or *the opposite of.* For example, *disorder* means *not in order. Unaware* means *not aware.*

The suffix *-ly* means *in such a way.* It is usually used to change an adjective into an adverb, as in the words *quickly* and *happily.*

Read each sentence from "Hiram Revels—The First African American Senator." Underline the word in each sentence that has the prefix *un-* or *dis-* or the suffix *-ly.* Write the meaning of the word on the line.

1. Back then, African Americans were treated badly.

   _____

2. Still, the laws in the South were unfair toward all African Americans.

   _____

3. Because he was unable to go to college in the South, Revels went to colleges in Indiana and Ohio.

   _____

4. He became highly educated.

   _____

5. There were many newly freed African Americans.

   _____

6. Revels disliked rules that were unfair for African Americans.

   _____

Name _____

> • A **present-tense verb** must agree with its **subject pronoun** in simple and compound sentences: *They dive* into the pool.
>
> • Add *-s* or *-es* to most present-tense action verbs only when using the singular pronouns *he, she,* and *it*: *She dives* into the pool.

Circle the verb that agrees with the subject pronoun in each sentence. Write the sentence on the line.

1. She (read, reads) a story to us every day.

_____

2. It (make, makes) us laugh to hear funny stories.

_____

3. It (take, takes) us twenty minutes to walk to the library.

_____

4. He (look, looks) for books about monkeys.

_____

Connect to Community

Talk to a parent or another trusted adult about your town library. Write about why libraries are important. Check your work for pronoun-verb agreement. Include questions with interrogative words like *who, what, when, where, how* and *why* to grab the attention of your reader.

_____

_____

_____

Name _____

> • Do not add *-s* or *-es* to a present-tense verb when using the plural pronouns *we, you,* and *they* or the singular pronouns *I* and *you*.
>
> • Subject pronouns and their verbs must agree in simple and compound sentences.

A. Choose the correct verb in parentheses to complete each sentence. Write the verb on the line.

1. We _____ helping Mom with our garden.   (like, likes)

2. She _____ lettuce, tomatoes, and cucumbers.   (grow, grows)

3. I _____ pull the weeds, and my brother waters.   (help, helps)

4. He _____ how to plant seeds, too.   (know, knows)

5. Do you _____ a garden at your house?   (want, wants)

B. Reread this paragraph from "Juanita and the Beanstalk." Circle the pronoun in the underlined sentence. Then rewrite the sentence in the present tense on the lines.

"I don't want to sell Pepe!" cried Juanita. <u>She petted the goat lovingly</u>. But she was an obedient girl and would not disobey her mother. Reluctantly, she took Pepe to town. On her way she met an old man who patted Pepe kindly.

_____

_____

Name _____

- A present-tense verb must agree with its subject pronoun in simple and compound sentences.

- Add *-s* or *-es* to most present-tense action verbs only when using the singular pronouns *he, she,* and *it.*

- Do not add *-s* or *-es* to a present-tense verb when using the plural pronouns *we, you,* and *they* or the singular pronouns *I* and *you.*

Choose the correct verb to complete each sentence. Write the verb on the line.

1. I (like, likes) Career Day at school. _____

2. We (hear, hears) speakers, like Mr. Jace, talk about their jobs. _____

3. He (work, works) on jets and airplanes. _____

4. I (think, thinks) that would be a hard job to do. _____

5. They (tell, tells) our class about the importance of reading. _____

6. I (see, sees) a speaker dressed like an astronaut. _____

7. She (explain, explains) what she does on space walks. _____

8. I (hope, hopes) to be a writer when I grow up. _____

 **In your writer's notebook, write about what you would like to be when you grow up. Reread your work when you are done. Make sure your pronouns and verbs agree.**

Name _____

> • A present-tense verb must agree with its subject pronoun in simple and compound sentences.
>
> • Add *-s* or *-es* to most present-tense action verbs only when using the singular pronouns *he, she,* and *it.* Do not add *-s* or *-es* to a present-tense action verb when using the plural pronouns *we, you,* and *they* or the singular pronouns *I* and *you.*

Rewrite the sentences below. Make sure that the pronouns and verbs agree with each other.

1. I sees a huge spider web on my bike!

   _____

2. He paint pictures of sailboats on the lake.

   _____

3. They hikes the Grand Canyon every August.

   _____

4. It rain almost every afternoon in Florida.

   _____

5. Do you swims at the Oak Park Water Club?

   _____

Name _____

A. Read the paragraph. Then answer the questions.

(1) My friend Jenny and I go to the library every week.
(2) We return our old books before looking for new ones. (3) The librarian often helps us. (4) He knows where all the books in the library are.

1. What is the verb that agrees with the singular pronoun *He* in sentence 4?

   A where

   B knows

   C books

   D are

2. Which sentence contains a plural subject pronoun?

   F Sentence 1

   G Sentence 2

   H Sentence 3

   J Sentence 4

B. Read the student draft and look for revisions that need to be made. Then answer the questions.

(1) My favorite book is *Alice's Adventures in Wonderland.* (2) It is about a girl who follows a rabbit down a hole. (3) She discover a new world with many unusual characters. (4) They takes her on adventures and shows her many strange things.

3. What is the correct way to write sentence 3?

   A She discovers a new world with many unusual characters.

   B It discover a new world with many unusual characters.

   C They discovers a new world with many unusual characters.

   D No change needed in sentence 3.

4. What is the correct way to write sentence 4?

   F They take her on adventures and shows her many strange things.

   G They take her on adventures and show her many strange things.

   H They takes her on adventures and show her many strange things.

   J No change needed in sentence 4.

Name _____

Fold back the
paper along
the dotted line.
Use the blanks
to write each
word as it is
read aloud.
When you finish
the test, unfold
the paper. Use
the list at the
right to correct
any spelling
mistakes.

1. _____
2. _____
3. _____
4. _____
5. _____
6. _____
7. _____
8. _____
9. _____
10. _____
11. _____
12. _____
13. _____
14. _____
15. _____

Review Words 16. _____
17. _____
18. _____

Challenge Words 19. _____
20. _____

1. basket
2. rabbit
3. lesson
4. letter
5. invite
6. bedtime
7. mammal
8. number
9. fellow
10. chapter
11. follow
12. problem
13. chicken
14. butter
15. napkin
16. hoping
17. dances
18. dropped
19. suppose
20. stubborn

Name _____

> If a syllable ends in a consonant, it is a **closed syllable** and the vowel sound is usually short. In words with a vowel-consonant-consonant-vowel (VCCV) spelling pattern, the word is usually divided between the two consonants. Read these words aloud: *sum/mer, rep/tile.*

RULE REVIEW

Alphabetize words by sorting them by where the first letter appears in the alphabet. The words *bear, car,* and *apple* are sorted as *apple, bear, car.* If two words begin with the same letters, sort by the first letter they don't share: *stay, step, stop.*

A. Write the spelling words with the matching spelling patterns.

basket	letter	mammal	chapter	chicken
rabbit	invite	number	follow	butter
lesson	bedtime	fellow	problem	napkin

ll

1. _____

2. _____

mm

3. _____

bb

4. _____

ss

5. _____

tt

6. _____

7. _____

B. Alphabetize these spelling words to the third letter: *invite, chapter, basket, chicken, bedtime, problem, number, napkin.*

_____

_____

_____

Name _____

If a syllable ends in a consonant, it is a **closed syllable** and the vowel sound is usually short. In words with a vowel-consonant-consonant-vowel (VCCV) spelling pattern, the word is usually divided between the two consonants. Read these words aloud: *sum / mer, rep / tile.*

A. Write the spelling words with the matching spelling patterns.

basket	latter	lesson	problem	Sunday
rabbit	invite	chapter	army	ladder
hello	number	follow	butter	pepper

ll

1. _____

2. _____

dd

3. _____

tt

4. _____

5. _____

pp

6. _____

bb

7. _____

ss

8. _____

B. Write these spelling words in alphabetical order: *basket, invite, number, chapter, problem, army, Sunday.*

_____

_____

Name _____

A. Read aloud the spelling words in the box. Then write the spelling words with the matching spelling patterns.

basket	rascal	mammal	chapter	chicken
rabbit	suppose	bottom	method	retreat
napkin	bedtime	fellow	problem	chimney

ll   *mm*   *pp*

1. _____   3. _____   5. _____

tt   *bb*

2. _____   4. _____

B. Alphabetize these words to the fourth letter: *basket, napkin, rascal, bedtime, chapter, method, problem, chicken, retreat, chimney.*

_____

_____

_____

C. Compare the words *fellow* **and** *follow*. **How are the words alike? How are they different?**

_____

_____

_____

Name _____

basket	letter	mammal	chapter	chicken
rabbit	invite	number	follow	butter
lesson	bedtime	fellow	problem	napkin

A. Write the spelling word that goes with the other two words.

1. plate, placemat, _____   4. bird, reptile, _____

2. lunchtime, daytime, _____   5. postcard, e-mail, _____

3. squirrel, chipmunk, _____

B. Write the spelling word that best completes each sentence.

6. I had toast with _____ and jam for breakfast.

7. Can the repair shop fix the _____ with the car engine?

8. The last _____ in this book is very exciting.

9. I will _____ all my friends to my birthday party.

10. Mom puts vegetables into a big _____ at the market.

11. A good _____ for life is learning to be patient.

12. Our house _____ is 24 Oak Lane.

13. Dad says, "A good _____ uses good manners."

14. A _____ can live for seven or eight years.

15. If Jim knows the way, we should _____ him to the show.

Name _____

There are six misspelled words in the paragraph below. Underline each misspelled word. Write the words correctly on the lines.

The first leson in chaptur two is all about animals and their habitats. I read about the rabit, a quiet and shy animal. He is part of the mamul group and can be found in forests, meadows, and even deserts. Sometimes people keep them as pets and call them bunnies. There was a photo in the book of a bunny that slept in a bakset next to his owner's bed. This pet liked to folow his owner all over the house.

1. _____   4. _____

2. _____   5. _____

3. _____   6. _____

Writing Connection **Write a story about what it would be like to keep a rabbit for a pet. Use at least four spelling words.**

_____
_____
_____
_____
_____
_____
_____
_____
_____

Name _____

Remember

A closed syllable is a syllable that ends in a consonant. Closed syllables usually have a short vowel sound. When a word has a vowel-consonant-consonant-vowel (VCCV) spelling pattern, the syllable division is usually between the two consonants. Read these words aloud: *doctor (doc/tor), runner (run/ner), traffic (traf/fic).*

basket	letter	mammal	chapter	chicken
rabbit	invite	number	follow	butter
lesson	bedtime	fellow	problem	napkin

A. Circle the spelling word in each row that rhymes with the word in bold type. Read the spelling word aloud and write it on the line.

1. **better**   ladder   letter   batter   _____

2. **habit**   bedtime   heater   rabbit   _____

3. **yellow**   fellow   follow   yelled   _____

4. **flutter**   chapter   butter   platter   _____

5. **camel**   mammal   maple   model   _____

6. **swallow**   swell   flowing   follow   _____

B. Write each spelling word. Draw a line between the syllables.

7. **basket** _____

8. **lesson** _____

9. **invite** _____

10. **bedtime** _____

11. **number** _____

12. **chapter** _____

13. **problem** _____

14. **chicken** _____

15. **napkin** _____

Name _____

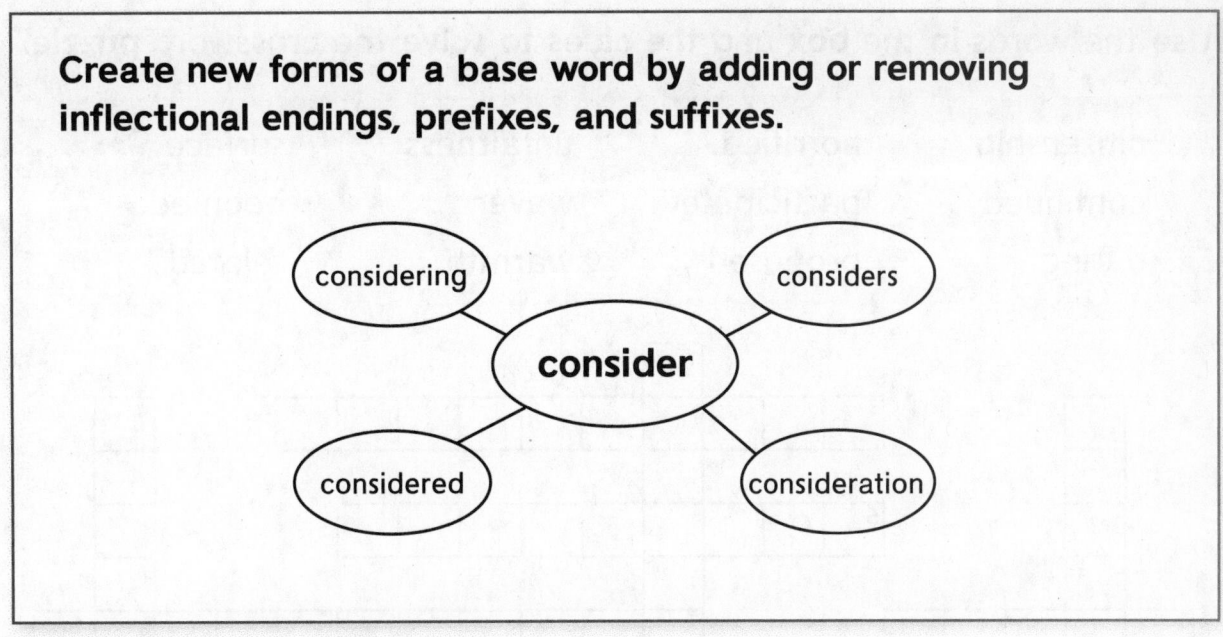

Create new forms of a base word by adding or removing inflectional endings, prefixes, and suffixes.

considering

considers

consider

considered

consideration

Look at your notes from *Clever Jack Takes the Cake*. Choose one word and write the word on the bottom layer of the cake below. Then write related words on the other layers. Use a print or digital dictionary to help you think of related words.

Name _____

Use the words in the box and the clues to solve the crossword puzzle.

citizenship	horrified	unfairness	surface
continued	participate	waver	boomed
daring	proposed	warmth	related

Across

3. Lack of honesty or justice

5. Kept going

6. Go back and forth

7. Membership of a country

8. From the same family

10. Suggested or asked

11. Heat

12. Grew or expanded suddenly

Down

1. Join in

2. The outside of something

4. Very scared

9. Brave

Name _____

> • A **possessive pronoun** takes the place of a possessive noun: *That is Jane's backpack. That is her backpack.*
>
> • A possessive pronoun shows who or what owns something: *That notebook belongs to him. That is his notebook.*
>
> • Use these possessive pronouns before nouns: *my, his, her, its, our, your, their.*

A. Write the possessive pronouns on the line.

1. My family won a trip to Chicago. _____

2. We wrote an essay telling our reasons for wanting to go. _____

3. Dad spent most of his childhood there. _____

4. Mom used to visit her grandmother in Chicago. _____

5. Mom and Dad want us to see their favorite landmarks. _____

B. Reread this paragraph from "When Corn Was Cash." Circle one possessive pronoun.

> Life is easier today. We have a system of money. We have stores that sell everything we need. But people still like to barter. The next time your school has a swap meet, think about trading in some of your old games and toys. Bartering is fun, and it helps people clean out their closets!

 **In your writer's notebook, write about a city you have visited or would like to visit. When you're done, reread your work. Make sure you used possessive pronouns correctly.**

Name _____

> • Some possessive pronouns that can stand alone are *mine, yours, his, hers, ours,* and *theirs*: *That book is* **mine**.
>
> • **Reflexive pronouns** are used when the subject and the object of a sentence are the same: *I drove* **myself** *to the store*. Reflexive pronouns include *myself, yourself, himself, herself, itself, ourselves* and *themselves*.

A. Read the sentences and the possessive pronouns in parentheses. Write the correct possessive pronoun on the lines.

1. The students in _____ class are painting.   (our, ours)

2. I am almost finished with _____.   (my, mine)

3. Have you finished _____?   (your, yours)

4. Staci showed me _____ painting.   (her, hers)

B. Read the sentences and the reflexive pronouns in parentheses. Write the correct reflexive pronoun on the lines.

5. The class read quietly to _____.   (himself, themselves)

6. Karen poured _____ a glass of water.   (herself, myself)

7. I bought _____ a new computer.   (myself, themselves)

8. You should cook _____ dinner.   (ourselves, yourself)

 **In your writer's notebook, write about something you created. Say why you're proud of what you made. Review your work when you're done to make sure you used possessive and reflexive pronouns correctly.**

Name _____

> - A possessive pronoun replaces a possessive noun. Use these possessive pronouns with nouns: *my, your, his, her, its, our, their.*
> - Use these possessive pronouns alone, without a noun: *mine, yours, his, hers, ours, theirs.*

Replace each underlined possessive noun with the correct possessive pronoun. Write the new sentences on the lines.

1. Jana left <u>Jana's</u> backpack on the bus.

_____

2. Frank and Pia studied <u>Frank's and Pia's</u> spelling words together.

_____

3. Tim asked Clara, "Is this <u>Clara's</u> notebook?"

_____

4. Jason gave me <u>Jason's</u> camera and asked me to take a picture.

_____

Writing Connection **Write about your favorite thing that you own. Say why you like it. Check your work for any errors.**

_____

_____

_____

_____

_____

Name _____

> • A possessive pronoun replaces a possessive noun. Use the pronouns *my, your, his, her, its, our,* and *their* with nouns. Use the pronouns *mine, yours, his, hers, its, ours,* and *theirs* by themselves.
>
> • Nouns and pronouns must agree when used in simple and compound sentences.

A. Proofread the paragraph. Circle any incorrect pronouns.

Mine brother and I visited our grandparents on theirs farm last summer. They have a vegetable garden, and they raise sheep. Theirs dogs help herd the sheep. My grandmother uses hers tomatoes to make delicious soup. Mine grandfather uses the sheep's milk to make cheese. We like the cheese sandwiches he makes from its. Theirs farm is a busy place in the summer. My brother and I had the best time on ours vacation.

B. Rewrite the paragraph with the correct pronouns.

_____

_____

_____

_____

_____

_____

Name _____

A. Read the paragraph. Then answer the questions.

(1) My mother asked my brother and me to clean our rooms. (2) I finished cleaning mine quickly. (3) Then I helped my brother clean his room. (4) I picked up all his books. (5) I was proud of myself for helping him.

1. What is the possessive pronoun in sentence 4?

   A I
   B picked
   C his
   D books

2. What is the reflexive pronoun in sentence 5?

   F I
   G myself
   H for
   J him

B. Read the student draft and look for revisions that need to be made. Then answer the questions.

(1) Mine sister and I visited our aunt and uncle at theirs ranch. (2) They have horses and ponies. (3) Our aunt rides hers favorite horse every day. (4) We got to ride the ponies and feed them hay. (5) What fun we had on our visit!

3. What is the correct way to write sentence 1?

   A Mine sister and I visited ours aunt and uncle at theirs ranch.
   B My sister and I visited our aunt and uncle at theirs ranch.
   C My sister and I visited our aunt and uncle at their ranch.
   D No change needed in sentence 1.

4. What is the correct way to write sentence 3?

   F Ours aunt rides hers favorite horse every day.
   G Our aunt rides her favorite horse every day.
   H Ours aunt rides her favorite horse every day.
   J No change needed in sentence 3.

Name _____

Fold back the
paper along
the dotted line.
Use the blanks
to write each
word as it is
read aloud.
When you finish
the test, unfold
the paper. Use
the list at the
right to correct
any spelling
mistakes.

1. _____
2. _____
3. _____
4. _____
5. _____
6. _____
7. _____
8. _____
9. _____
10. _____
11. _____
12. _____
13. _____
14. _____
15. _____

Review Words
16. _____
17. _____
18. _____

Challenge Words
19. _____
20. _____

1. tries
2. tried
3. trying
4. dries
5. dried
6. drying
7. hurries
8. hurried
9. hurrying
10. studies
11. studied
12. studying
13. plays
14. played
15. playing
16. chapter
17. bedtime
18. letter
19. obeyed
20. worrying

Name _____

When a word ends in a consonant and *y*, change the *y* to an *i* before adding the endings *-es* or *-ed*: *fry, fries, fried*. When a word ends in a vowel and *y*, do not change the *y* to an *i*: *spray, sprays, sprayed*. Never change the *y* to an *i* when adding *-ing*: *frying, spraying*.

DECODING WORDS

The inflectional ending *-ing* usually forms the last syllable in a word. For words that end in *y*, the syllables usually divide between the *y* and *i*: *dry/ing, carry/ing*.

Read aloud the spelling words in the box. Then write the spelling words that match the spelling patterns.

drying	playing	dried	hurrying	plays
tried	hurries	trying	studied	dries
hurried	tries	studies	studying	played

change *y* to *i* and add *-es*

1. _____
2. _____
3. _____
4. _____

change *y* to *i* and add *-ed*

5. _____
6. _____
7. _____
8. _____

add *-ing*

11. _____
12. _____
13. _____
14. _____
15. _____

add *-s* or *-ed*

9. _____
10. _____

Name _____

> When a word ends in a consonant and *y*, change the *y* to an *i* before adding the endings *-es* or *-ed*: *fry, fries, fried.* When a word ends in a vowel and *y*, do not change the *y* to an *i*: *spray, sprays, sprayed.* Never change the *y* to an *i* when adding *-ing*: *frying, spraying.*

DECODING WORDS

The inflectional ending *-ing* usually forms the last syllable in a word. For words that end in *y*, the syllables usually divide between the *y* and *i*: *dry/ing, carry/ing.*

Read aloud the spelling words in the box. Then write the spelling words that match the spelling patterns.

tries	crying	flying	flies	dried
played	plays	cried	cries	tried
trying	drying	dries	stays	playing

change *y* to *i* and add *-es*	change *y* to *i* and add *-ed*	add *-ing*
1. _____	5. _____	11. _____
2. _____	6. _____	12. _____
3. _____	7. _____	13. _____
4. _____	**add *-s* or *-ed***	14. _____
	8. _____	15. _____
	9. _____	
	10. _____	

Name _____

A. **Read aloud the spelling words in the box. Then write the spelling words that match the spelling patterns.**

worrying	studying	studied	studies	trying
tried	dried	replied	hurries	obeying
obeyed	drying	hurrying	dries	tries

change _y_ to _i_ and add -_es_

1. _____

2. _____

3. _____

4. _____

change _y_ to _i_ and add -_ed_

5. _____

6. _____

7. _____

8. _____

add -_ed_

9. _____

add -_ing_

10. _____

11. _____

12. _____

13. _____

14. _____

15. _____

B. **Compare the words _tried_ and _trying_. How are they alike? How are they different?**

_____

_____

_____

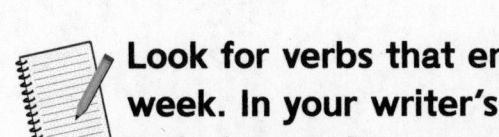 **Look for verbs that end in _y_ in the selections you read this week. In your writer's notebook, practice adding the endings -_ed_, -_ing_, and -_s_ or -_es_ to the verbs you find.**

Name _____

tries	studying	hurries	trying	hurried
playing	dried	plays	studied	played
studies	drying	hurrying	dries	tried

A. Write the spelling word that best completes each sentence.

1. Last year, my brother _____ for the Trenton Panthers.

2. Pioneers _____ apples so they would last longer.

3. My friend and I are _____ for the weekly spelling test.

4. Dad is _____ to fix the broken chain on my bike.

5. We _____ to catch the train before it pulled away.

6. My sister _____ in the library for her history test.

7. We are _____ the wet beach towels on the clothes line.

8. The baby _____ to walk for the first time.

9. Sam was _____ to reach his classroom before the bell rang.

10. The school band is _____ a lively march.

B. Write the spelling word that means the same thing as the words written below.

11. attempts to _____   14. learns about _____

12. makes less wet _____   15. does for fun _____

13. rushes or speeds _____

Name _____

Underline the six misspelled words in the paragraphs below. Write the words correctly on the lines.

My class has been studeing the presidents. I picked up many interesting facts. I read that Thomas Jefferson plaed chess. It's well known that Abraham Lincoln studied to be a lawyer, and he hid things in his stovepipe hat.

George Washington liked to eat cake with nuts and dryied fruits. And John F. Kennedy enjoyed plaing with his children. Do you suppose they tryed to play hide and seek in the White House? I'll always wonder.

1. _____   4. _____

2. _____   5. _____

3. _____   6. _____

Writing Connection **What do you think makes a good president? Write your ideas. Use at least four spelling words.**

_____

_____

_____

_____

_____

_____

_____

Name _____

Remember

> When a word ends in a consonant and the letter *y*, change *y* to *i* before adding the inflectional endings -*es* or -*ed*: *fry, fries, fried*. Do not change *y* to *i* when adding -*ing*: *frying*.
>
> In most cases, when a word ends in a vowel and the letter *y*, do not change the *y* to an *i* before adding any inflectional endings: *spray, sprays, sprayed, spraying*.

drying	dries	plays	hurrying	hurries
playing	studying	hurried	studied	played
trying	tries	studies	dried	tried

Combine each word and ending. Read the spelling word aloud and then write it on the line.

1. dry + s _____

2. study + ed _____

3. try + ing _____

4. hurry + ing _____

5. dry + ed _____

6. try + ed _____

7. play + ed _____

8. hurry + ed _____

9. play + ing _____

10. study + s _____

11. try + s _____

12. study + ing _____

13. play + s _____

14. hurry + s _____

15. dry + ing _____

Name _____

> **Homographs** are words that are spelled the same but have different meanings. They are sometimes pronounced differently. For example, the word *lead* can refer to a kind of heavy metal, or it can be a verb meaning *to manage or oversee*. When you come across a homograph in a text, use nearby words and context clues to figure out which meaning the author is using.

A. Read the sentences below. Underline the context clues to help you understand the meaning of the homograph in bold. Then write the meaning of the word on the line.

1. He tried hard to win the race, but he only came in **second** place.

   _____

2. The quick flash of lightning lit up the dark room for less than a **second**.

   _____

3. The factory is able to **produce** thousands of cars every year.

   _____

4. The fruits and vegetables in the **produce** aisle looked very fresh.

   _____

B. Write two sentences on the lines. In your first sentence, use the word *bat* to refer to the wooden club used in baseball. In your second sentence, use *bat* to refer to the flying animal.

_____

_____

_____

_____

Name _____

Read each sentence below. Write the base word of the underlined word. Then write the meaning of the underlined word.

1. We rode the train from Texas to Utah so that we could see trees, mountains, rivers, and all other parts of the beautiful <u>scenery</u>.

    _____

2. After I took a sip of the smoothie, the flavor of blueberry was <u>unmistakable</u>. I would know it anywhere!

    _____

3. The performer can do many things, but her <u>specialty</u> is singing.

    _____

4. We were <u>overjoyed</u> and smiling ear to ear when our parents said we could adopt a puppy.

    _____

5. I thought that my new shoes would hurt my feet, but instead they were quite <u>comfortable</u>.

    _____

6. The <u>uninformed</u> guests did not know where they were supposed to sit.

    _____

7. She was <u>relieved</u> to know that she earned an A even though her last project had received a B.

    _____

Name _____

> • A **contraction** is a shortened form of two words: *she is = she's.*
>
> • An apostrophe replaces letters that are left out in a pronoun-verb contraction.
>
> • Some common contractions are *he's (he is), she's (she is), it's (it is), you're (you are), I'm (I am), we're (we are), they're (they are),* and *I've (I have).*

Rewrite each sentence and replace the underlined words with the correct contraction.

1. <u>I am</u> writing a report about animals and their habitats.

   _____

2. I think <u>it is</u> interesting to learn about where animals live.

   _____

3. Dad says that <u>he has</u> seen an eagle's nest.

   _____

4. <u>I have</u> only seen a picture of an eagle's nest high in a tree.

   _____

5. <u>They are</u> known for building huge nests.

   _____

 **In your writer's notebook, write about a kind of bird that you have seen where you live. Use pronoun-verb contractions in your writing. Reread your work for any errors.**

Name _____

- Contractions can be formed with a pronoun and a helping verb such as *is, have,* or *will.*
- Some contractions formed with the word *will* are *I'll (I will), he'll (he will), she'll (she will), we'll (we will), you'll (you will), it'll (it will),* and *they'll (they will).*

A. Underline the two words in each sentence that you can make into a contraction. Rewrite the sentence with the contraction.

1. We will have lots of fun at the park.

_____

2. I will give her a call right now.

_____

3. Do you think it will be ready by noon?

_____

B. Reread this paragraph from "Pedal Power." Underline the two words that you can make into a contraction. Then rewrite the sentence with the contraction on the lines.

> What do you think? Are inventions that use pedal power a good idea, or a waste of time? Think about the arguments for and against pedal power, and decide. Maybe one day you will invent a pedal-powered machine!

_____

_____

Name _____

> • Do not confuse possessive pronouns with contractions.
>
> • The words *it's, you're,* and *they're* are contractions. They each have an apostrophe that stands for letters that are left out.
>
> • The words *its, your,* and *their* are possessive pronouns. They do not have apostrophes.

A. Write C if the underlined word is a contraction. Write P if it is a possessive pronoun.

1. I hope <u>it's</u> not too late to enter the science fair. _____

2. Lin and Gary showed me <u>their</u> science project. _____

3. I want to ask if <u>they're</u> finished with it. _____

4. Have you planned <u>your</u> project yet? _____

5. I am certain that <u>you're</u> going to win. _____

B. Complete each sentence with the correct contraction or possessive pronoun in parentheses.

6. I like (your, you're) _____ new backpack.

7. (Their, They're) _____ going to pick us up at noon.

8. I don't think (it's, its) _____ going to rain today.

9. I think that (your, you're) _____ the best pitcher we have.

 **In your writer's notebook, write about your favorite subject in school. Check your work when you're done to make sure you didn't confuse contractions and possessive pronouns.**

Name _____

> • Do not confuse possessive pronouns with contractions.
>
> • The words *it's, you're,* and *they're* are contractions. They each have an apostrophe that stands for letters that are left out.
>
> • The words *its, your,* and *their* are possessive pronouns. They do not have apostrophes.

A. Proofread the paragraph. Circle any possessive pronouns or contractions that are not used correctly.

Ive' just read a book about the history of ice cream. Its interesting to learn how long ice cream has been around. The Persians were known for making they're frozen treats by pouring fruit juice over snow. I'am sure that was delicious. I learned that George Washington and Thomas Jefferson liked ice cream. They'are two of our founding fathers who visited ice-cream parlors in New York.

B. Rewrite the paragraph with the correct pronouns.

_____

_____

_____

_____

_____

_____

_____

_____

Name _____

A. Read the paragraph. Then answer the questions.

(1) I've just read a book about elephants. (2) It's interesting to learn about their behavior and how they live. (3) They're the largest land animals in the world. (4) They eat only plants and vegetables, not meat. (5) They use their tusks for defense and for digging for water.

1. What is the contraction in sentence 2?
   A It's
   B to
   C their
   D they

2. Which sentence contains a contraction that means *they are*?
   F Sentence 1
   G Sentence 2
   H Sentence 3
   J Sentence 4

B. Read the student draft and look for revisions that need to be made. Then answer the questions.

(1) Maria dreams of working in a zoo when she grows up. (2) Shell' feed the animals and make sure their happy and healthy. (3) She will give bananas to the monkeys and throw fish to the sea lions. (4) "I'am sure that I'will be a great zookeeper!" she thought to herself.

3. What is the correct way to write sentence 2?
   A Shell feed the animals and make sure theyre happy and healthy.
   B She'll feed the animals and make sure they're happy and healthy.
   C Shel'l feed the animals and make sure their happy and healthy.
   D No change needed in sentence 2.

4. What is the correct way to write sentence 4?
   F "I'm sure that I'll be a great zookeeper!" she thought to herself.
   G "Im' sure that Ill' be a great zookeeper!" she thought to herself.
   H "Im sure that Iwill' be a great zookeeper!" she thought to herself.
   J No change needed in sentence 4.

Name _____

Fold back the paper along the dotted line. Use the blanks to write each word as it is read aloud. When you finish the test, unfold the paper. Use the list at the right to correct any spelling mistakes.

1. _____
2. _____
3. _____
4. _____
5. _____
6. _____
7. _____
8. _____
9. _____
10. _____
11. _____
12. _____
13. _____
14. _____
15. _____

Review Words

16. _____
17. _____
18. _____

Challenge Words

19. _____
20. _____

1. pilot
2. diner
3. tiger
4. favor
5. lemon
6. planet
7. cover
8. shady
9. robot
10. tiny
11. label
12. cozy
13. silent
14. spider
15. frozen
16. tried
17. hurried
18. studying
19. melon
20. stomach

Name _____

An **open syllable** is when a syllable ends with a vowel. The vowel sound is usually long, as in the word *focus*. The consonant-vowel-consonant (CVC) spelling pattern can also form closed syllables, as in *river*. Read these words aloud: *focus* (*fo/cus*), *river* (*riv/er*).

DECODING WORDS

The word *hotel* has two syllables. The first syllable, *ho*, ends with a long *o*. It is an open syllable. The second syllable, *tel*, ends with a consonant and has a short *e* sound. It is a closed syllable. Blend the syllables: *ho/tel*.

Write the spelling words that contain the matching sounds.

pilot	favor	cover	tiny	silent
frozen	lemon	diner	label	shady
tiger	planet	robot	cozy	spider

long *a* in first syllable

1. _____

2. _____

3. _____

long *i* in first syllable

4. _____

5. _____

6. _____

7. _____

8. _____

9. _____

long *o* in first syllable

10. _____

11. _____

12. _____

short vowel in first syllable

13. _____

14. _____

15. _____

Name _____

> An open syllable is when a syllable ends with a vowel. The vowel sound is usually long, as in the word *focus*. The consonant-vowel-consonant (CVC) spelling pattern can also form closed syllables, as in *river*. Read these words aloud: *focus* (*fo / cus*), *river* (*riv / er*).

DECODING WORDS

The word *hotel* has two syllables. The first syllable, *ho*, ends with a long *o*. It is an open syllable. The second syllable, *tel*, ends with a consonant and has a short *e* sound. It is a closed syllable. Blend the syllables: *ho/tel*.

Write the spelling words that contain the matching sounds.

pilot	limit	model	tiny	silent
diner	lemon	ever	cover	spider
tiger	planet	robot	salad	frozen

long *i* in first syllable	short vowel in first syllable	long *o* in first syllable
1. _____	7. _____	14. _____
2. _____	8. _____	15. _____
3. _____	9. _____	
4. _____	10. _____	
5. _____	11. _____	
6. _____	12. _____	
	13. _____	

Name _____

A. Write the spelling words that contain the matching sounds.

pilot	lemon	shady	refocus	rumor
label	planet	robotic	cozy	frozen
favorite	cover	tiny	modern	melon

long *a* in first syllable

1. _____

2. _____

3. _____

long *i* sound in first syllable

4. _____

5. _____

long *e* in first syllable

6. _____

long *o* in first syllable

7. _____

8. _____

9. _____

long *u* in first syllable

10. _____

short vowel in first syllable

11. _____

12. _____

13. _____

14. _____

15. _____

B. Compare the words *label* and *planet*. How are the words alike? How are they different?

_____

_____

_____

Name _____

pilot	favor	cover	tiny	silent
shady	lemon	diner	label	spider
tiger	planet	robot	cozy	frozen

A. Write the spelling word that belongs with each group below.

1. restaurant, cafe, _____   4. star, moon, _____

2. lion, cheetah, _____   5. orange, lime, _____

3. insect, bug, _____

B. Write the spelling word that best completes each sentence.

6. Under the oak tree is a cool and _____ place for a picnic.

7. After the ice at the skating rink is _____, hockey season will begin.

8. The cabin is warm and _____ with a fire in the fireplace.

9. The jet _____ told us about his exciting job.

10. Can you do me a _____ and help me with this heavy box?

11. Put a _____ on the pot.

12. I have a toy _____ that I programmed to tell jokes.

13. Our kitten is _____ now, but he will grow quickly.

14. The owl was as _____ as a mouse as it landed in a tree.

15. Before I go to camp, I have to _____ my clothes.

Name _____

There are six misspelled words in the paragraph below. Underline each misspelled word. Then write the words correctly on the lines.

A tigur is an amazing animal. It is tiney when it is born, but it grows fast. The biggest one on the planeat weighs more than 1,000 pounds. As it prowls through the shadey forest looking for food, it is sielent. It has been given the labul of fierce, and I think that fits this animal perfectly.

1. _____   4. _____

2. _____   5. _____

3. _____   6. _____

Writing Connection **Write about an animal that you think is fierce. Use at least four spelling words.**

_____

_____

_____

_____

_____

_____

_____

_____

_____

_____

Name _____

Remember

An open syllable is when a syllable ends with a long vowel sound, as in the first syllable of the word *token* (*to/ken*). Words with a consonant-vowel-consonant (CVC) spelling pattern have a syllable division after the vowel if the vowel is long, or after the second consonant if the vowel is short: *focus* (*fo/cus*), *limit* (*lim/it*).

pilot	favor	cover	tiny	silent
diner	lemon	shady	label	spider
tiger	planet	robot	cozy	frozen

Fill in the missing syllable to make each spelling word complete. Read the spelling word aloud and then write it on the line.

1. _____ der _____

2. lem _____ _____

3. pi _____ _____

4. sha _____ _____

5. _____ zen _____

6. ti _____ _____

7. co _____ _____

8. la _____ _____

9. _____ er _____

10. si _____ _____

11. di _____ _____

12. _____ et _____

13. _____ bot _____

14. _____ vor _____

15. _____ ger _____

Name _____

Content words are specific to a field of study. *Electricity* and *wind* are science content words.

Authors use content words to explain a concept or idea. Use context clues to figure out what a content word means. You can also use a print or digital dictionary.

It's All in the Wind gives facts about wind energy. It also gives facts about why people support or do not support wind energy. The author uses content words that relate to this topic to help you understand how wind power works and why it is important.

With a partner, search for content words related to wind power. Write them on the blades of the wind turbines below.

Pick two words that you were able to figure out the meaning of by using context clues. Write the words and what they mean on the lines.

_____

_____

Name _____

> **Homophones** are words that are pronounced the same way but have different meanings. Homophones often have different spellings as well. Some examples of homophones include *tail* and *tale*, *blue* and *blew*, *right* and *write*, and *hear* and *here*.

Read each sentence below. Underline the context clues that help you understand the meaning of each homophone in bold. Then write the correct definition of the homophone on the line.

1. The lookout atop the mountain showed the best views I've ever **seen**.

   _____

2. I liked every part of the movie, but the ending was my favorite **scene**.

   _____

3. Cell phones started to become popular **in** the 1980s.

   _____

4. The travelers needed a place to sleep, so they stopped at an **inn**.

   _____

5. We watched the bald eagle **soar** high in the sky.

   _____

6. I felt good after running yesterday, but today my muscles are **sore**!

   _____

 **Pick a pair of homophones listed on this page, or think of a pair by yourself. In your writer's notebook, write two sentences. Use one of the homophones in one sentence, then use the other homophone in your second sentence.**

Name _____

> • An **adjective** is a word that describes a noun. It modifies, or limits or adds to the description of the noun. An adjective usually comes before the noun it describes: *The **red** ball.*
>
> • Some adjectives are descriptive. They tell what kind of person, place, or thing the noun is: *The **small** squirrel climbs the **tall** tree.*
>
> • Some adjectives tell how many: *I caught a **few** fish.*
>
> • Some adjectives are limiting, such as *this, that, these,* and *those.*

Underline each adjective. Circle the noun the adjective describes.

1. Gramps has a brown horse.

2. Rex is the name of this big animal.

3. I am a good helper when I visit Gramps.

4. I take Rex out for long rides.

5. I feed Rex juicy apples.

6. Gramps lets me polish the heavy saddle.

7. In June I will help him paint the old barn.

8. I chose a bright red.

9. I think Rex will like that color.

 **In your writer's notebook, write about some things you might see on a farm. Reread your work when you're done to make sure you used adjectives correctly.**

Name _____

> • The **articles** *a, an,* and *the* are special adjectives.
>
> • Use *an* before an adjective or singular noun that begins with a vowel: *an apple, an umbrella, an ocean.*
>
> • Use *the* before singular and plural nouns when referring to something specific: *the dogs, the door, the book.*

A. Write *a, an,* or *the* to finish each sentence.

1. I went to see _____ first game of the World Series.

2. I wrote _____ essay about my exciting day.

3. I took _____ baseball in hopes of getting it signed.

4. After _____ game, I found my favorite pitcher.

5. I told him that I was _____ big fan.

B. Reread this paragraph from *Looking Up to Ellen Ochoa.* Circle the articles in the underlined sentence.

> First, there is the ground crew. They inspect and repair the shuttle before each mission. <u>Next, Mission Control workers guide the astronauts through each moment of a mission and debrief them on procedures.</u> They are responsible for knowing how equipment is working. They communicate with astronauts to check on how they feel.

Name _____

> - Use commas to separate three or more words in a series: *I play the guitar, piano, and drums.*
> - Use a comma between the day and year in a date: *May 6, 2018.*
> - Use a comma after introductory words: *No, I haven't had lunch.*
> - Use commas to set off appositives which add extra information about a noun or pronoun. *Aline, the girl with red hair, is my sister.*

Rewrite each sentence. Add commas where they belong.

1. Wow this is a great book that I got at the library!

   _____

2. It tells all about snakes lizards and alligators.

   _____

3. The author was born on June 15 1979.

   _____

4. His other book the one about sharks is my favorite.

   _____

Writing Connection **Write about a book you recently read. Check your work to make sure you used commas correctly.**

_____

_____

_____

_____

_____

Name _____

- An adjective is a word that describes a noun.

- Some adjectives are descriptive. Some adjectives tell how many. Some adjectives are limiting, such as *this, that, these*, and *those*.

- Use a comma after introductory words, between the day and year in a date, and to separate three or more items in a series.

A. Proofread the passage. Circle any adjectives and articles that are not used correctly. Add commas where needed.

When I grow up I think I want to be a astronaut. A few years ago I thought about becoming an famous basketball player. A long time ago, my grandmother played on a all-girls team. She was born on May 3 1959. One time she told me, "This days were so much fun." But I think it would be fun to go on space missions, too. To become an astronaut means that I have to be a excellent student. I got the "A" on my last math test. Next week I need to study for spelling science and reading.

B. Rewrite the passage. Use the correct adjectives and articles. Use commas correctly.

_____

_____

_____

_____

_____

_____

Name _____

A. Read the paragraph. Then answer the questions.

(1) My dad made a treasure hunt for my sister and me.
(2) He gave us a list of things he hid in our backyard.
(3) They included a tall jar with pennies in it, a painted egg,
two seashells, and a red ball. (4) We had fun that day!

1. Which adjective in sentence 3 tells how many?

   A tall

   B painted

   C two

   D red

2. Which word in sentence 4 is an adjective?

   F We

   G had

   H that

   J fun

B. Read the student draft and look for revisions that need to be made. Then answer the questions.

(1) Mom Dad and I went to my aunt's house for dinner. (2) She
made an roast chicken for dinner and a apple pie for dessert.
(3) Then we worked together on a jigsaw puzzle.

3. What is the correct way to write sentence 1?

   A Mom Dad, and I went to my aunt's house for dinner.

   B Mom, Dad, and I went to my aunt's house for dinner.

   C Mom, Dad, and I, went to my aunt's house for dinner.

   D No change needed in sentence 1.

4. What is the correct way to write sentence 2?

   F She made an roast chicken for dinner and an apple pie for dessert.

   G She made a roast chicken for dinner and a apple pie for dessert.

   H She made a roast chicken for dinner and an apple pie for dessert.

   J No change needed in sentence 2.

Name _____

Fold back the paper along the dotted line. Use the blanks to write each word as it is read aloud. When you finish the test, unfold the paper. Use the list at the right to correct any spelling mistakes.

1. _____
2. _____
3. _____
4. _____
5. _____
6. _____
7. _____
8. _____
9. _____
10. _____
11. _____
12. _____
13. _____
14. _____
15. _____

Review Words

16. _____
17. _____
18. _____

Challenge Words

19. _____
20. _____

1. disagreed
2. dislike
3. disappear
4. presale
5. preschool
6. precook
7. previous
8. rebuild
9. return
10. resell
11. reprint
12. unwrap
13. unlucky
14. untied
15. unbeaten
16. robot
17. tiny
18. label
19. unknown
20. recover

Name _____

> A prefix is a word part added to the beginning of a word. The prefixes *un-* and *dis-* mean *not* or *the opposite of,* as in *disorder* and *unprepared*. The prefix *re-* means *again*, as in *reset,* and *pre-* means *before*, as in *predate*.

disagreed	presale	return	unwrap	unlucky
rebuild	untied	dislike	reprint	preschool
unbeaten	resell	previous	precook	disappear

Read aloud the spelling words in the box. Then write the words that contain the prefixes below.

dis-

1. _____
2. _____
3. _____

pre-

4. _____
5. _____
6. _____
7. _____

re-

8. _____
9. _____
10. _____
11. _____

un-

12. _____
13. _____
14. _____
15. _____

 **Look back at the selections you read this week and look for words with the prefixes *pre-, dis-, un-,* and *re-*. Say the words you find aloud, and record them in your writer's notebook.**

Name _____

A prefix is a word part added to the beginning of a word. The prefixes *un-* and *dis-* mean *not* or *the opposite,* as in the words *disorder* and *unprepared.* The prefix *re-* means *again* (*reset*) and *pre-* means *before* (*predate*).

DECODING WORDS

Prefixes often form the first syllable in a word. Sound out the prefix, then the rest of the word. Use the prefix to figure out the word's meaning. For example, *preheat* (*pre/heat*) means *to heat before cooking.*

unhappy	prevent	rebuild	redo	unkind
resell	review	unlucky	dislike	prepaid
precook	untied	reprint	unfold	return

Read aloud the spelling words in the box. Then write the words that contain the prefixes below.

dis-	*re-*	*un-*
1. _____	5. _____	11. _____
pre-	6. _____	12. _____
2. _____	7. _____	13. _____
3. _____	8. _____	14. _____
4. _____	9. _____	15. _____
	10. _____	

 **Look back at the selections you read this week and look for words with the prefixes *pre-, dis-, un-,* and *re-.* Say the words you find aloud, and record them in your writer's notebook.**

Name _____

dislike	previous	rebuild	unwrap	unknown
reread	recover	disappear	precook	rearrange
untied	unbeaten	reenter	unafraid	unlucky

A. Read aloud the spelling words in the box. Then write the words that contain the prefixes below.

dis-

1. _____

2. _____

pre-

3. _____

4. _____

re-

5. _____

6. _____

7. _____

8. _____

9. _____

un-

10. _____

11. _____

12. _____

13. _____

14. _____

15. _____

B. Compare the words *dislike* and *unlucky*. How are they alike? How are they different?

_____

_____

_____

 **Look back at the selections you read this week and look for words with the prefixes *pre-, dis-, un-,* and *re-*. Say the words you find aloud, and record them in your writer's notebook.**

Name _____

disagreed	resell	previous	presale	precook
untied	preschool	rebuild	reprint	dislike
disappear	unlucky	return	unwrap	unbeaten

A. Write the spelling word that completes each sentence.

1. I like oranges and limes, but I _____ lemons.

2. I saw the latest movie, but I didn't see the _____ movie.

3. Once the Sun came out, the snow began to _____.

4. My friend bought movie tickets at the _____.

5. The wind damaged our treehouse, so we will _____ it.

6. I want to _____ the gift and see what's inside.

7. After missing the bus, I think this is an _____ day.

8. Mom takes my little sister to _____ every morning.

9. The puppy _____ my shoe and chewed the shoelace.

10. I will _____ the library book when I finish reading it.

B. Write a spelling word that matches each meaning.

11. not agreed _____

14. to print again _____

12. sell again _____

15. to cook before _____

13. not beaten _____

Name _____

There are six spelling mistakes in the paragraphs below. Underline the misspelled words. Write the words correctly on the lines.

Once there was a princess who went to prischool. She always forgot her lunch, and usually she forgot her homework, too. She thought she was a very unlukee princess. But her teacher desagreed. One day Miss Dora said, "I can make all this bad luck desappear, if you want."

The princess said, "Yes, please!" Miss Dora gave the princess a package. The princess unitied the red ribbon and began to unrap the package. Inside was a beautiful notebook and pencil. The princess wrote a note about bringing her homework and lunch to school. She never forgot them again.

1. _____ 4. _____

2. _____ 5. _____

3. _____ 6. _____

Writing Connection **Write about what you do to help you remember things. Use at least four spelling words.**

_____
_____
_____
_____
_____
_____
_____

Name _____

Remember

A prefix is a word part that is added to the beginning of a base word to create a new word. The prefix *re-* means *again,* as in the word *replay*. The prefix *pre-* means *before*, as in *preheat*. The prefixes *dis-* and *un-* both mean *not* or *opposite of*, as in the words *disobey* and *uncertain*.

reprint	unbeaten	previous	resell	unlucky
untied	preschool	unwrap	disagreed	dislike
disappear	precook	return	rebuild	presale

Write the missing syllable to make each spelling word complete. Then read the spelling word aloud, and write it on the line.

1. _____ appear _____

2. _____ lucky _____

3. _____ build _____

4. _____ tied _____

5. _____ school _____

6. _____ turn _____

7. _____ agreed _____

8. _____ print _____

9. _____ sale _____

10. _____ beaten _____

11. _____ sell _____

12. _____ wrap _____

13. _____ like _____

14. _____ cook _____

15. _____ vious _____

Name _____

> **Content words** are words specific to a field of study. Words like *space* and *astronomy* are science content words.
>
> You can figure out what a content word means by using context clues. You can also use a dictionary for help.

CONNECT TO CONTENT

Looking Up to Ellen Ochoa tells how Ellen Ochoa became the first female Hispanic American astronaut. The author uses science content words to help you understand more about the space program.

 **Go on a word hunt with a partner. Find content words related to astronauts and outer space. Write them on the lines.**

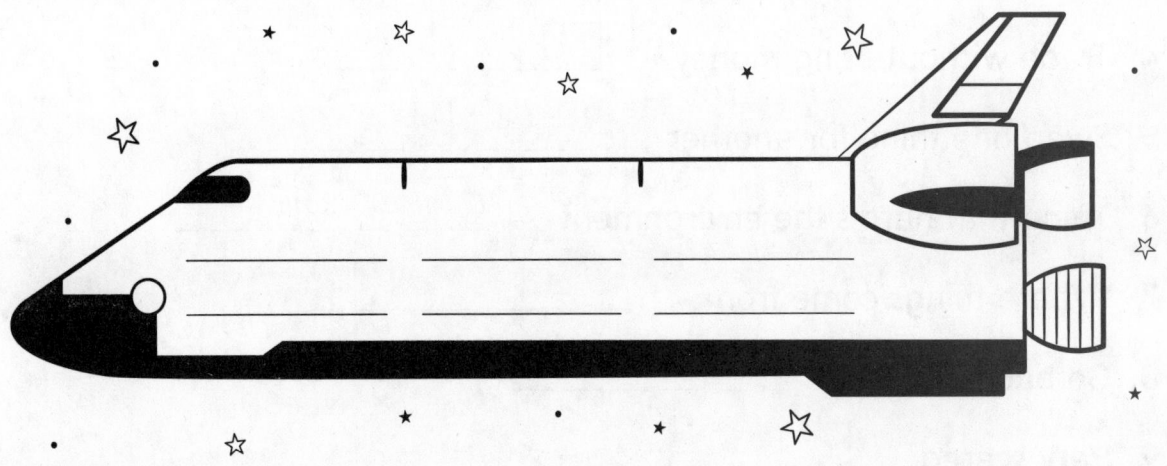

Pick two words that you were able to figure out the meaning of using context clues. Write the words and what they mean on the lines.

_____

_____

Name _____

Complete the puzzle with the vocabulary words. Use the letters in the boxes to solve the riddle below.

energy	natural	pollution	produce
renewable	replace	sources	barter
humble	waver	traditional	horrified

1. Something not made by people __ __ □ __ __ __ __

2. Small or modest □ __ __ __ __ __

3. Something used to power things __ __ □ __ __ __

4. Trade without using money □ __ __ __ __ __

5. Swap one thing for another __ __ __ □ __ __ __

6. Thing that harms the environment __ __ __ __ □ __ __ __ __

7. Where things come from __ __ __ __ __ □ __

8. Go back and forth □ __ __ __ __

9. Very scared □ __ __ __ __ __ __ __ __

10. Able to be replaced after use __ __ __ __ __ __ □ __ __ __

11. How something has always been __ __ __ __ __ __ __ __ __ __ □

12. Make or create something __ __ __ __ __ □ __

This is the largest animal to have ever existed. What is it?

□ □ □ □ □ □ □ □ □ □ □

Name _____

> - An adjective that compares is a descriptive adjective. You can use adjectives to compare two or more nouns.
> - Add *-er* to an adjective to compare two nouns: *The Arctic is* **colder** *than the tropics.*
> - Add *-est* to an adjective to compare more than two nouns: *Winter is the* **coldest** *of all four seasons.*

A. Circle the correct adjective for each sentence.

1. This pumpkin is (bigger, biggest) than the one I grew last year.

2. Mercury is the (smaller, smallest) of all the planets.

3. This is the (sweeter, sweetest) orange I've ever eaten.

4. That clap of thunder was even (louder, loudest) than the last one.

5. The yellow kitten is (furrier, furriest) than the striped one.

6. Of all the rabbits, the gray one was (quicker, quickest).

7. A river is usually much (wider, widest) than a creek.

B. Read the paragraph from "A Flight to Lunar City." Circle the adjective that compares in the underlined sentence.

> Now they were almost there! Robbie wriggled and squirmed. "Settle down!" Maria scolded. Sometimes Robbie was awfully wild, like a real puppy. <u>Maria was thinking about adjusting his Personality Profile Program to make him a little calmer.</u>

Name _____

- Some adjectives change their spelling when *-er* or *-est* is added.
- When an adjective ends in a consonant and *y*, change the *y* to *i* and add *-er* or *-est*: *happy/happier/happiest, cozy/cozier/coziest.*
- When an adjective ends in *e*, drop the *e* and add *-er* or *-est*: *pale/paler/palest, large/larger/largest.*
- When adjectives have a short vowel sound before a final consonant, double the final consonant and add *-er* or *-est*: *sad/sadder/saddest, thin/thinner/thinnest.*

A. Add *-er* or *-est* to each adjective. Write the correct form.

Add *-er*

1. big _____
2. sunny _____
3. silly _____
4. nice _____
5. blue _____

Add *-est*

6. funny _____
7. safe _____
8. fat _____
9. tiny _____
10. red _____

B. Write the correct form of each adjective in parentheses.

11. Yesterday was the (hot) _____ day all summer.

12. Shane was (fast) _____ than Tom.

13. This coat is (big) _____ than my old coat.

14. Tomorrow will be the (short) _____ day of the year.

15. It is (rainy) _____ today than it was yesterday.

Name _____

> • Some **adjectives** that compare do not add *-er* or *-est*.
>
> • The comparative form of *good* is *better*, and the superlative form is *best*.
>
> • The comparative form of *bad* is *worse*, and the superlative form is *worst*.
>
> • *Many* is an adjective that refers to more than one thing. *More* compares two things. *Most* compares more than two.

Circle the correct adjective for each sentence.

1. I like corn (better, best) than green beans.

2. Our city has (more, most) sunny days than rainy ones.

3. That was the (worse, worst) movie I've ever seen.

4. I think the Eagles are the (better, best) team in the country.

5. I did (better, best) on the last test than this one.

6. My cold is (worse, worst) today than it was yesterday.

7. Of all my friends, Maria has the (more, most) video games.

8. I think Mrs. Casa is the (better, best) teacher in the world.

9. We had (more, most) snow days this year than last year.

10. I just played my (worse, worst) game ever.

 **In your writer's notebook, compare your favorite and least favorite foods. When you're done, reread your work to make sure you used comparative and superlative adjectives correctly.**

Name _____

> • Add -er to an adjective to compare two nouns. Add -est to an adjective to compare more than two nouns.
>
> • The comparative form of *good* is *better,* and the superlative form is *best.* The comparative form of *bad* is *worse,* and the superlative form is *worst.*
>
> • *More* compares two things. *Most* compares more than two.

A. Proofread this passage. Circle any adjectives and articles that are not used correctly.

I think that Camp Woodbine is the better camp in the whole state. The camp has really good counselors. James is the nicer counselor of all of them. In the morning we get to choose our activities for the day. I like swimming most than rowing. I'm a fast swimmer, but my friend Patrick is fastest than I am. Last year we went hiking on the longer trail through the woods. I got the worser case of poison ivy ever!

B. Rewrite the passage. Use the correct adjectives and articles.

_____
_____
_____
_____
_____
_____
_____
_____

Name _____

A. Read the paragraph. Then answer the questions.

(1) My mom's cat had a litter of kittens. (2) The black kitten with the big eyes was smaller than the gray kitten. (3) The striped kitten was loudest. (4) They are all very cute.

1. Which adjective in sentence 2 compares two nouns?

   A black
   B big
   C smaller
   D gray

2. Which sentence contains a superlative adjective?

   F Sentence 1
   G Sentence 2
   H Sentence 3
   J Sentence 4

B. Read the student draft and look for revisions that need to be made. Then answer the questions.

(1) My family just moved from the city to the country. (2) I think the country is prettyer than the city. (3) The better thing of all about the country is the air is cleaner. (4) I miss my city friends, but we will still visit each other.

3. What is the correct way to write sentence 2?

   A I think the country is prettier than the city.
   B I think the country is more prettier than the city.
   C I think the country is prettiest than the city.
   D No change needed in sentence 2.

4. What is the correct way to write sentence 3?

   F The more better thing of all about the country is the air is cleaner.
   G The most better thing of all about the country is the air is cleaner.
   H The best thing of all about the country is the air is cleaner.
   J No change needed in sentence 3.

Name _____

Fold back the paper along the dotted line. Use the blanks to write each word as it is read aloud. When you finish the test, unfold the paper. Use the list at the right to correct any spelling mistakes.

1. _____
2. _____
3. _____
4. _____
5. _____
6. _____
7 _____
8. _____
9. _____
10. _____
11. _____
12. _____
13. _____
14. _____
15. _____

Review Words
16. _____
17. _____
18. _____

Challenge Words
19. _____
20. _____

1. able
2. purple
3. riddle
4. handle
5. eagle
6. puzzle
7. castle
8. little
9. pickle
10. towel
11. nickel
12. camel
13. travel
14. tunnel
15. squirrel
16. preschool
17. rebuild
18. unlucky
19. motel
20. couple

Name _____

When a word ends in *le* or *el*, the last syllable is usually formed by those letters and the consonant before them. This is called a **final stable syllable**. Examples include *cable* (*ca/ble*), *little* (*lit/tle*), *hotel* (*ho/tel*), and *channel* (*chan/nel*).

The word *turtle* has two syllables and a VCCCV spelling pattern. The syllables divide after the first consonant, creating a final stable syllable spelled *tle*. Blend the syllables and read the word aloud: *tur/tle*.

able	towel	castle	handle	travel
tunnel	eagle	little	puzzle	riddle
nickel	pickle	camel	squirrel	purple

Read the spelling words aloud. Then write the words that contain the matching final consonant spelling.

-le

1. _____   6. _____

2. _____   7. _____

3. _____   8. _____

4. _____   9. _____

5. _____

-el

10. _____

11. _____

12. _____

13. _____

14. _____

15. _____

 **Look back at the selections you read this week. Look for words with a final syllable spelled *le* or *el*. Read the words you find aloud, and record them in your writer's notebook.**

Name _____

When a word ends in *le, el,* or *al*, the last syllable is usually formed by those letters and the consonant before them. This is called a **final stable syllable**. Examples include *cable* (*ca/ble*), *viral* (*vi/ral*), *hotel* (*ho/tel*), and *channel* (*chan/nel*).

DECODING WORDS

The word *turtle* has two syllables and a VCCCV spelling pattern. The syllables divide after the first consonant, creating a final stable syllable spelled *tle*. Blend the syllables and read the word aloud: *tur/tle*.

able	eagle	ankle	bottle	travel
tunnel	little	puzzle	towel	purple
table	middle	pickle	camel	global

Read the spelling words aloud. Then write the words that contain the matching final consonant spelling.

-le

1. _____
2. _____
3. _____
4. _____
5. _____
6. _____
7. _____
8. _____
9. _____
10. _____

-el

11. _____
12. _____
13. _____
14. _____

-al

15. _____

Name _____

tunnel	icicle	pickle	motel	handle
terrible	nickel	camel	whistle	able
riddle	castle	single	towel	squirrel

A. Read the spelling words aloud. Then write the spelling words that contain the matching final consonant sound.

-le	-el
1. _____	10. _____
2. _____	11. _____
3. _____	12. _____
4. _____	13. _____
5. _____	14. _____
6. _____	15. _____
7. _____	
8. _____	
9. _____	

B. Compare the words *pickle* and *nickel*. How are they alike? How are they different?

_____

_____

_____

 **Look back at the selections you read this week. Look for words with a final syllable spelled *le* or *el*. Read the words you find aloud, and record them in your writer's notebook.**

Name _____

able	handle	castle	towel	travel
tunnel	eagle	nickel	little	purple
riddle	puzzle	pickle	camel	squirrel

A. Write the spelling word that goes with the other two words.

1. red, blue, _____

2. hawk, owl, _____

3. mansion, palace, _____

4. penny, dime, _____

5. tiny, small, _____

B. Write the spelling word that completes each sentence.

6. It is fun to _____ by trains and planes.

7. An earthworm digs a deep _____ underground.

8. Did the _____ bury an acorn under the tree?

9. I lost a piece of the _____ and can't finish it.

10. A _____ is a desert animal with a hump on its back.

11. Will you be _____ to go to the movie with me?

12. Dad asks me a _____ every night after dinner.

13. I eat a crisp, green _____ with my sandwich.

14. We need a _____ to wipe up the water we spilled.

15. I broke the _____ on my new suitcase.

Name _____

There are six spelling mistakes in the paragraph below. Underline the misspelled words. Write the words correctly on the lines.

Long ago, a king and queen lived in a big cassel. The king wore a long purpel cape and shiny crown. One day a squirle came along and saw the crown in the window. He grabbed it from the window and ran. The king chased him, but the animal ran deep inside a tunnle with the crown. The king wanted to find someone who was abel to crawl inside and get his crown. Finally, a litel boy said he would do it. In a few minutes, he came out with the king's crown.

1. _____   4. _____

2. _____   5. _____

3. _____   6. _____

Writing Connection **Write a story about a king and queen. Use at least four spelling words in your story.**

_____

_____

_____

_____

_____

_____

_____

_____

_____

Name _____

Remember

When a word ends with the letters *le* or *el,* the final syllable usually includes the consonant that comes before those letters. This is called a final stable syllable. For example, the letters *ble* form the last syllable in the word *possible*. The letters *bel* form the last syllable in the word *label*.

able	handle	castle	towel	travel
purple	eagle	little	nickel	tunnel
riddle	puzzle	pickle	camel	squirrel

Write the missing letters to make each spelling word complete. Read the spelling word aloud, and then write it on the line.

1. cam _____   _____

2. _____ ble   _____

3. rid _____   _____

4. tra _____   _____

5. tow _____   _____

6. squir _____   _____

7. pick _____   _____

8. han _____   _____

9. pur _____   _____

10. lit _____   _____

11. ea _____   _____

12. puz _____   _____

13. nick _____   _____

14. tun _____   _____

15. cas _____   _____

Name _____

> **Multiple-meaning words** are words that have more than one meaning. For example, a *school* is a place where you go to learn. But a *school* is also a word for a group of fish.
>
> When you come across a multiple-meaning word, use context clues and background knowledge to figure out which meaning the author is using.

Read the sentences below. Underline the context clues that help you figure out the meaning of each word in bold. Then write the meaning on the line. Use a dictionary and background knowledge for help.

1. The woman kept her money and valuable jewelry in a **safe**.

   _____

2. Amelia Earhart was the first female pilot to **fly** solo across the Atlantic.

   _____

3. The farmer grew corn and potatoes on his **land.**

   _____

4. Members of the audience were impressed with the actors in the **play**.

   _____

5. He could easily lift the box because it was very **light**.

   _____

6. The white **crane** flew from its nest to the river to catch a fish.

   _____

Name _____

Many English words have roots in Greek and Latin. For example, the Latin root *fin* meaning *end* is the root of the English words *final* and *finish*. Use your knowledge of roots to figure out the meaning of a new word. Here are some roots that may help you:

- The Latin root *mir* means "wonder" or "amazement."
- The Latin root *orb* means "circle" or "ring."
- The Greek root *hydro* means "water."

Use the Greek and Latin roots from the box above to find the meaning of each word in bold below. Write the meaning of the word on the line. Then use each word in a sentence of your own.

1. orbit _____

_____

_____

2. infinite _____

_____

_____

3. admire _____

_____

_____

4. hydrant _____

_____

_____

Name _____

> - An **adverb** describes an action verb. It modifies, or limits or adds to the description of the verb.
> - Adverbs can tell the place, time, or manner in which an action takes place. Adverbs answer the questions *where, when,* or *how.*
> - Most adverbs that tell how an action takes place end in *-ly*: *He walked **slowly**. The dog barked **loudly**.*

A. Draw one line under each adverb that tells how an action takes place. Circle the verb that the adverb describes.

1. Mom and I walked carefully down to the edge of the pond.

2. We eagerly ate our picnic lunch.

3. Mom pointed silently to a turtle sunning itself on a rock.

4. The turtle woke up quickly.

5. It looked around worriedly.

6. A frog jumped noisily in the water.

7. It swam briskly across the pond.

B. Read this paragraph from "Carlos's Gift." Underline the adverb and circle the verb in the underlined sentence.

> Carlos read the book that night. He found a photograph of the exact kind of bulldog puppy that he craved. He eagerly showed Mama the next morning.

Name _____

> • Some adverbs that tell where an action takes place are *there,*
> *ahead, outside, around, up, far, here, away, nearby, somewhere,*
> and *everywhere.*
>
> • Some adverbs that tell when an action takes place are *first, soon,*
> *always, early, next, today, later, tomorrow,* and *then.*

**A. Draw one line under each adverb that tells where an action
takes place. Circle the verb that the adverb describes.**

1. My family goes outside on weekends if the weather is nice.

2. Last week, we hiked far into the woods.

3. We climbed up several hills.

4. I ran ahead to the lake.

**B. Draw one line under each adverb that tells when an action
takes place. Circle the verb that the adverb describes.**

5. My dad always bakes a big cake for the school bake sale.

6. First, he buys all the ingredients for the cake.

7. Next, he mixes everything together.

8. Then he bakes the cake in the oven.

 **In your writer's notebook, write about an activity you like to
do outside. Use adverbs that tell how and when to describe
your actions. When you're done, use a dictionary to check
that you used and spelled adverbs correctly.**

Name _____

> - Use an adjective to describe a noun.
> - Use an adverb to describe a verb.
> - Don't mix up adjectives with adverbs that tell *how*.

Circle the word that correctly completes each sentence.

1. The dragon is an (important, importantly) part of Chinese New Year.

2. People dressed as a dragon dance (bold, boldly) down the street.

3. The costume is made of (colorful, colorfully) silk.

4. The dragon weaves (quick, quickly) in and out of the crowd.

5. The people shout (loud, loudly) to get the dragon's attention.

6. (Happy, happily) children wave to the dragon.

Connect to Community **Talk to a parent or another trusted adult about a parade or other celebration in your community. Write about what happens during the celebration and why it is important. Be sure to check your work for errors.**

_____

_____

_____

_____

_____

_____

Name _____

- Adjectives describe nouns. Adverbs describe verbs.
- Adverbs that tell *when* include *first, next,* and *then.* Adverbs that tell *where* include *here, there, up,* and *down.*
- Adverbs that tell *how* an action takes place usually end in *-ly.*

A. Proofread this passage. Circle any adjectives and adverbs that are not used correctly.

Today my grandfather and I made a beautifully kite. I helped him careful cut the paper into the right size and shape. We worked happy on the kite the entire morning. Sudden my mom called us in for lunch. I was surprised that the morning had gone by so quick. After we finished lunch, we went back to the garage and easy attached the long tail to the kite. We will let the glue dry slow overnight. We are hopefully that there will be a good breeze tomorrow so that we can fly our new kite.

B. Rewrite the passage. Use the correct adjectives and adverbs.

_____

_____

_____

_____

_____

_____

_____

Name _____

A. Read the paragraph. Then answer the questions.

　　(1) My older sister and I like to go to the beach together. (2) We walk slowly along the shore and look for interesting seashells. (3) Sometimes we see seagulls fly gracefully above the blue water. (4) There's so much to see and do at the beach!

1. Which word in sentence 2 is an adverb?
   A walk
   B slowly
   C look
   D interesting

2. Which word in sentence 3 is an adverb that tells *when*?
   F Sometimes
   G see
   H gracefully
   J blue

B. Read the student draft and look for revisions that need to be made. Then answer the questions.

　　(1) I got a new pair of eyeglasses today. (2) They fit perfect, and I can see so clear through them. (3) I can't wait to read my book. (4) First, but I need to do my homework.

3. What is the correct way to write sentence 2?
   A They fit perfectly, and I can see so clear through them.
   B They fit perfect, and I can see so clearly through them.
   C They fit perfectly, and I can see so clearly through them.
   D No change needed in sentence 2.

4. What is the correct way to write sentence 4?
   F Firstly, but I need to do my homework.
   G Then, but I need to do my homework.
   H But I need to do my homework first.
   J No change needed in sentence 4.

Name _____

Fold back the paper along the dotted line. Use the blanks to write each word as it is read aloud. When you finish the test, unfold the paper. Use the list at the right to correct any spelling mistakes.

1. _____
2. _____
3. _____
4. _____
5. _____
6. _____
7. _____
8. _____
9. _____
10. _____
11. _____
12. _____
13. _____
14. _____
15. _____

Review Words

16. _____
17. _____
18. _____

Challenge Words

19. _____
20. _____

1. explained
2. remain
3. reading
4. detail
5. presoak
6. monkey
7. brief
8. preteen
9. about
10. allowing
11. complain
12. enjoys
13. poison
14. repeats
15. unreal
16. able
17. castle
18. towel
19. repaid
20. approached

Name _____

> A **vowel team** is two or more letters that make one sound. The letters *ai* form long *a*. The letters *ea, ey, ie,* and *ee* usually form long *e*, and *oa* forms long *o*. The letters *ou* and *ow* form the vowel sound in *cow*, and *oy* and *oi* form the vowel sound in *coin*.

DECODING WORDS

The word *monkey* is a two-syllable word with a VCCV spelling pattern. The first syllable is a closed syllable spelled *mon*. The second syllable is an open syllable with the vowel team *ey*. Blend the sounds together: *mon/key*.

explained	detail	brief	allowing	reading
repeats	presoak	preteen	complain	remain
poison	monkey	about	enjoys	unreal

Read the spelling words aloud. Then write the words that contain the vowel team spelling patterns.

ai	*ea, ey, ie,* and *ee*	*oy* and *oi*
1. _____	6. _____	12. _____
2. _____	7. _____	13. _____
3. _____	8. _____	*ou* and *ow*
4. _____	9. _____	14. _____
oa	10. _____	15. _____
5. _____	11. _____	

 **Look back at the selections you read this week. Look for words with vowel teams. Read the words you find aloud, and record them in your writer's notebook.**

Name _____

A **vowel team** is two or more letters that make one sound. The letters *ai* and *ay* form long *a*. The letters *ea, ey, ie,* and *ee* form long *e,* and *oa* forms long *o*. The letters *ou* and *ow* form the vowel sound in *cow,* and *oy* and *oi* form the sound in *coin*.

DECODING WORDS

The word *monkey* is a two-syllable word with a VCCV spelling pattern. The first syllable is a closed syllable spelled *mon*. The second syllable is an open syllable with the vowel team *ey*. Blend the sounds together: *mon/key.*

away	remain	reading	streets	allow
enjoys	repeats	detail	chief	complain
explained	unreal	soaked	key	poison

Read the spelling words aloud. Then write the words that contain the vowel team spelling patterns.

ai and *ay*	*ea, ey, ie,* and *ee*	*ow*
1. _____	6. _____	12. _____
2. _____	7. _____	*oy* and *oi*
3. _____	8. _____	13. _____
4. _____	9. _____	14. _____
5. _____	10. _____	*oa*
	11. _____	15. _____

 **Look back at the selections you read this week. Look for words with vowel teams. Read the words you find aloud, and record them in your writer's notebook.**

Name _____

explained	detail	brief	approached	viewpoint
remain	monkey	replay	textbook	complain
repeatedly	preheated	preteen	allowing	enjoyment

A. Read the spelling words aloud. Then write the words that contain the vowel team spelling patterns.

ai and *ay*   *ea, ey, ie,* and *ee*   *ow*

1. _____   6. _____   11. _____

2. _____   7. _____   *oy*

3. _____   8. _____   12. _____

4. _____   9. _____   *oo*

5. _____   10. _____   13. _____

                                        oa

                                        14. _____

15. Which word has two vowel teams? _____

B. Compare the words *brief* and *preteen*. How are they alike? How are they different?

_____

_____

_____

 **Look back at the selections you read this week. Look for words with vowel teams. Read the words you find aloud, and record them in your writer's notebook.**

Name _____

explained	detail	brief	allowing	poison
remain	presoak	preteen	complain	repeats
reading	monkey	about	enjoys	unreal

A. Write a spelling word that goes with the other two words.

1. taught, showed, _____

2. writing, spelling, _____

3. chimp, ape, _____

4. deadly, chemical, _____

5. short, small, _____

B. Write the spelling word that completes each sentence.

6. To get out a stain, _____ the clothing before washing.

7. Please _____ in your seats when the bell rings.

8. The model ship we built has amazing _____.

9. Someone who is twelve years old is a _____.

10. I need to find a book _____ the solar system.

11. The ballpark is _____ us to bring in food.

12. The neighbors will _____ if we are too loud.

13. Dad likes baseball, but he _____ football more.

14. Our parrot _____ our words.

15. Being able to meet the president seemed _____.

Name _____

There are six spelling mistakes in the paragraph below. Underline the misspelled words. Write the words correctly on the lines.

I am supposed to write a breef book report abowt my favorite book. I like raeding a lot, but I don't know what to write. I explaned to my teacher that I've read so many books I can't choose just one. She said that she enjois many books, too. She asked if there was one book that really stands out. I thought about it and then said, "The book about the monkee that goes to school!"

1. _____   4. _____

2. _____   5. _____

3. _____   6. _____

Writing Connection **Write about your favorite book. Use at least four spelling words in your writing.**

_____

_____

_____

_____

_____

_____

_____

_____

_____

Name _____

Remember

A vowel team is when two or more letters form one vowel sound. The vowel team *ai* forms a long *a* vowel sound as in *rain*. The vowel teams *ea*, *ey*, *ie*, and *ee* usually form a long *e* sound. The letters *oa* form a long *o*. The letters *ou* and *ow* form the sound you hear in *cow*, and *oy* and *oi* form the sound in *coin*.

explained	detail	brief	allowing	poison
remain	presoak	preteen	complain	repeats
reading	monkey	about	enjoys	unreal

Write the missing letters to make each spelling word complete. Read the spelling word aloud and then write it on the line.

1. com _____   _____

2. rep _____   _____

3. r_____ding   _____

4. ex _____ ed   _____

5. all _____ ing   _____

6. pres _____ k   _____

7. p _____ son   _____

8. rem _____   _____

9. mon _____   _____

10. en _____   _____

11. de _____   _____

12. br _____   _____

13. pret _____ n   _____

14. ab _____   _____

15. un _____   _____

Name _____

Create new forms of a base word by adding or removing inflectional endings, prefixes, or suffixes.

```
        obsessing          obsesses

                  obsess

        obsessed          obsession
```

Use your notes from *King Midas and the Golden Touch*. Choose a word and write it on the treasure box below. Then write related words on the gold coins around the treasure box. Use a dictionary for help.

Name _____

Read the clues. Then unscramble each word by writing the letters in the correct order on the line.

communicated	motivated	research	creation
essential	payment	magnificent	specialist
goal	professional	serious	participate

	SCRAMBLED	**CLUE**	
1.	pecsiaistl	Expert	_____
2.	ssenteail	Very important or needed	_____
3.	pateciartip	Join with others	_____
4.	edvatiotm	Eager to do something	_____
5.	aymnetp	Amount paid for something	_____
6.	ccammuoinedt	Spoke with	_____
7.	loga	Target or dream	_____
8.	ionfessproal	Relating to a skilled job	_____
9.	usersoi	Very important	_____
10.	fiagmncenit	Very beautiful	_____
11.	tcraoien	Something you made	_____
12.	chresaer	Study to find facts	_____

Name _____

> • **Adverbs** can be used to compare two or more actions.
> • To compare actions using most one-syllable adverbs, add -er or -est: *slow/slower/slowest, hard/harder/hardest.*
> • *More* and *most* are used with adverbs that have two or more syllables to make comparisons: *more carefully, most silently.*

A. Circle the correct word to complete each sentence.

1. My brother runs (faster, fastest) than I do.

2. Jay solved the problem (more, most) quickly than Frank.

3. The first band played the song the (louder, loudest) of any of the bands.

4. Kara finished the test (quicker, quickest) than the other students.

5. Hurricanes are (more, most) common in fall than they are in spring.

6. Birds migrate (more, most) often before winter than after.

7. That piano recital lasted (longer, longest) than the last one.

B. Read these lines from "Theseus and the Minotaur." Circle the adverbs in the underlined sentence.

Narrator: At last the prince returned dragging the sword.

Prince Theseus: The Minotaur is destroyed. Let's go quickly and quietly back to the ship.

Narrator: The prince tapped on the door and the princess opened it. They all ran to their ship together and sailed away.

Name _____

- To make comparisons using the adverb *well*, use *better* and *best*:
  My dad cooks better than I cook, but my mom cooks best.

- To make comparisons using the adverb *badly*, use *worse* and
  *worst. I am worse than my sister at playing tennis, but my brother
  plays worst of all of us.*

**Write the correct form of the word in parentheses to complete each
sentence. Then write the sentence on the line.**

1. Jai scored _____ on the test than Ben scored. (well)

   _____

2. Jai scored _____ of all his friends on the test. (well)

   _____

3. Mom's flowers looked _____ during August than they
   did in July. (badly)

   _____

4. Mom's flowers looked _____ of all during the hot, dry
   months. (badly)

   _____

 **In your writer's notebook, write a story about two people who
play in a game or competition. Compare how they do using
adverbs. Check your work for errors when you're done.**

Name _____

> - Add *-er* or *-est* to the end of short adverbs to compare.
> - Use *more* and *most* with adverbs that have two or more syllables.
> - Adverbs that are used with *more* or *most* do not change their endings to make comparisons.

Circle the correct word or words to complete each sentence.

1. The scientists worked (more quickly, most quickly) than they had ever worked before.

2. That was the (more carefully, most carefully) planned expedition ever.

3. He travels to Texas (more often, oftener) than he travels to Florida.

4. It rains (more heavily, heavilier) in April than it does in August.

5. Some people wait (more patiently, most patiently) than others.

6. Jim swam the (most fastest, fastest) of all the swimmers.

7. The little bird sang (more sweetly, sweetlier) than the crow sang.

| Connect to Community | **Write about some of the differences between two seasons. Use adverbs to compare the two seasons you choose. Check your work for errors when you're done.** |

_____
_____
_____
_____
_____
_____

Name _____

- Add *-er* or *-est* to the end of short adverbs to compare.

- To make comparisons using the adverb *well,* use *better* and *best.* To make comparisons using *badly,* use *worse* and *worst.*

- Use *more* and *most* with adverbs with two or more syllables.

- Adverbs that are used with *more* or *most* do not change their endings to make comparisons.

A. Proofread this passage. Circle any adjectives and adverbs that are not used correctly.

I went to the First Street Market with my mom. She thinks the market has gooder vegetables than the one in Oak Hill. They have the most freshest fruits I've ever tasted. Mom chooses her fruits and vegetables carefullier than anyone I know. She slowlier sniffs each piece of fruit. She wants to buy the fruits and vegetables that are the riper. Mr. Able owns the market. He chooses his produce the more skillfully of all the market owners.

B. Rewrite the passage. Use the correct adjectives and adverbs.

_____

_____

_____

_____

_____

_____

_____

Name _____

A. Read the paragraph. Then answer the questions.

(1) I know a lot about big cats. (2) Lions roar the loudest of all big cats. (3) Cheetahs can run faster than any other mammal can. (4) Tigers can swim more skillfully than most other big cats.

1. What is the adverb that compares actions in sentence 3?
   A can
   B run
   C faster
   D any

2. Which sentence contains an adverb that does not change its ending to make comparisons?
   F Sentence 1
   G Sentence 2
   H Sentence 3
   J Sentence 4

B. Read the student draft and look for revisions that need to be made. Then answer the questions.

(1) The bird feeders in our backyard attract lots of birds. (2) The larger birds swoop down quicklier than the smaller birds. (3) Hummingbirds are the smaller birds of all.

3. What is the correct way to write sentence 2?

   A The larger birds swoop down more quicker than the smaller birds.
   B The larger birds swoop down more quick than the smaller birds.
   C The larger birds swoop down more quickly than the smaller birds.
   D No change needed in sentence 2.

4. What is the correct way to write sentence 3?

   F Hummingbirds are the more smaller birds of all.
   G Hummingbirds are the smallest birds of all.
   H Hummingbirds are the most smallest birds of all.
   J No change needed in sentence 3.

Name _____

Fold back the paper along the dotted line. Use the blanks to write each word as it is read aloud. When you finish the test, unfold the paper. Use the list at the right to correct any spelling mistakes.

1. _____

2. _____

3. _____

4. _____

5. _____

6. _____

7 _____

8. _____

9. _____

10. _____

11. _____

12. _____

13. _____

14. _____

15. _____

Review Words 16. _____

17. _____

18. _____

Challenge Words 19. _____

20. _____

1. severe

2. prepared

3. declare

4. later

5. writer

6. cellar

7. trailer

8. author

9. person

10. circus

11. garlic

12. partner

13. restore

14. sister

15. actor

16. explained

17. brief

18. enjoys

19. circular

20. editor

Name _____

> An *r*-controlled vowel syllable is formed when a vowel and the letter *r* remain in the same syllable, creating a new vowel sound. Some *r*-controlled vowel syllables are *er* as in *permit*, *ere* as in *here*, *ir* as in *circle*, *or* as in *corn*, and *ar* as in *carpet* or *care*.

severe	later	trailer	circus	restore
prepared	writer	author	garlic	sister
declare	cellar	person	partner	actor

Read the spelling words aloud. Then write the spelling words that match the spelling of the *r*-controlled vowel syllable.

er
1. _____
2. _____
3. _____
4. _____
5. _____

ir
6. _____

or
7. _____
8. _____
9. _____

ar
10. _____
11. _____
12. _____
13. _____

ere
14. _____

15. **Which word has two *r*-controlled syllables? Which ones?**

_____

Name _____

An *r*-controlled vowel syllable is formed when a vowel and the letter *r* remain in the same syllable, creating a new vowel sound. Some *r*-controlled vowel syllables are *er* as in *permit*, *ere* as in *here*, *ir* as in *circle*, *or* as in *corn*, and *ar* as in *carpet* or *care*.

SPELLING TIP

Pay attention to spelling patterns to help you decide if a *c* or *g* is hard or soft. When *c* comes before the letters *i* or *e*, it usually has a soft /s/ sound as in *center*. When *g* comes before the letters *a, u,* or *o,* it usually has a hard /g/ sound as in *gum*.

sister	doctor	silver	author	dirty
remark	later	cellar	artists	severe
winter	better	actor	report	circus

Read the spelling words aloud. Then write the spelling words that match the spelling of the *r*-controlled vowel syllable.

er

1. _____
2. _____
3. _____
4. _____
5. _____

ir

6. _____
7. _____

ar

8. _____
9. _____
10. _____

or

11. _____
12. _____
13. _____
14. _____

ere

15. _____

 **Look back at the selections you read this week. Look for words with *r*-controlled vowel syllables. Read the words aloud, and record them in your writer's notebook.**

Name _____

circular	dancer	trailer	expert	market
restore	later	partner	circus	further
feather	cellar	author	border	desert

A. Read the spelling words aloud. Then write the spelling words that match the spelling of the _r_-controlled vowel syllable.

er
1. _____

2. _____

3. _____

4. _____

5. _____

6. _____

ir
7. _____

or
8. _____

9. _____

ar
10. _____

11. _____

both _ir_ and _ar_
12. _____

both _ar_ and _er_
13. _____

both _or_ and _er_
14. _____

both _ur_ and _er_
15. _____

B. Compare the words _feather_ and _author_. How are they alike? How are they different?

_____

_____

_____

 **Look back at the selections you read this week. Look for words with _r_-controlled vowel syllables. Read the words aloud, and record them in your writer's notebook.**

Name _____

severe	later	trailer	circus	restore
prepared	writer	author	garlic	sister
declare	cellar	person	partner	actor

A. Write a spelling word that matches each meaning.

1. the underground part of a building _____

2. the opposite of brother _____

3. someone who works with another _____

4. to state or make known _____

5. singular of people _____

6. someone who writes books _____, _____

B. Write the spelling word that best completes each sentence.

7. You can go on ahead, and we'll catch up _____.

8. We will hitch a _____ to the back of the truck.

9. Are you _____ to take the big test?

10. Some people like to _____ old homes.

11. Do you want to be a movie _____?

12. The _____ set up a huge tent at the fairgrounds.

13. We go to the basement during _____ weather.

14. The _____ in this sauce smells great.

Name _____

There are six spelling mistakes in the paragraph below. Underline the misspelled words. Write the words correctly on the lines.

What would you like to be when you grow up? My sistur can't make up her mind. When she was little she wanted to be a clown in a curcus. Then her teacher told her she was a good writor, so she decided to become an auther. Latur, after she had been in a play, she told us that she planned to be an acter. I wonder what she will want to be next week.

1. _____   4. _____

2. _____   5. _____

3. _____   6. _____

Writing Connection **Write about a job you would like to do someday. Use at least four spelling words in your writing.**

_____

_____

_____

_____

_____

_____

_____

_____

Name _____

Remember

A vowel followed by the letter *r* creates an *r*-controlled vowel syllable. For example, the letters *er* create the vowel syllable in the word *dinner*. Other *r*-controlled vowel syllables are *er* as in *here*, *ir* as in *circle*, *or* as in *corn*, *ar* as in *cart,* and *ar* as in *care*.

severe	later	trailer	circus	restore
prepared	writer	author	garlic	sister
declare	cellar	person	partner	actor

Write the missing syllable to make each spelling word complete. Read the spelling word aloud, then write it on the line.

1. sis _____   _____

2. pre _____   _____

3. cel _____   _____

4. la _____   _____

5. re _____   _____

6. trail _____   _____

7. _____ son   _____

8. wri _____   _____

9. de _____   _____

10. se _____   _____

11. au _____   _____

12. _____ cus   _____

13. _____ lic   _____

14. _____ ner   _____

15. ac _____   _____

Name _____

A **compound word** is formed when two small words are put together to make one bigger word. For example, the words *sun* and *light* create the word *sunlight*. Figure out the meaning of an unfamiliar compound word by breaking it into smaller words.

A. Underline the compound word in each sentence. Then write the meaning of the compound word on the line.

1. I asked the salesperson in the store if she had the shirt in a smaller size.

_____

2. I stayed overnight at my friend's house and went home the next day.

_____

3. Before he left for school, he put his books and papers in his backpack.

_____

4. I went to the bay to watch the sailboats glide across the water.

_____

B. Underline the compound word that appears in each sign. Then write the meaning of the compound word on the line.

5.

6.

_____   _____

_____   _____

Name _____

Read each sentence below. Write the base word of the word in bold on the line. Then write the definition of the word in bold.

1. When I caught the flu last winter I felt so **miserable**.

   _____

2. I'll always remember my **unforgettable** camping trip in the Rocky Mountains.

   _____

3. My friend had heard about the new rules, but I was **uninformed**.

   _____

4. I thought the rabbit might be afraid of the deer, but it did not seem **threatened**.

   _____

5. Knowing that I can do anything I set my mind to makes me feel **empowered**.

   _____

6. I had hoped we would have sunny weather for the picnic, but **unfortunately** it rained.

   _____

Name _____

> • A **preposition** is a word that shows a relationship between a noun or a pronoun and another word: *I swam in the ocean.*
>
> • Common prepositions include *in, on, at, over, under, to, from, for, with, by, of, into, before, after,* and *during.*
>
> • The noun or pronoun that follows a preposition is the **object of the preposition**. In the sentence *I swam in the ocean,* the object of the preposition is *the ocean.*

Underline the preposition in each sentence. Then write it on the line.

1. My dad brought home plans for a picnic table. _____

2. We will build it in the backyard. _____

3. First, we will drive to Jon's Lumber Yard and buy the wood. _____

4. It is across town. _____

5. I think it is by the old skating rink. _____

6. Dad said that we could go after lunch. _____

7. He is making a list of the supplies we need. _____

8. It will be fun building the table from the wood we buy. _____

9. We will get everything we need at Jon's Lumber Yard. _____

10. I climb into Dad's big truck, and we are ready. _____

 **In your writer's notebook, write about something you have built or would like to build. When you're finished writing, read over your work to make sure you used prepositions correctly.**

Name _____

> • A **prepositional phrase** is a group of words that includes a preposition, the object of the preposition, and any words in between, such as *at the sandy beach* and *by the tall tree*.
>
> • When a pronoun follows a preposition, it should be an object pronoun, such as *me, you, him, her, it, us,* and *them*.

A. Underline the prepositional phrases in the following sentences.

1. Last weekend, Uncle Dan and I went on a hike.

2. A few years ago, Uncle Dan hiked across the country.

3. He took photographs along the way.

4. His photos were made into a book.

5. We have his book on our bookshelf.

6. He took some amazing pictures during his long hike.

7. One photo shows some hikers near the top of Mt. Everest.

B. Reread these lines from "Ollie's Escape." Underline one prepositional phrase.

He slithered his way to the office
as teachers jumped out of his way.
But Principal Poole
is the boss of the school.
We wondered just what he would say.

Copyright © McGraw Hill. Permission is granted to reproduce for classroom use. Text Credit: From *Reading, Rhyming, and 'Rithmetic* by Dave Crawley. Illustrated by Liz Callen. Copyright © 2010 by Dave Crawley and Liz Callen. Published by Wordsong, an imprint of Boyds Mills Press. Reprinted by permission.

Name _____

• A comma is used to separate an introductory word from the rest of a sentence: *Yes, let's go hiking. Dad, will you carry the water?*

• An introductory word could be a name, an adverb, or another word that should be separated from the rest of the sentence.

• An interjection is followed by a comma. If it expresses strong emotion, it is followed by an exclamation point. *Oh, I don't care. Wow! That's a great idea!*

Rewrite each sentence. Add a comma or exclamation point after the introductory words.

1. Yes we had a great time on our camping trip.

_____

2. First we set up our tent and unpacked our supplies.

_____

3. Wow we went canoeing down Green River.

_____

4. Mom what was your favorite part of the trip?

_____

 **In your writer's notebook, write step by step instructions that explain how to do something that you know well. Use words like *first, next,* and *then.* When you're done, reread your work to make sure you included commas after introductory words.**

Name _____

> A prepositional phrase is a group of words that includes a preposition, the object of the preposition, and any words in between, such as *near the snowy mountain* and *in the water*.

A. Proofread the passage below. Add commas where they are needed. Underline any incorrect prepositional phrases.

The people at my neighborhood started a community garden. Yes it's one of the first community gardens on our city. Dad do you remember what year it was started? Lately lots of reporters have come out to write stories to it. We donate lots of the vegetables to the local shelter. Wow they are always in need of help from the community. Therefore it is important for all of us to do what we can.

B. Rewrite the passage. Use commas and prepositional phrases correctly.

_____

_____

_____

_____

_____

_____

 **In your writer's notebook, write about other ways people can help their community. Write your thoughts in cursive, and remember to leave spaces between words. Check for errors in your prepositional phrases.**

Name _____

A. Read the paragraph. Then answer the questions.

(1) Yesterday, I looked everywhere for my necklace and could not find it. (2) I looked under the bed, on my desk, and on the shelves in my room. (3) No luck! (4) Then, my little sister walked into my room. (5) She was wearing my necklace!

1. Which is the preposition in sentence 1?
   A afternoon
   B for
   C my
   D it

2. How many prepositional phrases does sentence 2 contain?
   F 1
   G 2
   H 3
   J 4

B. Read the student draft and look for revisions that need to be made. Then answer the questions.

(1) I am going with a picnic at my swim team today. (2) First, we'll play tag and maybe some cards. (3) After that we will jump with the pool and have a race. (4) My best friend Hannah will probably win because she's so fast. (5) We'll eat dinner when the races are over. (6) I'm sure we'll be hungry!

3. What is the correct way to write sentence 1?
   A I am going at a picnic to my swim team today.
   B I am going on a picnic with my swim team today.
   C I am going in a picnic for my swim team today.
   D No change needed in sentence 1.

4. What is the correct way to write sentence 3?
   F After that, we will jump with the pool and have a race.
   G After that we will jump for the pool and have a race.
   H After that, we will jump in the pool and have a race.
   J No change needed in sentence 3.

Name _____

Fold back the paper along the dotted line. Use the blanks to write each word as it is read aloud. When you finish the test, unfold the paper. Use the list at the right to correct any spelling mistakes.

1. _____
2. _____
3. _____
4. _____
5. _____
6. _____
7. _____
8. _____
9. _____
10. _____
11. _____
12. _____
13. _____
14. _____
15. _____

Review Words

16. _____
17. _____
18. _____

Challenge Words

19. _____
20. _____

1. careful
2. cheerful
3. helpful
4. colorful
5. harmful
6. pitiful
7. painless
8. priceless
9. helpless
10. sleepless
11. rainless
12. helplessly
13. peacefully
14. carefully
15. wisely
16. later
17. declare
18. partner
19. wonderful
20. cloudless

Name _____

A **suffix** is a word part added to the end of a word to create a new word. The suffix -ful means full of, -less means without, and -ly means in this way. The suffixes -ful and -less can change a noun into an adjective: joy/joyful; noise/noiseless. The suffix -ly makes an adjective an adverb: joyful/joyfully.

Copyright © McGraw Hill. Permission is granted to reproduce for classroom use.

DECODING WORDS

If a word ends in a consonant and y, change the y to an i before adding the suffixes -ful, -less, or -ly. For example: happy/happily, pity/pitiful. Note that this usually changes the vowel sound as well. When you add -ful to plenty, the long e changes to a short i: plen/ti/ful.

careful	peacefully	cheerful	harmful	colorful
painless	sleepless	priceless	rainless	carefully
wisely	helpless	pitiful	helplessly	helpful

Read the spelling words aloud. Then write the spelling words that contain the suffixes below. Some words have more than one suffix.

-ful	-less	-ly
1. _____	9. _____	15. _____
2. _____	10. _____	16. _____
3. _____	11. _____	17. _____
4. _____	12. _____	18. _____
5. _____	13. _____	
6. _____	14. _____	
7. _____		
8. _____		

Name _____

A **suffix** is a word part added to the end of a word to create a new word. The suffix -ful means "full of"; -less means "without"; and -ly means "in this way." The suffixes -ful and -less can change a noun into an adjective: joy/joyful; noise/noiseless. The suffix -ly makes an adjective an adverb: joyful/joyfully.

careful	harmful	painless	sleepless	hopeful
restless	careless	wisely	rainless	cheerful
helpful	handful	helpless	weekly	priceless

Read the spelling words aloud. Then write the spelling words that contain the suffixes below.

-ful	-less	-ly
1. _____	7. _____	14. _____
2. _____	8. _____	15. _____
3. _____	9. _____	
4. _____	10. _____	
5. _____	11. _____	
6. _____	12. _____	
	13. _____	

Name _____

careful	colorful	carefully	cloudless	peacefully
wisely	harmful	priceless	helplessly	graceful
ungrateful	rainless	wonderful	pitiful	angrily

A. Read the spelling words aloud. Then write the words with the suffixes below. Some words have more than one suffix.

-ful	-less	-ly
1. _____	10. _____	14. _____
2. _____	11. _____	15. _____
3. _____	12. _____	16. _____
4. _____	13. _____	17. _____
5. _____		18. _____
6. _____		
7. _____		
8. _____		
9. _____		

B. Compare the words *careful* and *carefully*. How are they similar? How are they different?

_____

_____

_____

_____

Name _____

careful	colorful	helpful	sleepless	peacefully
rainless	helpless	priceless	cheerful	carefully
painless	pitiful	harmful	helplessly	wisely

A. Write the spelling word that matches each definition below.

1. without sleep _____

2. full of color _____

3. without pain _____

4. in a wise way _____

5. full of cheer _____

B. Write the spelling word that best completes each sentence.

6. A desert is a mostly _____ place.

7. The _____ little dog was wet and dirty.

8. I like to be _____ and wash the dishes for my mom.

9. It is important to be _____ when using scissors.

10. After the busy day, I slept _____.

11. The gold coins were so rare that they were considered _____.

12. Not getting enough exercise can be _____ to your health.

13. The puppies are _____ because they are born with their eyes closed.

14. I walked _____ down the icy sidewalk.

15. She looked on _____ as I began to fall.

Name _____

There are six misspelled words in the paragraph below. Underline each misspelled word. Write the words correctly on the lines.

Once there was a man who was always cheerfel. He wore a colorfil jacket everywhere he went because it made him feel happy. As he traveled about, he looked for ways to be helpfull to others. One day he was resting peacefullee in the shade of a tree when he heard a pityfull cry. He saw a tiny kitten mewing helplissly up in the branches. Quickly, he climbed to the top and rescued the kitten. From that day on, the man and the kitten traveled together.

1. _____   4. _____

2. _____   5. _____

3. _____   6. _____

Writing Connection

Write about someone who is cheerful. Use at least four spelling words in your writing.

_____

_____

_____

_____

_____

_____

_____

_____

Name _____

Remember

A suffix is a word part that is added to the end of a word to create a new word with a new meaning. The suffixes *-ful* and *-less* can change a noun into an adjective: *joy/joyful, noise/noiseless*. The suffix *-ly* can change an adjective into an adverb: *joyful/ joyfully, helpful/helpfully*.

careful	colorful	painless	sleepless	peacefully
cheerful	harmful	priceless	rainless	carefully
helpful	pitiful	helpless	helplessly	wisely

Write the missing suffix or suffixes to make each spelling word complete. Read the spelling word aloud. Then write it on the line.

1. color ____ _____

2. price _____ _____

3. peace __ __ _____

4. pain _____ _____

5. harm _____ _____

6. wise _____ _____

7. help ___ ___ _____

8. care __ __ _____

9. rain _____ _____

10. sleep _____ _____

11. help _____ _____

12. piti _____ _____

13. care _____ _____

14. cheer _____ _____

15. help ____ _____

Name _____

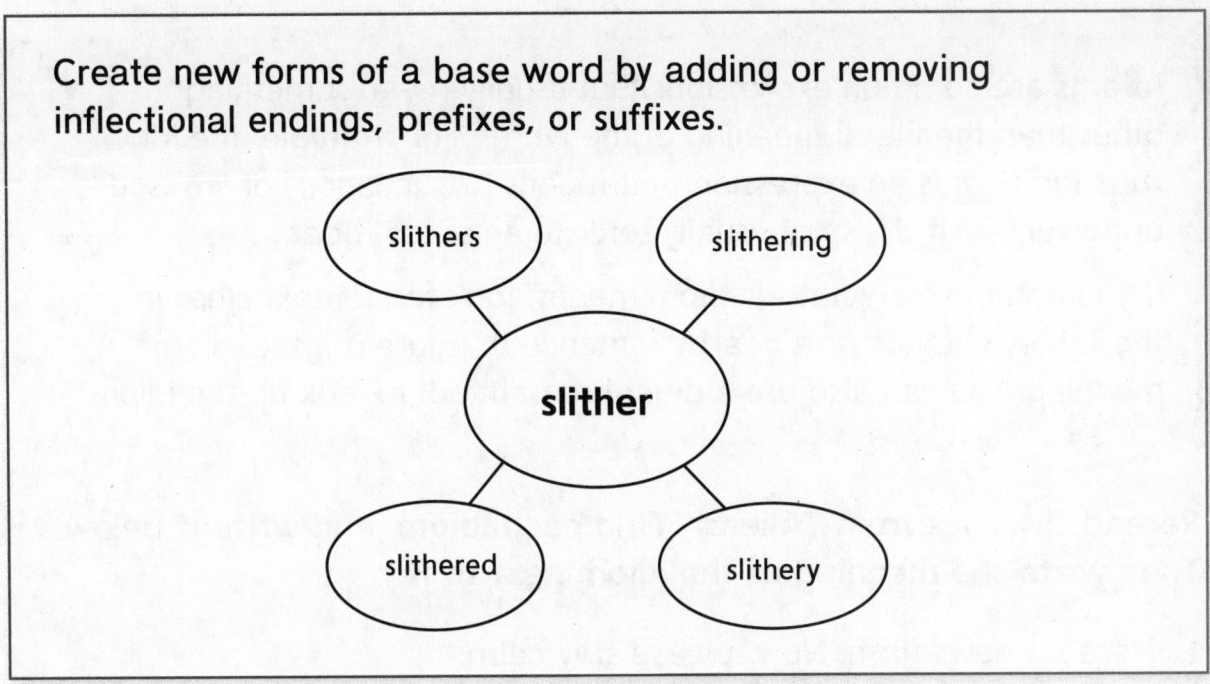

Create new forms of a base word by adding or removing inflectional endings, prefixes, or suffixes.

slithers

slithering

slither

slithered

slithery

Use your notes from "Ollie's Escape." Choose one word and write it on the biggest coil of the snake below. Then write related words on the other coils. Use a dictionary to help you think of new words.

Name _____

> **Idioms** are common expressions that usually mean something other than the literal meaning of the words. For example, the idiom *miss the boat* is an expression that means "lost chance" or "missed opportunity." It does not usually refer to an actual boat.
>
> If you don't know what an idiom means, look for context clues in the same sentence or a nearby sentence to figure out the idiom's meaning. You can also use a digital search tool to look up the idiom.

Reread the lines from "Aliens!" Find each idiom, and write it below. Then write the meaning of the idiom next to it.

1. Here's a news flash. Now, please stay calm:
   there are *aliens* around.

   _____

   _____

2. We didn't want to tell you boys,
   we thought it might just freak you out.

   _____

   _____

3. But Mom was clever enough to say,
   "Did something go down while I was away?"

   _____

   _____

 **In your writer's notebook, write about something you learned that surprised you. Include one of the idioms used above in your writing, or include an idiom you can think of yourself.**

HANDWRITING

Table of Contents

Cursive Writing Position: Left- and Right-Handed Writers 362
The Cursive Alphabet 363
Size and Shape 364
Letters *i t* 365
Letters *e l* 366
Letters *o a* 367
Letters *c d* 368
Letters *n m* 369
Connectives 370
Letters *u w* 371
Letters *b f* 372
Letters *h k* 373
Letters *g q* 374
Letters *j p* 375
Letters *r s* 376
Letters *y z* 377
Letters *v x* 378
Size and Shape 379
Letters *A O* 380
Letters *C E* 381
Letters *L D* 382
Letters *B R* 383
Letters *T F* 384
Letters *S G* 385
Letters *I J* 386
Spacing Letters and Words 387
Letters *N M* 388
Letters *H K* 389
Letters *P Q* 390
Letters *V U* 391
Letters *W X* 392
Letters *Y Z* 393
Transition to Two Lines 394
Practice with Small Letters 395
Practice with Tall Letters 396

Name _____ Date _____

Cursive Writing Position

Left-Handed Writers

Sit tall. Place both arms on the table.

Keep your feet flat on the floor.

Slant your paper.

Hold your pencil with your first two fingers and your thumb.

Right-Handed Writers

Sit tall. Place both arms on the table.

Keep your feet flat on the floor.

Slant your paper.

Hold your pencil with your first two fingers and your thumb.

Name _____ Date _____

The Cursive Alphabet

Aa Bb Cc Dd

Ee Ff Gg Hh

Ii Jj Kk Ll

Mm Nn Oo Pp

Qq Rr Ss Tt

Uu Vv Ww Xx

Yy Zz

Size and Shape

Tall letters touch the top line. **Make your writing easy to read.**

h *d* *l* *t*

Short letters touch the middle line.

o *a* *n* *m* *c* *u* *w*

These letters go below the bottom line.

g *f* *z* *j* *p* *y*

Circle the letters that are the right size and shape and sit on the bottom line.

a *w* *xh* *n* *d*

g *P* *e* *b* *l*

q *o* *f* *m* *s*

i t

Trace and write the letters. Then trace and write the word.

i i i i i i i

t t t t t t t

it it it it it

e l

Trace and write the letters. Then write the words.

e   e   e   e   e   e   e

l   l   l   l   l   l   l

ill   lit   tie   tile

Name _____ Date _____

o a

Trace and write the letters. Then write the words.

$\mathcal{O}$ $\mathcal{O}$ $\mathcal{O}$ $\mathcal{O}$ $\mathcal{O}$ $\mathcal{O}$ $\mathcal{O}$

a a a a a a a

toe   *toll*   *tail*   *ate*

tote   *oil*   *oat*   *lot*

c d

Trace and write the letters. Then write the words and the phrases.

c c c c c c c c

d d d d d d d

coat deed code

dime dance time

n m

Trace and write the letters. Then write the words.

n n n n n n

m m m m m m

name   note   moat

mitten   tame   nine

Connectives

Trace the connectives.

air tie her like

an and end sand

glad just yell

zebra you yarn

gap lazy game

five pick jam

feel plan quite

u w

Trace and write the letters. Then write the words.

_w_   _w_   _w_   _w_   _w_   _w_

_w_   _w_   _w_   _w_   _w_   _w_

wait   wit   would

undo   uncle   lute

b f

Trace and write the letters. Then write the words and the phrases.

b   *b b b b b b*

f   *f f f f f f*

boat   fall   bubble

fine food bat ball

Name _____   Date _____

h k

Trace and write the letters. Then write the words.

chick   hatch   hook

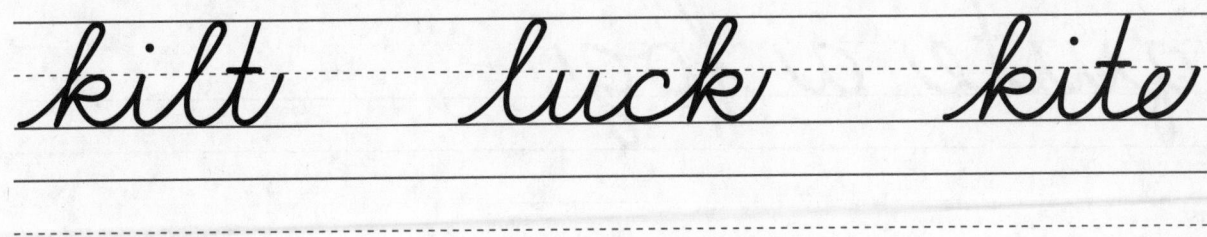

kilt   luck   kite

g q

Trace and write the letters. Then write the phrases.

g g g g g g g

q q q q q q q

quacked good game

quite a fog

j p

Trace and write the letters. Then write the phrases.

j j j j j j j

p p p p p p p

jump for joy

picture perfect

r s

Trace and write the letters. Then write the phrases.

r   *r*   *r*   *r*   *r*   *r*   *r*   *r*   *r*

s   *s*   *s*   *s*   *s*   *s*   *s*   *s*

rose blossom

stars and stripes

y z

Trace and write the letters. Then write the phrases.

y   *y* *y* *y* *y* *y* *y*

z   *z* *z* *z* *z* *z* *z*

zip code   zoom in

pretty azaleas

v x

Trace and write the letters. Then write the phrases.

v   *v*   *v*   *v*   *v*   *v*   *v*

x   *x*   *x*   *x*   *x*   *x*   *x*

x marks the spot

vim and vigor

Size and Shape

All uppercase letters are tall letters.
Tall letters should touch the top line.

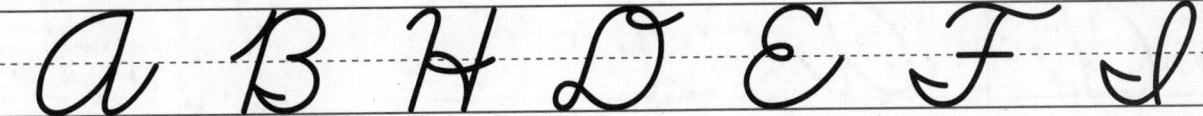

Letters with descenders go below the bottom line.

J Z Y

You can make your writing easy to read.

Look at the letters below. Circle the letters that are the correct size and shape.

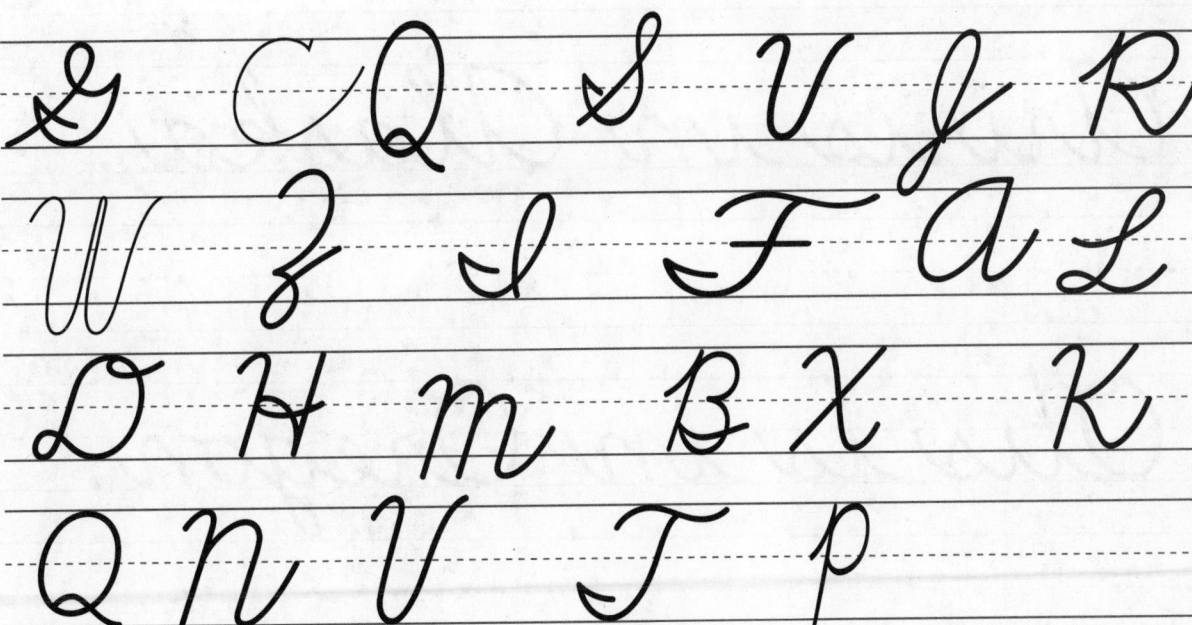

A O

Trace and write the letters. Then write the sentences.

a a a a a a

O O O O O O

Ari is in Alaska.

Otis is in Oregon.

C E

Trace and write the letters. Then write the sentences.

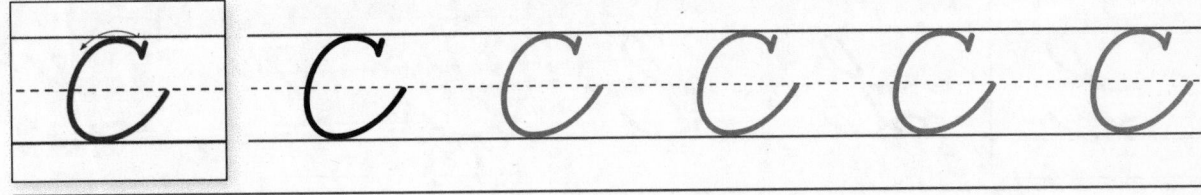

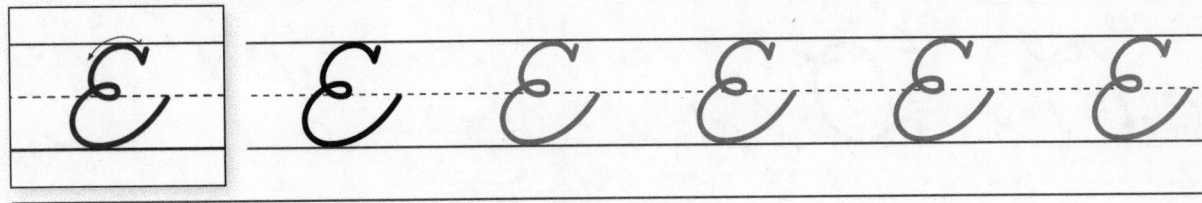

Cece visits China.

Ed is in England.

L D

Trace and write the letters. Then write the sentences.

$\mathscr{L}$ | $\mathscr{L}$ $\mathscr{L}$ $\mathscr{L}$ $\mathscr{L}$ $\mathscr{L}$

$\mathscr{D}$ | $\mathscr{D}$ $\mathscr{D}$ $\mathscr{D}$ $\mathscr{D}$ $\mathscr{D}$

Dad did a dance.

Leo dined at Del's.

B R

Trace and write the letters. Then write the sentences.

B B B B B B

R R R R R R

Bill is in Brazil.

Rose is in Russia.

Name _____ Date _____

T F

Trace and write the letters. Then write the sentences.

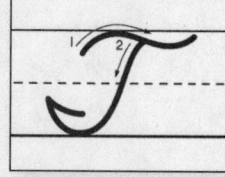 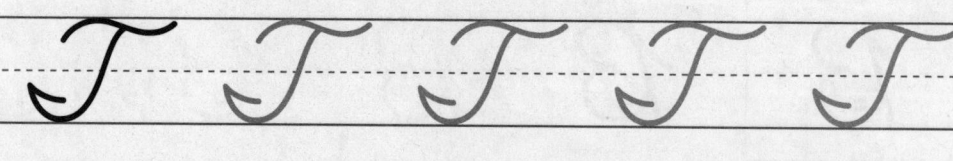

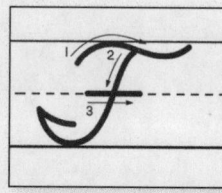

Theodore Roosevelt
won. Friends cheer.

S G

Trace and write the letters. Then write the sentences.

 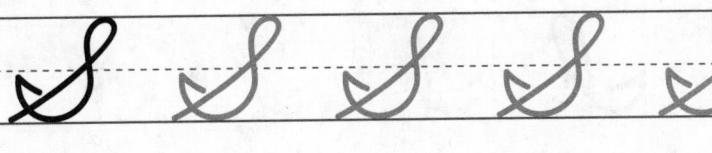

Sal Sr. met Gail.

Greg is our guest.

I J

Trace and write the letters. Then write the sentences.

I I I I I I I I

J J J J J J J J

Ida is in India.

Jack is in Japan.

Name _____ Date _____

Spacing Letters and Words

You can make your writing easy to read. Letters should not be too close
or too far apart.

These letters are

spaced just right.

Draw a slanted line between these words to check that the spacing is as
wide as a small o. Then copy the sentences.

The flowers are

in bloom.

Smell the flowers!

N M

Trace and write the letters. Then write the sentences.

n n n n n n n

m m m m m m m

Nebraska Nevada

Minnesota Maine

H K

Trace and write the letters. Then write the sentences.

H H H H H H H H

K K K K K K K

Hank likes Haiti.

Kai likes Kansas.

P Q

Trace and write the letters. Then write the sentences.

P P P P P P P P

Q Q Q Q Q Q Q Q

Quebec Quin Quito

Pittsburgh Plano

V U

Trace and write the letters. Then write the sentences.

V *V* *V* *V* *V* *V* *V*

U *U* *U* *U* *U* *U* *U*

Viv is in Vermont.

Ute lives in Utah.

W X

Trace and write the letters. Then write the words.

$\mathcal{W}$ $\mathcal{W}$ $\mathcal{W}$ $\mathcal{W}$ $\mathcal{W}$ $\mathcal{W}$

$\mathcal{X}$ $\mathcal{X}$ $\mathcal{X}$ $\mathcal{X}$ $\mathcal{X}$ $\mathcal{X}$

Will Waco Wales

Xavier Xia X-axis

Y Z

Trace and write the letters. Then write the words.

Y Y Y Y Y Y Y

Z Z Z Z Z Z Z

Yolanda Yukon

Zena Zen Zachary

Transition to Two Lines

Write the sentences. In the last two rows, write the sentences without the guidelines.

A robin has wings.

Ostriches run fast.

Parrots can talk.

Ducks lay eggs.